# Biopsychosocial medicine

# Biopsychosocial medicine

## An integrated approach to understanding illness

Edited by

Peter White
Department of Psychological Medicine
St Bartholomew's Hospital
London

OXFORD
UNIVERSITY PRESS

# OXFORD
UNIVERSITY PRESS

Great Clarendon Street, Oxford OX2 6DP

Oxford University Press is a department of the University of Oxford.
It furthers the University's objective of excellence in research, scholarship,
and education by publishing worldwide in

Oxford New York

Auckland Cape Town Dar es Salaam Hong Kong Karachi Kuala Lumpur Madrid
Melbourne Mexico City Nairobi New Delhi Taipei Toronto Shanghai

With offices in

Argentina Austria Brazil Chile Czech Republic France Greece Guatemala
Hungary Italy Japan South Korea Poland Portugal Singapore Switzerland
Thailand Turkey Ukraine Vietnam

Oxford is a registered trade mark of Oxford University Press
in the UK and in certain other countries

Published in the United States
by Oxford University Press Inc., New York

A catalogue record for this title is available from the British Library

Library of Congress Cataloguing in Publication Data

Biopsychosocial medicine : an integrated approach in understanding
  illness / edited by Peter White. – 1st ed.
  Includes bibliographical references and index.
  1. Holistic medicine   2. Medicine and psychology   3. Social medicine
  I. White, Peter
     [DNLM:   1. Psychophysiologic Disorders–etiology   2. Holistic Health
  3. Psychophysiologic Disorders–Therapy   4. Social Medicine   5. Stress,
  Psychophysiological–complications   WM 90 B618 2005]
  R733.B565 2005     616´0019–dc22     2004024509
  ISBN 0–19–853033–1 (Hbk: alk. paper)
  ISBN 0–19–853034–X (Pbk: alk. paper)

10 9 8 7 6 5 4 3 2 1

Typeset by EXPO Holdings Sdn Bhd., Malaysia.
Printed in Great Britain
on acid-free paper by
Biddles Ltd., King's Lynn

This book is dedicated to Caroline, Tom and Sara.

# Foreword

Simon Wessely

## The greatest benefit to mankind

Why do we bother with all this psycho social business? Medicine should be about dealing with disease and sorting out the body. All the rest is social work. Even psychiatry, which romantics might argue ought to be concerned with the world beyond nerve, muscle, and synapse, is only neurology in waiting. One day, when the combined talents of our geneticists, neuroscientists, and imagers have made the brain reveal its secrets, psychiatry too will come into the domain of real medicine, at which point proper doctors will feel more comfortable dealing with them than they do now.

It is a seductive view, isn't it? And it is one shared by a considerable number of our colleagues. It is seductive, precisely because it works. The biomedical model, which I have just been parodying, delivers. Old people with fading cognitive abilities used to be derided and ignored as senile. But as our knowledge of the neurobiology of Alzheimer's has been transformed, so has our care of sufferers, and at last there are genuine hopes for progress in treatment. Likewise, no amount of prayer, incantation, amulets, or spiritual devotion could make any impression on the scourge of the great infections, but immunization and antibiotics managed it. And, to use an example beloved of several of the contributors to this book, psychotherapy failed to cure peptic ulcers, but discovering and then eradicating *H pylori* did the trick. Let there be no mistake—modern scientific medicine is, as the late Roy Porter wrote, for once without his tongue in cheek, the 'greatest benefit of mankind'.

## The dangers of hubris

But it is easy to be swept away by this rhetoric, powerful though it is. Moving away from this *Boy's Own* story of medical progress, the stories of Pasteur, Koch, Fleming, and others that inspired me as a child and influenced my own career choice (inspired by the combined influences of a hagiography of Marie Curie, episodes of Dr Kildare, and our own family doctor), we can see gaps, and increasingly large ones at that.

Even on its own terms, modern medicine has not been entirely a story of progress. Most of the great infections have been mastered. But treatable conditions such as childhood gastroenteritis and malaria continue to claim the lives of millions. HIV is now manageable, but in most of the world it isn't managed.

Likewise, I seem to have spent much of the last decade sitting on grant-giving bodies, doling out small and not so small fortunes to subjects such as psychiatric genetics which has yet to improve the care of a single patient. Antidepressants promised a new era in the biological treatment of depression but, despite their widespread use, the prevalence of that condition seems to be increasing world wide, and our latest thinking sees it as a life long condition that requires management rather than cure, much as we see diabetes.

Yet at the same time the behaviour therapies have changed the care of the phobic patient in ways in which psychoanalysts could only dream of, the cognitive therapies are more effective at reducing relapse in depression than drugs alone, and the strange marriage of the two, cognitive behaviour therapy, has transformed the management of many chronic symptomatic conditions.

And what about the much vaunted *H pylori*? A seminal advance, but it has not meant the end of abdominal pain. 'Non ulcer dyspepsia' continues to be a common complaint in gastroenterology clinics and general practice, and does not respond to *H pylori* eradication.

## Psycho and social—why do we bother?

Since the beginnings of a recognizable scientific medicine in the mid 19th century every generation has lauded its scientific titans, and rightly so. They have transformed our understanding of, and ability to combat, disease. A strictly reductionist approach works, not just in gaining Nobel prizes, but also in improving the state of man. But equally, every generation has also faced up to the limitations of this same strictly reductionist approach to the teaching and practice of medicine. The biomedical approach works, but not well enough it seems.

George Engel, who figures considerably in the subsequent pages, highlighted these limitations in his seminal article of 1977 in which he coined the term 'biopsychosocial' , and the reader will learn much about this if they progress. Edward Shorter and the subsequent discussants place Engel in his historical context. They show that his intellectual dissatisfaction with a narrow view of medicine was not new, but his articulation of that disquiet came at a good time, when many others in and beyond medicine were coming to similar conclusions. Mike Fitzpatrick, as an *engagé* young doctor, came to Engel at the same time as he came to McKeown, Illich, and others. I remember reading the same authors together with Szasz and Laing with the same effect. Something was not quite right in the state of medicine, and it fell to Engel to articulate the problem. Szasz, Laing, and Illich have faded with time, because their critiques were too radical, babies were disappearing with bathwaters wherever you looked. But Engel had 'got something', as we say. We needed, he argued, better to integrate mind and body, and to include the social context of illness as well.

It all sounds obvious, something few could argue with. But as this volume shows, on closer examination there is more to this than meets the eye. And, as the chapters contributed by Professors Marmot, Steptoe, Lightman, and Davey Smith, galacticos all, showed, argue we did. It was then that your chairman would have earned his money, if any had been on offer.

That psychological and social factors contribute to disease is clear. Cancer and heart disease are the biggest killers in this country. The commonest cause is smoking. Eliminate smoking and you eliminate nearly all lung cancer. But what are the causes of smoking? Clearly these are rooted in our psychological life and social surroundings. Likewise alcohol related disease. Obesity and lack of exercise are rightly targeted as major public health problems—and no amount of reductionistic medicine is going to make us eat less or run more. No one in their right minds, not even government, would dream of tackling these issues without firming anchoring policy and intervention in the social sphere.

No argument there. Likewise, when it comes to patient experience, something we now call 'Quality of Life', there was no dispute amongst our galacticos that here we are dealing with a psychological construct *par excellence*. We know that ESR, CRP, and so on tell us little about how a patient with rheumatoid arthritis (RA) is coping with life. 'Objective' measures of swollen joints are poor predictors of when or if someone with RA will return to work. Mansel Alyward, lately medical supremo of the Department of Work and Pensions, pointed out that millions of people are registered disabled but still work, and even more millions of people without obvious markers of disease do not. Objective markers of disease do not seem to predict what we would like them to predict. Beck Depression Inventories provide a cheaper and more accurate guide.

When I teach medical students I remind them it is possible to live a happy, fulfilled life and have cancer. It is not possible to do so and have depression. Quality of Life (QOL) is all the rage now, and instruments to measure come thicker and faster than new directives from the Department of Health, but we in psychiatry have been measuring it for years with our GHQs and Beck Inventories. If only David Goldberg or Aaron Beck had thought to include 'QOL' in the titles of their measures, neither would have needed to go back to the day job.

Psychological issues matter, and matter greatly, particularly if you are concerned with how your patient is feeling, rather than how their CRP is behaving. When people talk in the vernacular about their reductionist bodies, they are still often actually talking about their feelings, albeit in metaphorical disguise. New Zealand psychologist Keith Petrie recently asked people to rate the strengths of that contemporary *zeitgeist*, their immune system. Rating of 'immune strength' bore no relationship to the actual measures the researchers made of immune function, but correlated near perfectly with measures of well-being and mood.

## Psycho and social—can we have too much of a good thing?

Where the titans clashed was not over the influence of psychological and social variables on psychological and social functioning, nor the importance of both. But does bio psycho social mean more than that? What role does the psycho and social play in the bio?

Sir Michael Marmot is perhaps the most distinguished epidemiologist today working on this issue, although he would modestly dispute that description. But to use a much abused word for once accurately, the Whitehall studies that he has guided are seminal. What they have shown is how social differentials, both at work and home, are major determinants of disease outcome. Not just depression or well-being, but hard outcomes such as heart disease sufficient to satisfy the most Gradgrind of practitioners impatient for the facts, just the facts. He and his team (and in fairness many other groups across the world) have shown that this is not simply due to the influence of the behavioural factors that I mentioned earlier, such as smoking and alcohol, which are clearly socially patterned and associated with 'hard' outcomes such as death and disease.

So can we say that the psychological is a direct determinant of the physical outcome? Professors Lightman and Steptoe say yes, and point to a series of elegant observations and experiments in which they can show how our early social environment affects the organization of our central nervous system, or how psychological variables, stress in the vernacular, affects cardiovascular functioning. If these observations are to be accepted, then we have proof at last that psychosomatic disease is a reality—that the psyche can affect the soma directly, as opposed to via tobacco and ethanol.

But consensus is rarely as exciting as dissension. The dissenting voice that punctured the biopsychosocial consensus was that of George Davey Smith, *enfant terrible* of epidemiology, and a man with an envious ability to go without sleep whilst combining immense statistical erudition with a deep knowledge of the historical origins of social medicine.

Davey Smith's argument centred on that old epidemiological spoilsport, confounding. In particular, he showed how in a series of observational studies, in which people were measured for a particular exposure—for example beta carotene, and then followed up over time, levels of the exposure correlated with subsequent heart disease, and that this association persisted despite every attempt to remove it by statistical adjustment for any number of known confounders.

But you can only adjust for the confounders you are aware of, or remembered to measure. The only certain way to deal with all confounding is to make sure that they are randomly distributed between your two groups—and this can only happen via the agency of the randomized controlled trial. Davey Smith showed how observed associations often did not match up to the rigours of randomization. The most likely reason for the previously reported associations was not a casual relationship, but was very likely due to some as yet unknown confounding.

And Davey Smith found plenty of examples in our field. And to add to the problem of confounding, he introduced the issue of bias. And unfortunately the psychosomatic literature is full of examples of such bias. Case control studies that link life events with peptic ulceration, stress in pregnancy with having offspring with Down's Syndrome, or life events and the relapse of breast cancer all come to mind. In all the original observations appear flawed, because of unrecognized bias. Thus are paradigms made and unmade.

As the impartial chairman I was fortunately not called on to take sides in this argument. As a psychiatrist working in the general hospital I feel that I have avoided what Nancy Frasure Smith, a name much in evidence in the following pages, calls the 'seduction of death', the belief that unless we can show evidence that we can influence 'hard' outcomes, we are not doing our job, and are not 'proper' doctors like those cardiologists or oncologists. I have never believed that—and have always felt that trying to influence psychological and social outcomes is a very good and satisfying career for a doctor on its own terms, even if in the public eye people like myself and many of the other participants in the meeting will never achieve the respect, acclaim, and rewards given to our more glamorous colleagues.

But no one interested in this field can afford to ignore these arguments. Our experimental medicine remains too crude to come to a definitive answer as yet, even given the skills and technologies available to Professors Lightman and Steptoe and many of my colleagues at the Institute of Psychiatry. Instead, we must beware of glibly accepting measures of 'stress' without carefully considering what they are actually measuring. We must also be very cautious indeed how we interpret any observed associations between psychosocial experience and 'hard' outcomes. The most likely links will be, as Davey Smith says, via confounding and bias, and these are the explanations we should first reach for before we seize upon the psychosomatic. I myself hazard a guess that there are genuine links between psyche and soma along the lines laid out by Steptoe, Lightman, and others, but the case remains unproven. Davey Smith believes the world to be simpler than it appears, in contrast to Engel, who believed it was more complex that we could imagine. I would love the answers to be simple, but I suspect they will not be.

## On the soma side of the street

So did George Engel manage to unite mind, body, and environment? Within the conference, the answer was generally positive, although one could argue that 'we would say that, wouldn't we?'. Perhaps in their choice of participants and Chairman the organizers had loaded the dice, but for most of us the intellectual objections to a solely dualistic approach to disease and illness remain compelling.

But the next day, liberated from the intoxicating environment provided by our hosts at the Novartis Foundation, I returned to the real world of clinical practice, which remains as firmly dualistic as ever. I myself work in the most dualistic of London addresses, Denmark Hill. For those unfamiliar with London topography, I should point out that Denmark Hill is actually a street that dissects the London Borough of Camberwell. On the left hand side is the vast complex that is the Maudsley Hospital and the Institute of Psychiatry. On the right hand side is a major teaching hospital, King's College Hospital and its associated medical school. Perhaps 3,000 people work on the campus on opposite sides of the road. I am one of the few who work on both sides. The vast majority belong to the mind on the left or the body on the right, with only a handful avoiding dualism by having a presence on both sides.

Of course, it is not quite that simple. It would spoil my rhetorical flourish to admit that the Institute of Psychiatry is overflowing with imagers, geneticists, and neuroscientists of every shape and form, nor of my colleagues in psychiatry and psychology who deliver services to the nooks and crannies of the general hospital. But nevertheless, the divide exists.

Patients make intensely dualistic choices, and services are organized to encourage this. Working in the environments that I do, I can see the consequences of those choices. My own speciality is in those grey areas that lie uncomfortably between medicine and psychiatry—one might place our professional space right in that dangerous zone in middle of the street, and at times it certainly feels that way. Professors Chalder, Creed, Main, Sharpe, and White inhabit the same grey zone. We currently call these the unexplained symptoms and syndromes, the latest in a long line of failed attempts to find satisfactory descriptive labels for these conditions. Many of the patients that I see first tell me about their soma—their overwhelming fatigue, pain, weakness, tremor, abdominal disturbances, and so on. I tend to see these patients on the right side of the Hill, within the general hospital. Others talk more about their sadness, fear, anger, frustration, anxiety, and occasional despair. I see them more often on the left, Maudsley side of the street. But if I ask these patients about their physical symptoms, it is a rare person who does not admit to them. Likewise, if I gently probe my patients on the King's side, and if they have decided to trust me, they will soon admit to complex emotional lives and distress. Two decades of research have shown beyond reasonable doubt that when it comes to symptoms, mind and body are inexplicably intertwined—if you have a lot of 'physical' symptoms, you will almost invariably endorse similar levels of 'psychological symptoms', and vice versa.

But there are considerable differences between the populations we see on the two sides of Denmark Hill. In the general hospital setting many are at best suspicious, and at worst dismissive, of any attempts to link soma and psyche, and deeply distrustful of the entire psychiatric enterprise. Whilst on the Maudsley side of the road, and indeed in general practice, we often see the opposite. Patients may react with disdain to any suggestion of a somatic intervention, such as antidepressants, preferring instead to see counsellors. There are tales of randomized trials that set out to compare antidepressants with the talking treatments that have failed to deliver because so many potential participants expressed too strong a preference for the counselling arm. We don't know how effective it is, but it is certainly popular. Dualism remains alive and well in Denmark Hill as elsewhere.

But I have done it again—used a rhetorical device that oversimplifies a complex reality. On the soma side of the street, to paraphrase the *Tin Pan Alley* song, our cancer patients lobby intensively for better psychological care. Our renal patients are delighted with the single session of psychiatric time we are able to provide, and our dermatology chest, gastroenterological, and liver patients likewise. A new combined medical and psychiatric service for people with diabetes is proving immensely popular, and is producing data suggesting the service is improving care of both mind and body.

And on the psyche side of the street, for some the objections to somatic therapies are not so much ideological ('don't mess with my brain') but practical and often realistic concerns about side-effects, withdrawal, and the risk of dependence.

But the widespread acceptance of psychological therapies (and also, as Professor Furnham pointed out, alternative therapies) in the oncology clinic does not represent the end of dualism. Cancer patients do not lobby for psychologists because they believe that psychological factors are why they developed cancer in the first place (which is certainly progress given that in previous times there have been scientists who have made those erroneous claims). They do so because they feel that it is safe and permissible to engage with psychological therapies precisely because their doctors do not hold with psychosomatic theories of cancer. Once the physical basis of disease is established, then one can explore the psychological in safety, but not before.

Compare and contrast this with the well known reluctance of sufferers from chronic fatigue syndrome (CFS) to do the same. Here is a group who are not demanding better access to psychotherapy. Instead, the principal focus of some activists is the reverse—to reduce and even eliminate all traces of the psychological from the CFS clinic, and even the planet itself if some ultras had their way. The difference between these CFS sufferers and those with cancer is the former are not confident that the somatic basis of their problems has been established beyond doubt, even if they are convinced that it will in time. Worse, they suspect, and with good reason, that their doctors are not confident either, and if pushed might well endorse a psychosomatic contribution to ill health. In these circumstances it would be foolhardy to lobby for better psychiatry, since that would only increase their sense of stigma and rejection.

## Conclusion

It is an irony, and one that even the august contributors to this volume do not fully confront, that perhaps the best way to improve the psychological support for, and understanding of, patients with a range of illnesses, is not to try to combine mind and body. George Engel was right in theory, but wrong in practice. Medical care remains dualistic, perhaps more so than ever. In the clinic, but not the conference hall or laboratory, we seem best able to tackle the social and psychological only when we have solved the physical first.

# Preface

The biomedical approach to ill-health has given human beings immense benefit, and this will accelerate now we are able to identify the genetic basis of diseases and even observe the workings of the brain. At the same time there is a paradox. While we have never been as healthy or lived for as long as we now do, we seem to have more concerns about our health and suffer from more chronic disability than ever before.

Why is this? This book was written because some people believe that medicine is currently travelling up a 'blind alley' in its attempt to help patients improve their health and reduce their disability. This blind alley is the biomedical approach to healthcare, in spite of the great benefits it has given us. The biomedical approach or model assumes that ill-health and disability is directly caused by diseases and their pathological processes. The evidence, some of which will be reviewed in this book, suggests that the biomedical model may not explain much chronic ill-health and even less the disability associated with it. For instance it is quite common to have a disease without a symptom, such as high blood pressure caused by an unknown kidney disease. Equally it is common to have symptoms without any apparent disease, such as a chronic pain disorder.

There is an alternative. This is an approach that extends the biomedical approach by taking into account "the patient, the social context in which he lives, and . . . the physician role and the health care system."[1] The biopsychosocial approach, a term invented by George Engel,[1,2] is one that incorporates thoughts, feelings, behaviour, their social context, and their interactions with both physiology and pathophysiology into its approach to ill-health and disability. Such an approach does not abandon the biomedical model, but extends it.

But does the biopsychosocial model fit the evidence any better? Is it really more useful? Is it more effective in helping patients regain their health and former capabilities? What are the barriers to its better implementation and how might they be overcome?

This book attempts to answer these questions. It arose out of a two day conference held at the Novartis Foundation, in London, on the last day of October and the first day in November 2002. Because the biopsychosocial approach is better established in psychiatry and healthcare for medically unexplained

symptoms, we concentrated on examining the relevance of the biopsychosocial approach to chronic medical diseases.

The conference was a joint venture between the Novartis Foundation and
One Health. One Health is a not-for–profit company that was established in
order to promote a system of healthcare based on the biopsychosocial model
of ill-health. The conference was co-organized by Dr. Greg Bock, Deputy
Director of the Novartis Foundation, and myself, ably assisted by staff at
Novartis. Twenty eight international experts in the field were invited (see the
list of contributors). Twelve talks were given followed by an equal time spent
in discussion. This book includes those talks, edited and updated since the
conference in order to incorporate the latest relevant research findings in the
field. The discussions and some of the presentations were audiotaped and
transcribed by Jamie Cooke. The discussions have only been edited for the
sake of clarity, since I wanted to keep them as close as possible to the original
discussions, in order to keep them as spontaneous as they were on the day.

1. Engel GL. The need for a new medical model: a challenge for biomedicine.
   *Science* 1977; **196**: 129–36.

2. Engel GL. The clinical application of the biopsychosocial model. *Am J
   Psychiatry* 1982; **137**: 535–44.

Professor Peter White,
Chairman of One Health
*December 2004*

# Acknowledgements

I would like to thank all the speakers and discussants at the conference. Their involvement and dedication have made this book. Greg Bock gave great support and advice, as did his staff at the Novartis Foundation. The whole conference was ably chaired by Professor Simon Wessely alone, with ample asides, witticisms, and his usual insightful observations, which all helped to keep us to the task throughout the two days. I am also grateful to him for his enlightened and challenging Foreword to the book. Jamie Cooke undertook the difficult task of writing and initially editing the transcriptions.

My fellow directors of One Health gave good advice and great support. They are Professors Trudie Chalder, Bob Lewin, Chris Main, and Dr. Brian Marien. The Patron of One Health, Greville Mitchell, made this all possible. He is an influential and far-sighted philanthropist whose dedication, determination, and generosity have led to the establishment of One Health and thus this book. One Health is supported by the Andrew Mitchell Christian Charitable Trust.

Richard Marley first agreed to publish the book on behalf of Oxford University Press, and Martin Baum took over the task of steering the book through its various stages, assisted by Carol Maxwell.

# Contents

# Contributors
## (either speakers or discussants)

**Professor Mansel Aylward**
Professor of Psychosocial and
Disability Research
Director, The Centre for
Psychosocial and
Disability Research
Cardiff University
Cardiff CF10 3YG, UK

**Dr Gregory Bock**
Deputy Director
Novartis Foundation
41 Portland Place
London W1B 1BN, UK

**Professor Trudie Chalder**
Professor of Cognitive Behavioural
Psychotherapy
Department of Psychological
Medicine
Institute of Psychiatry
Guy's, King's & St Thomas' School of
Medicine
Weston Education Centre
Cutcombe Road, London SE5 9RJ,
UK

**Professor Francis Creed**
Professor of Psychological
Medicine
School of Psychiatry and
Behavioural Medicine
Rawnsley Building
Manchester Royal Infirmary
Oxford Road
Manchester M13 9WL, UK

**Professor George Davey Smith**
Professor of Clinical Epidemiology
Department of Social Medicine
University of Bristol
Canynge Hall
Whiteladies Road,
Bristol BS8 2PR, UK

**Professor Douglas A Drossman**
Professor of Medicine and Psychiatry
Co-Director, UNC Center for
Functional GI
and Motility Disorders
Division of Gastroenterology and
Hepatology
Department of Medicine
University of North Carolina
Chapel Hill, NC 27599–7080, USA

**Professor Glyn Elwyn**
Department of Primary Care
School of Medicine
University of Wales Swansea
Grove Building, Singleton Park
Swansea SA2 8PP, UK

**Dr Michael Fitzpatrick**
General Practitioner
Barton House Health Centre
233 Albion Road
London N16 9JT, UK

**Professor Adrian Furnham**
Professor of Psychology
Department of Psychology
University College London
Gower Street
London WC1E 6BT, UK

**Professor Peter Halligan**
Professor of Neuropsychology
School of Psychology
Cardiff University
PO Box 901
Cardiff CF10 3YG, UK

**Professor Jos Kleijnen**
Director
Centre for Reviews and
Dissemination
NHS Centre for Reviews and
Dissemination,
University of York
York YO10 5DD, UK

**Professor Robert Lewin**
British Heart Foundation Research
Unit
Department of Health Sciences
Room 28
University of York
Heslington
York YO10 5DD, UK

**Professor Stafford Lightman**
Professor of Medicine and Director
of the Henry Wellcome Laboratories
for Integrative Neuroscience and
Endocrinology
Henry Wellcome Laboratories for
Integrative Neuroscience and
Endocrinology Dorothy Hodgkin
Building
Whitson Street
Bristol BS1 3NY, UK

**Professor Kate Lorig**
Stanford Patient Education Research
Centre Stanford School of Medicine
1000 Welch Road
Suite R04
Palo Alto, CA 94304, USA

**Professor Chris J Main**
Professor of Clinical and
Occupational Rehabilitation
Unit of Chronic Disease
Epidemiology Stopford Building
University of Manchester
Oxford Road
Manchester, M13 9PT, UK

**Professor Helge Malmgren**
Professor of Theoretical
Philosophy
Department of Philosophy
Göteborg University
Box 200
SE-405 30 Göteborg, Sweden

**Dr Brian Marien**
Back Pain Service/Health Psychology
Unit
King Edward VII Hospital
Midhurst
West Sussex GU29 0BL, UK

**Professor Sir Michael Marmot**
Professor of Epidemiology and
Public Health
International Centre for Health and
Society
University College London
Gower Street
London WC1E 6BT, UK

**Mr Greville Mitchell**
Andrew Mitchell Christian
Charitable Trust
4 College Terrace
The Grange
St Peter Port
Guernsey
Channel Islands TY1 2PX, UK

**Professor Peter Salmon**
Professor of Clinical Psychology
Department of Clinical Psychology
University of Liverpool
Whelan Building
PO Box 147
Brownlow Hill
Liverpool L69 3GB, UK

**Professor Michael Sharpe**
Professor of Psychological Medicine
and Symptoms Research
Department of Psychiatry
School of Molecular and Clinical
Medicine
University of Edinburgh
The Kennedy Tower
Royal Edinburgh Hospital
Morningside Park
Edinburgh EH10 5HF, UK

**Professor Edward Shorter**
Hannah Chair in the History of
Medicine
University of Toronto
88 College Street
Room 207
Toronto, ON, M5G 1L4, Canada

**Professor Stephen Stansfeld**
Professor of Psychiatry
Department of Psychiatry
3rd Floor
BMS Building
Barts and the London, Queen Mary
University of London
University of London
Mile End Road
London E1 4NS, UK

**Professor Andrew Steptoe**
British Heart Foundation Professor
of Psychology

Psychobiology Group
Department of Epidemiology and
Public Health
University College London
1–19 Torrington Place
London WC1E 6BT, UK

**Professor Michael Von Korff**
Senior Investigator
Center for Health Studies
Group Health Cooperative of Puget
Sound
1730 Minor Avene
Suite 1600
Seattle, WA 98101, USA

**Professor Gordon Waddell**
Centre for Psychosocial and
Disability Research
University of Cardiff
Cardiff CF10 3AT, UK

**Professor Simon Wessely**
Co Director
King's Centre for Military Health
Research Professor of
Epidemiological and Liaison
Psychiatry
Institute of Psychiatry
King's College London
Weston Education Centre
Cutcombe Rd
London SE5 9RJ, UK

**Professor Peter White**
Professor of Psychological Medicine
Department of Psychological
Medicine
Bart's and the London, Queen Mary
School of Medicine and Dentistry
St Bartholomew's Hospital
London EC1A 7BE, UK

# 1 The history of the biopsychosocial approach in medicine: before and after Engel

Edward Shorter

## Summary

Historically, physicians have always tended to take the patient's personality and social circumstances into consideration, so George Engel's 'biopsychosocial model' involves something more than mere attentiveness to the doctor–patient relationship and its inherent therapeutic qualities. Engel, an internist, was also steeped in psychoanalysis and originally pleaded for the adoption of dynamic insights in fields outside of psychiatry. Yet spanning internal medicine and psychiatry as he did, he embraced more a consultation–liaison (C–L) model of psychiatry than a psychodynamic one. Then in the 1960s his focus began to shift from the doctor–patient dyad to the system of medical care itself. In his famous 1977 article where he enunciates the biopsychosocial model, he adopts quite an innovative strategy, shifting the 'social' from the patient's social context to the role of the health care system itself in engendering and relieving illness. This kind of systemic thinking, however, put the biopsychosocial model directly in conflict with the alternative 'medical model'. In the debates about whether the biopsychosocial model should be adopted, resource issues have figured almost as prominently as patient-care issues. Recently however, the case for the biopsychosocial model has become strengthened as the provision of pharmacotherapy—always the core of the medical model—appears increasingly inadequate as a solution to most patients' problems.

## Introduction

Recently, the biopsychosocial model has become a concept to conjure with. Indeed it has become so endowed with warm and fuzzy vibes that the President of the American Psychiatric Association recently called for the appointment of a psychiatrist, rather than a psychologist, to head the Yale Child Study Center.

This was on the grounds that a psychiatrist would be 'a person that is specifically trained in the biopsychosocial model ... so that he or she can point the institution into the future.'[1]

One sees that the term 'biopsychosocial' has come a long way from its origins. But *pace* American Psychiatric Association President Richard Harding, biopsychosocial thinking is by no means coterminous with a modern medical education. Indeed, the term is most often used by those who oppose the latest salient advances of biological thinking in medicine and long for the return of a more holistic epoch. Especially in psychiatry, invocation of the biopsychosocial model is becoming a way to back-pedal from biological psychiatry and psychopharmacology and to restore the lost primacy of psychotherapy. At stake in the issue really is not how the patient is actually treated, or the quality of the doctor–patient relationship, but the nature of the discipline of psychiatry itself. The debate about the biopsychosocial model is, in other words, much more political than therapeutic.

How did this biopsychosocial model arise, that today is poised like a dagger at the heart of biological psychiatry? How was the biopsychosocial approach launched with such optimism, yet failed to become the central approach in internal medicine some decades later?

## The origins of the biopsychosocial model

It has always been apparent to physicians, in an insight that different generations gain in their own ways, that the body, the patient's personal history, and their current social circumstances all play a role in the pathogenesis of illness and in the patient's interpretation of their symptoms. This is the implicit biopsychosocial model: the recognition that material lesions, life experiences, and current social situation all matter in the presentation of illness; they influence what the physician sees in the consulting room. The tissue changes or the biochemical lesions are the 'bio-', the personal growth and development the 'psycho-', and the current life situation the 'social'. Holistic concepts go back to Hippocrates and these Hippocratic notions represent an implicit recognition of what much later generations would begin to articulate as 'models'.[2]

These implicit insights first become explicit in the era of therapeutic nihilism of the late nineteenth century, when physicians quite correctly began to realize there was little they could cure and thus sought psychological means of supporting their patients. Among the originators of the 'patient-as-a-person' movement was the Viennese internist Hermann Nothnagel, who sought in the 1880s to resurrect Hippocratic holistic thinking and see the patient's presentation of illness as the product of a range of circumstances, not just biology. As he said in his inaugural lecture in 1882, 'I repeat once again, medicine is about treating sick people and not diseases.' [3]

The London physician—and later Chair of Medicine at University College London—Russell Reynolds described in 1869 a young female patient who had experienced a psychogenic 'paralysis' of the lower limbs. Her family had recently undergone financial hardship; she had been obliged to take a job as governess, walking long distances back and forth, all the while nursing an ailing father:

> Thus she lived and worked on for many dreary weeks, with paralysis constantly upon her mind, her brain overdone with thought and feeling, her limbs wearied with walking, and her heart tired out with the effort to look bright and be so ... Her legs 'became heavier day by day' and she at last reached the state in which I found her when she was carried to the hospital.[4]

Reynolds's analysis represents, of course, an implicit acknowledgment of the biopsychosocial model.

William Osler, the very icon of modern internal medicine, has been quoted as saying, 'The good physician treats the disease but the great physician treats the patient who has the disease.'[5] Indeed, this rich vein in American internal medicine continued through the 1920s and 1930s, in the form of such books as Harvard Professor of Medicine Francis Weld Peabody's *The care of the patient* (1927) and Hopkins Internist George Canby Robinson's *The patient as a person* (1939).[6] Although forgotten today, these specialists in internal medicine were once very much associated with the idea that the patient was more than 'a sack of enzymes', that personal history and social circumstances mattered as well, both in the pathogenesis of illness and in its treatment.

What could subsequent generations have contributed to these more or less enduring insights in medicine about the nature of an implicit biopsychosocial model?

## George Engel and the biopsychosocial model

The term 'biopsychosocial model' is associated indelibly with the name of George Engel, the internist, psychiatrist, and psychoanalyst. Since 1946 Engel had preached the indissoluble nature of mind–body links at the University of Rochester and presented the term itself to a broad scientific public in a 1977 article in *Science*.[7] Born in New York in 1913, Engel had graduated as a doctor of Medicine from Johns Hopkins University in 1938. After doing his internship at Mount Sinai Hospital in New York for 3 years (and being a Medicine Resident at the Peter Bent Brigham Hospital in Boston for 1 year), Engel joined the Medicine Service of the Cincinnati General Hospital in 1942.

In Cincinnati, he came into contact with a small group of psychiatrists who later formed part of the leadership of the psychoanalytically influenced approach to psychosomatic medicine in the USA: John Romano, Milton Rosenbaum, and Maurice Levine (also members of this intense little group were Albert Sabin in pediatrics, Arthur Mirsky in medicine, and Charles Aring in neurology).[8] Yet it was Romano who had the greatest impact on Engel with his views on psychoanalysis as the wave of psychiatry's future.[9] Of Romano, Engel later fondly wrote, 'Little by little he introduced me to the mysteries of mind, so painlessly that I could for some time continue to believe I was merely acting as a medical consultant to the psychiatric service.'[10]

But it was Levine who introduced Engel to Franz Alexander's Chicago Institute for Psychoanalysis. After an introduction to psychoanalytic training at the New York Psychoanalytic Institute in 1949–50, Engel was associated for 5 years, until 1955, with the Chicago Institute. Thus Engel the internist came to have his feet firmly planted in American psychoanalysis.

Meanwhile, in 1946 he had followed Romano to Rochester, where the latter had just established the Department of Psychiatry. Engel would remain at Rochester, jointly appointed in psychiatry and medicine, until his retirement in 1983. Engel helped make Rochester the pioneer centre for cross-training medical undergraduates in the mind–body relationship.[11]

Engel's background in medicine and psychoanalysis would have naturally inclined him to look for cross-links among primary somatic illness, personal development, and life situation. Thus the concept of biopsychosocial model begins to feature early in his work.

On the occasion of opening a new building in 1951, for the Institute for Psychosomatic and Psychiatric Research of Chicago's Michael Reese Hospital, Roy Grinker asked Engel to contribute a piece to the volume commemorating the occasion. Engel noted of 'the concept of health and disease', that the satisfaction of instinctual needs may occur simultaneously 'at biological, psychological and social levels', as well as at different developmental levels.[12] So the language was there as early as 1951.

Engel incorporated this implicit model into all his clinical research as well as into abstract theorizing about instinct. For example, in 1956 he asked why patients with ulcerative colitis often seemed to develop headaches when the bowel illness was quiescent. His theory was that when headaches appeared in these patients, 'there was evidence of strong conscious or unconscious aggressive or sadistic impulses'. When bleeding occurred, 'the patient was feeling to varying degrees helpless, hopeless, or despairing'. The bottom line, not entirely convincing to all gastro-enterologists, was 'Bleeding ... characteristically occurs in the setting of a real, threatened, or fantasized loss, leading to psychic helplessness.'[13] Yet unlike many members of the Chicago school, who considered psychic events to be primary, Engel believed that organicity itself could be primary, the psyche merely explaining the timing of the symptoms; so, mind and body inter-related, rather than the former dominating the latter. This distinction was crucial in later getting the biopsychosocial model adopted by non-psychiatrists.

During the 1960s, Engel's clinical work began ever more to approximate his famous model, taking him even further from conventional psychoanalysis. By 1968 he had worked out a theory of conversion phenomena implicating the autonomic nervous system: '... There becomes established a vicious cycle in which the physiological concomitants of an affect ... also become a vehicle for the expression of an unconscious wish', as seen, for example, in blushing. 'Interaction with local predisposing factors may result in localized lesions.' This is pretty conventional Franz Alexander-style psychosomatics. Yet Engel added another pathway: There can be 'fantasies aroused by the experiencing of somatic changes which have no primary psychologic meaning.' Contrary to the standard psychoanalytic wisdom, Engel said there are 'more complex psychosomatic inter-relationships, where the final organic process may be reached through a number of different sequences.'[14] This was the internist speaking and the logic would shortly have a significant impact on the conceptualizing of the mind–body relationship across the board in American medicine.

As noted, it was in his 1977 article in *Science* that Engel's biopsychosocial model was enunciated as such and this time with all the trappings of psychoanalysis left (almost entirely) behind. Would psychiatry do well to emulate the medical model he asked rhetorically? No, he thought not. It was not merely psychiatry but all medicine that was in crisis as a result of applying the 'biomedical model' where the biopsychosocial model should serve. The biomedical model meant the reduction of both illness to measurable biological parameters and therapy to a rejigging of the numbers of these parameters (the assumption that this is what most American physicians in the 1960s and 70s actually did is breathtaking in its sweep).

In psychiatry in particular, two opposing schools of thought had evolved. One, led by Thomas Szasz, was exclusionist, asserting that there was no such thing as psychiatric illness and that psychiatry was a non-discipline that should be removed from medicine in favour of helping so-called patients cope with 'problems of living'. The other postulated school of psychiatry, no less attractive in Engel's depiction, was said to reduce the complex world of psychiatric symptoms and subjective feelings to brain 'dysfunction'. This reductionist approach, scoffed Engel, 'assumes that the language of chemistry and physics will ultimately suffice to explain biological phenomena.' Engel compared the commonalities in diabetes and schizophrenia, both possessing perhaps a primary somatic cause, yet requiring for their successful treatment a clinical understanding of the patients' subjectivity. The psychiatrist had to grasp the verbal expression of his patient's illness to penetrate to the heart of the disease. Both diabetes and schizophrenia had in common that 'conditions of life and living' help determine onset and course. Thus Engel called attention to 'the advantages of a biopsychosocial model.' To be effective, a model 'must also take into account the patient, the social context in which he lives and ... the physician role and the health care system.' This then was the third and innovative element in biopsychosocial: social had shifted from the patient's personal social context—self-evident in medicine since time immemorial—to the role of the health care system itself in engendering and relieving illness.

Engel's text hummed with the buzz-words of medical sociology: the doctor must consider what 'well' and 'sick' mean as well as the 'biological indices' that also define disease. 'The doctor's task,' explained Engel to anyone who might have thought it consisted of making house calls or providing care, 'is to account for the dysphoria and the dysfunction which lead individuals to seek medical help, adopt the sick role, and accept the status of patient-hood.' Engel closed with a blast at those psychiatrists who had already adopted the biomedical model.[15]

Engel specifically acknowledged Freud and Hopkins psychiatrist Adolf Meyer in the genesis of his own biopsychosocial thinking[16] (some authors argue that Engel's work represented a rejection of psychoanalysis, yet I do not think the core articles sustain that interpretation[17]). It is unlikely that Freud can be displayed as the father of the biopsychosocial model, if only because the founder of psychoanalysis was never particularly interested in organic disease—and Engel the internist was. As for Meyer, his thinking in general was so scattered that he could be said to be the father of everything, or nothing.[18] The citation to Meyer's work that Engel gave, for example, was to a one-and-a-half-page article in 1917 in the *Journal of the American Medical Association* on the graduate teaching of psychiatry. Meyer was keen that his own 'psycho-biology' model was integrated into teaching programmes and that trainees enter into the study of 'the patient as a person'.[19] Yet in those days, as we have seen, the air was thick with talk of treating 'the patient as a person' and Meyer owns no patents here.[20]

The impact of Engel's 1977 *Science* article was enormous. It placed the biopsychosocial model firmly on the undergraduate teaching agenda of the world's medical schools and on the educational programme of residency training in psychiatry in many places. The cutting edge was not psycho-analysis, nor personal development, but 'the system' and how it can make people sick as well as better.

## The biopsychosocial model after Engel

The great recent popularity of the biopsychosocial model may be attributed to the usefulness Engel assigned to it as a lance in power struggles. In the struggle to carve up scarce resources, biopsychosocial thinking has done yeoman service in the following kinds of turf struggles.

There has been great debate about whether psychiatry is just another specialty *comme toutes les autres* or whether instead it should offer holistic care in a primary care setting. The biopsychosocial model insists that psychiatry has a privileged role in primary care and is not just a sister discipline alongside referral specialties, such as nephrology. In hospital care, as Georgetown University psychiatrist Thomas Wise points out, 'The consultation–liaison psychiatrist is most often the messenger of the biopsychosocial approach... .'[21] In C–L psychiatry, of course, the psychiatrist, unlike the nephrologist, is in demand on many services.

It has been a particular grievance of C–L and primary care advocates that post-graduate training in psychiatry has swum against this particular stream. Robert Weiss, at the Columbia University Center for Community Health Systems, deplores that, after the 1960s, 'Most psychiatry departments in medical schools moved very quickly into the building of a competing empire with other departments as specialization in all of medicine became the accepted mode of training ... Psychiatry moved more and more into a separatist position in most institutions.'[22] According to the biopsychosocial model, psychiatry should be bringing the care of the whole person together, rather than just carving off the mind into a watertight specialty of its own. Incorporating psychiatry as a fundamental part of community care in centres such as Weiss's—or enlarging the C–L services of a hospital psychiatry department—has considerable resource implications.

Second, the discussion has been greatly agitated over the relative role of 'biological' versus 'clinical' research. The biopsychosocial model, of course, preferred the latter, seeing biology as the reductionist darling of the biomedical model. Clinical research, by contrast, was thought to favour interdisciplinarity, boundary demolition, and the promotion of wholeness. Yale's Morton Reiser, for example, in a George Engel Festschrift, characterized schizophrenia as a stress disorder, with a constitutionally weakened brain the 'target organ'.[23] Investigating such a hypothesis would involve social scientists, psychologists, and clinicians from all over the map, as opposed to studying serotonin reuptake after the administration of fluoxetine. Here the resource decisions for a National Institute of Mental Health 'study session' would be considerable.

Third, perhaps the fiercest debate arising from the post-Engel agenda of biopsychosocial thinking is over psychopharmacology versus psychotherapy as the preferred treatment modality in psychiatric care (recognizing of course that both are necessary). Advocates of Engel-style thinking seem to endorse an almost visceral rejection of 'pills' and of psychiatric therapeutics resting upon the assumption of organicity. For decades, this approach had been dismissed as the medical model, a term in use even before Engel's biopsychosocial model. In the early 1940s, for example, psychoanalytically oriented colleagues at Harvard had scorned psychiatrist Mandel Cohen's quantitative model of anxiety attacks on the grounds that it employed the medical model.[24]

In the eyes of biopsychosocial advocates, more recent villains of the piece included psychiatrist Arnold Ludwig of the University of Kentucky, who in a prominent 1975 *Journal of the American Medical Association* article argued for the medical model and mocked the ' "model muddlement" currently prevalent in psychiatry';[25] yet for biopsychosocial fans the *bête noire* without comparison was the late Samuel Guze of Washington University of St Louis, himself a pioneer of biological thinking although not necessarily of psychopharmacology. In the medical model that Guze urged with great insistence upon psychiatry, precisely what united psychiatry with the rest of medicine was a scientifically based system of psychotropic medication and a systematic diagnostic classification—namely the Diagnostic and Statistical Manual (*DSM*).[26] Said Duncan Double of the Norfolk Mental Health Care National Health Service Trust, one of the opponents of Guze's medical model, 'This attempt to make psychiatric diagnosis more reliable was associated with a return to a biomedical model of mental illness. The approach has been called neo-Kraepelinian ... .'[27] So, for biopsychosocial, anything but neo-Kraepelinianism would do.

The resource issues in psychopharmacology versus psychotherapy are awesome, because they involve the pharmaceutical industry, which has, in fact, become almost an equal partner in the elaboration of psychiatric diagnosis. Yet one can argue for a simpler, more valid system of diagnosis than *DSM*—one less lucrative for industry[28]—without surrendering one whit of the biological paradigm. Nonetheless, it is historically the case that biopsychosocial-style thinking has become a lance in the struggle to help extract the pharmaceutical industry from psychiatry (there are, however, other ways to diminish the influence of industry without returning everybody to the couch).

Why not just be eclectic and take the best of what each camp has to offer? Behind the resistance to the biopsychosocial model lies a real fear that psychiatry might become demedicalized. That would entail a material loss to its practitioners, as work wanders away to psychiatric social workers and psychologists. And it would betoken an intellectual loss, as the content of the discipline drifts off to antipsychiatry. For better or worse, the medical model promises to keep psychiatry within medicine. And even though Engel the internist desired that as well,[29] there are proponents of the biopsychosocial model who have other goals in mind.

It is intriguing to inquire why the biopsychosocial model failed to catch on after Engel's heyday in the 1960s and 1970s. The reason is that the biopsychosocial model failed to address the stunning success of pharmacotherapy in the last quarter century. Engel had the misfortune to be preaching a humane approach to patients just as the pharmacopoeia was exploding with effective new drugs in a range of diseases in all of the non-surgical specialties. Especially in psychopharmacology, physicians harvested a series of triumphs from the anxiolytics to the antipsychotics. One bears in mind that it had been for 'functional' illness—thought by some to be psychogenic—that Engel's approach held its greatest appeal. And for a while, the riddle of psychogenicity seemed tamed with the benzodiazepines and the selective serotonin re-uptake inhibitors. So Engel's message was really drowned in several decades of drug hype, some of which was true, some of which was not.

Now that some of the weaknesses of the pharmacological approach to illness have been revealed, there is in medicine a much greater receptiveness to non-pharmacological approaches to the problem of illness, especially functional ones. Chronic fatigue syndrome turns out not to be responsive to psychoactive drugs, but seems to yield more readily to cognitive and behavioral therapies—biopsychosocial country. This is quite ironic. A hundred years later, post-modern medicine has really found no more effective approach to the problem of functional illness than did William Osler. Osler emphasized the therapeutic use of the doctor–patient relationship and that is precisely the message that the biopsychosocial model has for us today.

## References

1. Rosack J. Angry response follows appointment of psychologist to head Yale Center. *Psychiatric News* 17 May 2002; pp. 2 and 41 (quote).
2. On Hippocrates, see Porter R. *The greatest benefit to mankind: a medical history of humanity.* New York: Norton; 1997.
3. Neuburger M, Nothnagel H. *Leben und Wirken eines deutschenKlinikers.* Vienna: Rikola; 1922. On Nothnagel, see Lesky E. *Die Wiener medizinische Schule im 19. Jahrhundert.* Graz: Böhlau; 1978. On these aspects of the history of the doctor–patient relationship, see Shorter E. Primary care. In: Porter R, ed. *The Cambridge illustrated history of medicine.* Cambridge: Cambridge University Press; 1996. pp. 118–53.
4. Quoted in Shorter E. *From paralysis to fatigue: a history of psychosomatic illness in the modern era.* New York: Free Press; 1992.

5. Quoted in Farrar CB. *The four doctors. Proceedings of the Seventh Annual Psychiatric Institute, September 16, 1959.* Princeton, New Jersey: New Jersey Neuro Psychiatric Institute; 1959 (quote p. 110).

6. Peabody FW. *The care of the patient.* Cambridge, Massachusetts: Harvard University Press; 1927. Canby Robinson G. *The patient as a person.* New York: The Commonwealth Fund; 1939.

7. George L. Engel. The need for a new medical model: a challenge for biomedicine. *Science* 1977; **196:** 129–36.

8. Ader R, Schmale AH Jr. George Libman Engel: on the occasion of his retirement. *Psychosom Med* 1980; **42** (**suppl.**): 79–101.

9. Romano J. Basic orientation and education of the medical student. *JAMA* 1950; **143:** 409–12.

10. Engel GL. A reconsideration of the role of conversion in somatic disease. *Comp Psychiat* 1968; **9:** 316–26 (quote p. 316).

11. For details of Engel's life see American Psychiatric Association. *Biographical directory of fellows and members.* New York: Bowker; 1963. *American men and women of science, 1992–93.* 18th ed. New Providence, New Jersey: Bowker; 1992.

12. Engel GL. Homeostasis, behavioral adjustment and the concept of health and disease. In: Grinker RR, ed. *Mid-century psychiatry: an overview.* Springfield, Illinois: Charles C. Thomas; 1953. pp. 33–59 (quote p. 54.)

13. Engel GL. Studies of ulcerative colitis, IV: the significance of headaches. *Psychosom Med* 1956; **18:** 334–46 (quotes pp. 335 and 344).

14. Engel GL. A reconsideration of the role of conversion in somatic disease. *Comp Psychiat* 1968; **9:** 316–26 (quotes pp. 324 and 325).

15. Engel GL. The need for a new medical model: a challenge for biomedicine. *Science* 1977; **196:** 129–36 (quotes pp. 129–132).

16. Engel GL. The need for a new medical model: a challenge for biomedicine. *Science* 1977; **196:** 129–36 (quotes pp. 134 and 135).

17. McLaren N. A critical review of the biopsychosocial model. *Austr NZ J Psychiat* 1998; **32:** 86–92 (especially p. 91).

18. For an analysis of Meyer's work, see Shorter E. *A history of psychiatry.* New York: Wiley; 1997.

19. Meyer A. Progress in teaching psychiatry. *JAMA* 1917; **69:** 861–2. Theodor Lidz attempts to presents Meyer's 'psychobiological thinking' as an influential contribution in Lidz T. Adolf Meyer and the development of American psychiatry. *Am J Psychiat* 1966; **123:** 320–32. Yet Meyer's own psychobiological views were nothing more than an accumulation of the platitudes of the day; see Meyer A. The Philosophy of Psychiatry, 1942. In: Winters E, ed. *Collected Papers of Adolf Meyer.* Baltimore: Johns Hopkins Press, 1951; 3: pp. 478–91.

20. For a brief effort to give a coherent account of Meyer's ideas see the encomium of his colleague at Hopkins and fellow Swiss-national Oskar Diethelm: Diethelm O. Panikreaktion vom Standpunkt psychobiologischer Psychiatrie. In: Prinzhorn H, ed. *Die Wissenschaft am Scheidewege von Leben und Geist: Festschrift Ludwig Klages zum 60. Geburtstag.* Leipzig: Barth; 1932. pp. 58–64. Diethelm argues that Meyer differs from Kraepelin in his efforts to individualize diagnosis through integration of the patient's personality.

21. Wise TN. Teaching psychosomatic medicine: utilizing concurrent perspectives. *Psychother Psychosom* 1993; **59:** 99–106 (quote p. 102).

22. Weiss RW. The biopsychosocial model and primary care. *Psychosom Med* 1980; **42 (suppl.):** 123–9 (quote p. 124).

23. Reiser M. Implications of a biopsychosocial model for research in psychiatry. *Psychosom Med* 1980; **42 (suppl):** 141–51.

24. Healy D (interviewer). Mandel Cohen and the origins of the Diagnostic and Statistical Manual of Mental disorders, third editon: DSM-III. *Hist Psychiat* 2002; **13:** 209–30 (see p. 213).

25. Ludwig AM. The psychiatrist as physician. *JAMA* 1975; **234:** 603–4.

26. Guze SB. *Why psychiatry is a branch of medicine.* New York: Oxford University Press; 1992.

27. Double D. The limits of psychiatry. *BMJ* 2002; **324:** 900–4 (quote p. 903).

28. Healy D. *The creation of psychopharmacology.* Cambridge, Massachusetts: Harvard University Press; 2002.

29. Engel GL. From biomedical to biopsychosocial: being scientific in the human domain. *Psychosomatics* 1997; **38:** 521–8.

## Discussion

*White:* It is interesting that in describing the history of the biopsychosocial (BPS) approach you see it, as did Engel apparently, as being very as much an either/or situation. Did any of the earlier proponents of the BPS approach see it differently, as an evolution of the biomedical model into a BPS model?

*Shorter:* That is a thoughtful question. But the word 'evolution' is really the last word that would come to the lips of the proponents of the medical model, who see their own concept—that of medicalizing psychiatry—as progressive. What they absolutely do not want is for the medical model that has been gained for psychiatry at such cost (in the struggle against pyschoanalysis) to somehow be diluted with the inrush of psychoanalysis through the back door, to fuzzy-ize their profession all over again.

*Wessely:* You used that phrase 'medical model' frequently in your paper. As far as I can see, it is only ever used within psychiatry. The people who we might think are the proponents of the medical model don't seem to use the term.

*Shorter:* In North American psychiatry it is used as a positive term and not just as a term of opprobrium. This goes back to the influence of the St Louis school within American psychiatry and within biological psychiatry in particular. *DSM* comes partly out of the St Louis school. The people that worked so hard to put *DSM III* through against the resistance of the analysts within the American Psychiatric Association used the term 'medical model' with pride. People such as Gerry Klerman were happy to identify themselves with the medical model. It wasn't that they took up arms against the BPS model—in fact, they didn't use the term at all—but they were certainly taking up arms against the analysts.

*Wessely:* They probably wouldn't have noticed the emergence of the BPS model.

*Shorter:* I've never seen a reference to it in the writings of Robert Spitzer or Gerry Klerman.

*Wessely:* If you were giving a talk entitled 'The history of the medical model' as opposed to the BPS model, where would you root that? Who thought up that term and does anyone in medicine ever say, 'We are going to use the medical model'? I suspect it may only be used to describe what we are not doing in psychiatry, or should be doing in psychiatry.

*Shorter:* I don't know a good historical answer to that. It would be delicious to know if the term 'medical model' was used in psychiatry in the 1920s. The first reference I have seen to it is from 1942.

*Main:* I want to put to you a different type of BPS model, which comes from the pain and disability literature. This doesn't have its origins—except for some conceptual allegiance—to the very interesting thinking of Engel, but has really developed quite differently from the behavioural cognitive tradition. Here, the medical model is often used in the field of back pain to talk about the pathological biomechanical basis of the pain. This is a very different sort of model that is more empirically based. There is a sense in which it might be interesting as part of the next 2 days to talk about whether we have gone in a different direction in models of pain. By and large, we have left psychopathological models behind.

*Shorter:* In the pain field, is the term 'medical model' used pejoratively?

*Main:* No, it is used descriptively.

*Waddell:* It's the other way round: to the vast majority of clinicians the term BPS is pejorative.

*Elwyn:* There is a contrast here with general practice, which has taken the ideas of Engel and created patient-centred medicine. The ideas of Levenstein, MacWhinney, and Moira Stewart have been the basis of a teaching curriculum.[1] They use 'medical model' in exactly the same way as psychiatrists, in a pejorative fashion.

*Marmot:* If you think about the relationship between molecules and what goes on in the mind, most people would probably reject the idea of a 'ghost in the machine' and say that what takes place in the mind has a clear relation to molecules: it has a molecular underpinning. But then the assumption is that it presumably works the other way: mental representations of what goes on in the outside world affect molecules. When you described Engel's ideas, I wasn't clear about which he thought was more important: molecules influencing behaviour, or behaviour influencing molecules?

*Shorter:* He died 2 years ago; it would have been interesting to have heard his own response to that question. Perhaps Doug Drossman, who knew him, can explain his own views. My impression from Engel's writing is that he saw the traffic as going almost equally in both directions.

*Drossman:* That is exactly right. He told me that he wasn't competing with the concept of what he called the biomedical model, which encompassed reductionism and dualism and the idea there is an altered molecule that explains everything. He tried to embrace this model and suggested that this was an essential component of health care medicine and illness, but with this you have to bring in the influence of the social and psychological environment to the degree that that environment can also affect molecules. He was looking at this as an integrative kind of approach.

*Davey Smith:* I would like to try to think about why interest in the BPS model arose as it did. You talked about the late nineteenth century, when there clearly were antecedents of the BPS model in the USA and the UK. In the USA we can think of James Putnam's emphasis on 'not the disease only, but also the man'[2] and Oliver Wendell Holmes with his lovely descriptions of the inevitably male physician going to see a patient, where Holmes said he would rather the physician took his wife along, as she would understand the psychological and social reasons for sickness. All the male physician did, Holmes said, was prescribe tablets and collect the bills. Holmes famously suggested 'if all drugs were cast into the sea, it would be so much the better for man and so much the worse for the fish.'[3]

So what was going on? Perhaps the acceptance of the germ theory, although a triumph for understanding the cause of disease, was not a triumph for the image of clinical medicine. There weren't any effective treatments to deal with these infectious agents, which would encourage clinical nihilism and perhaps a concentration on issues other than somatic medicine.

Then we move forward to Engel's 1977 paper.[4] Although, as you pointed out, Engel had by this stage been writing for some 20 years, it was the 1977 paper that was the first to have any real influence. The way he presented it was that what he said applied to all of medicine and not just psychiatry. We should bear this in mind in our discussions and not just take the BPS model back into psychiatry, where many people in somatic medicine would be happy to see it go. In his *Science* paper, Engel contends that all medicine is in crisis and the reason for this is the adherence to a model of disease that is no longer adequate. Why did this 1977 paper resonate so clearly with its medical audience? The reason is that it appeared at a time when the therapeutic optimism that followed the introduction of antibiotics and safe surgery was receding, because the diseases that were now seen to be the leading causes of morbidity and mortality once infection had been 'conquered'—in particular coronary heart disease in men and breast cancer in women—were not responsive to treatment. Thomas McKeown had summarized 20 years of his work in two high-impact books in 1976 that seriously questioned the contribution of medicine to falling mortality rates during the nineteenth and twentieth centuries.[5,6] John Powles' 1973 article on 'The limitations of modern medicine' was also influential.[7] On the popular front, Ivan Illich's *Medical nemesis* was published around this time.[8]

Thus a view was emerging that medicine wasn't working any more, in terms of making people less sick and able to live longer.[5–8] Engel's article fell into this subcultural mood, perhaps not dissimilar to that at the end of the nineteenth century, and the rest is history.

One of the historical ironies is that if you step back and take a broader perspective, 1977 was precisely the time when—until then—understandable therapeutic nihilism should have started to wane. Look at the major killers of the time. Thrombolytics were being introduced to treat coronary heart disease and these had a substantial effect on increasing survival among people who had experienced heart attacks. Beta-blockers were also being introduced in post-myocardial infarction treatment. In the prevention field, blood pressure-lowering medications without serious side-effects were shown to reduce the risk of coronary heart disease and stroke by 30 per cent. For breast cancer, tamoxifen was introduced, which had a dramatic effect on survival. *Helicobacter pylori* was identified in 1983 and peptic ulcer—the classic BPS disease, but one for which cognitive behavioural therapy rather disturbingly had no effect—could now be cured. What is interesting is the continuing resonance of the BPS model, despite the fact that its basis in disillusion with therapeutic medicine should be shrinking. The historical reasons why people were initially interested in it started to disappear just as the model was introduced and when a new period of therapeutic optimism would have been an objective reading of the situation.

*Shorter:* I think that's an excellent résumé and I endorse your comments.

*Chalder:* Part of the problem of the BPS model is that it is so broad and non-specific to render it almost completely meaningless. It is theoretical and it doesn't lead us anywhere. What does the term 'psychological' mean here?

*Shorter:* It does lack a certain determinant quality in its broadness and yet others argue that this is precisely what medicine requires: a broadening of the focus, getting away from looking at the body as a sack of enzymes.

*Wessely:* In your paper, you firmly placed the emergence of the BPS model within the boundary disputes happening in psychiatry. You gave a pretty strong impression that Engel was a 'new Labour' modernizer of psychoanalysis. He was an analyst, but he was repackaging it for the period. He thought that the old Alexander-type thinking was clearly outdated and verging on the ludicrous. Medicine had already moved on and perhaps the model's lack of influence in medicine as opposed to psychiatry was because of this. Have I summarized your argument correctly? You locate this within the internecine dispute within American psychiatry, trying to get rid of the analytic dragon.

*Shorter:* The BPS model was much more sympathetic to psychotherapy than the medical model. The medical model has struggled valiantly against analysis. Engel himself doesn't so much repudiate psychoanalysis as just sort of wander away from it.

*Wessely:* I'm suggesting that he didn't repudiate it at all, he just repackaged it.

*Shorter:* It is not that he reconceptualizes psychoanalysis. I think he simply loses interest in it.

*Drossman:* I don't think he was either refuting or reinforcing analysis as much as what he called a 'paradigm shift', which was moving it from the concept of linear causality to one of a systems approach. This is why it is such a complex research model because you are shifting from regression to path analysis. You are really having to look not so much at what is the aetiology, but the degree to which the biology, genetics, social environment, or the person's psyche might be impacting on their behaviour in the face of the illness. This is where I think the shift was: not a single cause, but a bunch of interacting systems.

*Wessely:* Is not George Davey Smith's point correct that the real paradigm shift has been the discovery of *H. pylori*?

*Drossman:* That is a great example of where the BPS might play a role. Prior to that we had some misinformation about personality style being predictive of these diseases. Now all of a sudden we find a biological organism that we can remove and then get rid of ulcers. The assumption is that the organism is necessary and sufficient for the expression of the disease, but this is not quite the case. Fifty per cent of people over the age of 60 harbour *H. pylori* but they don't all have the disease. This shifts us back into the environment or the host: what is it about the host that might lead to the clinical expression of the disease? Susan Levenstein has done some work looking at this and has showed that altered psychological states may be involved with the clinical expression of disease. The same is true for tuberculosis: lots of people can harbour the infection but the social environment may be what predicts the expression of the disease itself.

*Davey Smith:* The question then becomes one of why do some people get the disease and not other people. This is one obvious strand of the BPS model. Whether or not you look for psychological or social factors there, or at factors such as age of infection or coinfection, is an important issue for understanding disease aetiology. However, in terms of public health or overall population levels of well-being, this is not necessarily the right way to go. In fact, it can be misleading. If you look at people who have smoked 20 cigarettes a day since the age of 16, only around 15 per cent of them develop lung cancer. You could say that what is really interesting is why these 15 per cent develop lung cancer and you could look at the genetic or psychological factors predicting this. But the fact of the matter is that if no one smoked there would be virtually no lung cancer. It can be diversionary to start focusing on these individual-level factors. Exactly the same applies to peptic ulcer. If you look at Iceland and the UK, where good data exist for the reductions in peptic ulcer, these followed cohort-specific reductions in *H. pylori* infection. This is what is determining the level of disease in populations and if we are interested in improving the overall level of health this is what we should focus on.

*Sharpe:* Following on from that argument, psychological and social factors are self-evidently important because that is why people smoke and that is why they get lung cancer!

On another matter it was interesting that in your talk you focused quite rightly on Engel's role, in terms of turf disputes in psychiatry. Do you know anything about the role of psychologists within medicine? There is probably more resistance within psychiatry to bringing in psychology than there is from medicine. My experience of medicine, in both primary and secondary care, is that they are keen on psychology. Inter-disciplinary competition is not an issue seen. Therefore if we restrict this debate to the confines of psychiatry we miss part of the picture. What is the history of the role of psychology in relation to medicine?

*Shorter:* There is currently a huge turf war in the USA for the rights of psychologists to prescribe. The psychiatrists, the American Psychiatric Association, are resisting this with great bitterness. The psychologists are pressing towards this. Any traditional affiliation you think the psychologists might have had for psychotherapy to the exclusion of pills has vanished. American psychologists are being recruited to the medical model almost as firmly as American psychiatry has been recruited to that model. But this is an area with enormous resource implications and is much more a turf struggle than an intellectual struggle.

*Fitzpatrick:* As a GP I have an interesting experience of the *H. pylori* story. Its eradication in the indigenous white working class population has been very effective. Our Turkish and Bangladeshi immigrants all come back after their *H. pylori* treatment with a recurrence of symptoms. This is a familiar scenario in general practice. I also wanted to take issue with George's characterization of this historical trend. I don't think it is true that a new era of therapeutic optimism supplanted the 1970s period of doubt about medical progress, notwithstanding the advances that have taken place. What we had in the 1970s was essentially a radical critique. It was also largely confined to the medical world itself. What happened in the 1980s was a generalization of doubt. Even though the scientific biomedical advances occurred, there was a generalization of doubt about the scope of biomedicine, which afflicted both the medical profession and increasingly the general public. Through the 1980s there was a growing loss of confidence in medicine across the board and this had widespread consequences, including an uptake of the BPS model at all sorts of levels. This included the government at one level as a stick to beat the whole of the medical world. It also included general practice: it reorganized in the 1980s in Britain around two things—Michael Balint and the pyschoanalytic input, and radical epidemiology. In many ways these were explicitly derived from the BPS model. At the same time, moving in parallel with this there has been a growing scepticism in the general public about psychiatry.

*Davey Smith:* I don't disagree with any of that. I didn't say that a new era of therapeutic optimism supplanted the 1970s period of doubt, I said that rationally it should have done so. It is ironic that the BPS model came to prominence in 1977 just as treatment started to improve. What is remarkable within my discipline, public health, is the number of people who carry on quoting McKeown as showing that medicine has no influence on population health. The irony is the ideas spread at the time when much of the material basis for those ideas was disappearing.

*Lorig:* There is another trend that is a little broader than all of this. In the 1960s and early 1970s we started to see that the major cause of illness and death was chronic illness as opposed to acute. Engel came out of the acute illness medical model and saw this transition to the chronic. Chronic disease, by its definition, is not curable. Therefore there are medical interventions to assist with the disease, but you also have a large portion of the population that has quality of life issues which to a great extent are what the psychosocial piece of that attached to. There are also a large number of people in the population who are depressed going along with their chronic illness not as a pathological illness. As we look at these models and what happened historically we have to look at them in the chronic/acute context.

*Salmon:* I'm struck that BPS language and thinking have been embraced by many disciplines with no particular link to Engel. In many cases this has been part of an increasing scope and power of those disciplines. Medical education has increased tremendously in scope, for example, by including these ideas. There seem to be two strands in what you are saying about the popularity of the BPS model. One is to see Engel as setting up an intellectual hare running: it's a scientific issue—people cite his articles because there were important scientific issues in them. The other current in what you are saying is that it is about 'turf' or power and if Engel hadn't written that we would have found something else to cite to substantiate the claims to 'turf' that we want to make. I suppose it is back to the two views of history. Is it about individuals doing things, or is it about political factors?

*Shorter:* Are there great men who shape history, or are there unopposable currents that sweep us all along? I think the latter. Engel was made by his times and he just happened to hit on a catchy phrase for concepts that had been articulated in medicine for a long time.

## References

1. Stewart M, Brown JB, Weston WW, McWhinney IR, McWilliam CL, Freeman TR. *Patient-centred medicine: transforming the clinical method.* Thousands Oaks, California: Sage; 1995.

2. Putnam JJ. Not the disease only, but also the man. *Boston Med Surg J* 1899; **141**: 53–7.

3. Quoted in Shryock RH. *The development of modern medicine.* Philadelphia: University of Philadelphia Press; 1936.

4.  Engel GL. The need for a new medical model: a challenge to biomedicine. *Science* 1977; **196:** 129–36.

5.  Mckeown T. *The modern rise of population.* New York: Academic Press; 1976.

6.  Mckeown T. *The role of medicine.* Oxford: Nuffield Foundation; 1976.

7.  Powles J. On the limitations of modern medicine. *Science Med Man* 1973; **1:** 1–30.

8.  Illich I. *Medical nemesis: the expropriation of health.* London: Penguin; 1977.

# 2 The theoretical basis of the biopsychosocial model

Helge Malmgren

## Summary

This chapter addresses the philosophy behind the biopsychosocial model, moving it on from George Engel's original description. I start by summarizing five aetiological problems that the biopsychosocial model must address, with a focus on the core issue of the relationship between mind and body (the mind–body problem). To understand this, I first define consciousness (awareness) in three dimensions: cognitive, experiential, and functional. I go on to consider the nature of the unconscious and then address the mind–body problem, suggesting that a consideration of the relationship between computer software and hardware is a useful analogy. Both are necessary to describe and understand the workings of a computer, even though without the hardware no software would function. Similarly descriptions and measures of both mind and body are necessary in order to understand human beings, even though the mind is 'supervenient', or completely dependent on the brain. We are fortunate in the study of humans to be able to use information from first-, second-, and third-person perspectives. All are necessary for a complete understanding.

## Introduction

I have been asked to speak about the theoretical basis of the biopsychosocial model. This topic can be interpreted in two different ways: either narrowly as the theoretical basis of Engel's actual model,[1–3] or more broadly as the theoretical issues involved in any similar approach trying to integrate biological, psychological, and social factors, especially in the field of so-called psychosomatic illnesses.

There are several reasons why I have chosen the broader approach. One is that an explicit biopsychosocial approach is not particularly common among people working with psychosomatic issues. Two alternative theoretical frameworks are stress theory (Selye) and coping theory (Lazarus). In a recent Medline search, I found 1200 references using the term 'biopsychosocial' but 7500 with 'psychosomatic', 50 000 with 'coping', and no less than 204 000 with the term 'stress'. A combined search for 'psychosomatic and coping' delivered 550 references but 'psychosomatic and biopsychosocial' only 50. There is likely to be a lot of biopsychosocial thinking going on in psychosomatics outside the 50 papers that explicitly use Engel's framework.

## The systems perspective and 'linear' models

Another reason why I chose the broader perspective is that Engel's own model can be criticized in several ways from a philosophical viewpoint. Inspired by *General system theory*,[4] Engel conceptualizes nature as a hierarchy of systems, but he does not go into any detail about the interactions between systems at different levels. He does not explain what really happens when, for example, there is an interaction between the personal and the social level, or the biochemical and the personal level. Also, I think that Engel's attack on 'linear causal models' in traditional biomedical thinking is at least partly misguided. It is true that representatives of the medical sciences sometimes imply that a symptom or a disease has a single cause; too much unicausal thinking is inherent in this (cf. the *Helicobacter* example below). Usually, however, talk about 'the cause of disease X' presupposes a whole field of background factors that are taken for granted, so use of such phrases cannot be taken as proof of unicausal thinking. One must not forget that at least since the days of Claude Bernard,[5] biologists and physicians have been used to thinking in terms of complex causal systems. It is too simplistic to suggest that mainstream biomedical researchers—for example, cell biologists or geneticists—usually think 'linearly' (in the sense of using unicausal models). In quite a different sense, linear thinking can truly be said to be the paradigm of much medical research today, namely, in the sense of linear statistical models (as opposed to nonlinear ones). However, linearity in this sense (which is compatible with a multivariate, systems approach) was certainly not Engel's primary concern.

My most important objection to Engel's model, however, is that it does not attempt to give a detailed account of mind–body relations. Common sense tells us that mental events and processes can influence bodily ones and vice versa. However, there are philosophical arguments against the possibility of such an interaction and these arguments have to be carefully analysed. Without a proper understanding of the role of mind and consciousness in the genesis and shaping of somatic events and processes, one cannot adequately address psychosomatic issues. And it is not sufficient for such an understanding that one thinks in terms of layered systems and multifactorial causality, because deeper philosophical issues are involved. McLaren even goes as far as saying that Engel's model is not a model at all as it only formulates the *need* for understanding the influence of non-biological factors on biological ones, without contributing to that understanding.[6]

## Five core issues

So, this chapter will address the general methodological problems involved in the biopsychosocial model and the emphasis will be on mind–body interactions and consciousness. It is important in this context to keep a number of issues that are often confused apart. These include

(1)  genetic versus environmental influences ('nature versus nurture');

(2)  single-factor versus multifactor causality;

(3)  somatic versus mental causes (the core mind–body problem);

(4)  reasons versus causes;

(5)  conscious versus non-conscious influences.

All these issues are relevant to the biopsychosocial model and conceptual mistakes on each point may be deleterious. For example, a simplistic single-factor concept of causation (2) seems to have led many to take the discovery of the essential role of *Helicobacter pylori* as showing that peptic ulcer is not in any sense a psychosomatic disease; however, because not everybody with a *Helicobacter* infection develops an ulcer, there is an obvious place for psychosocial factors as possibly contributing or even necessary causes.[7] But although each point on the list above is important, it is at least equally important to keep them apart in the discussion.

As already mentioned, although (2) (single versus complex causality) is very important in the biopsychosocial model, one cannot solve the core mind–body problem (3) by means of the concept of multifactorial causality. Saying that a mental factor is a *partial* cause of a somatic disorder carries with it exactly the same philosophical problems as saying that it is a *complete* cause (more about this point below).

Most importantly, the nature–nurture controversy (1) is distinct from the core mind–body problem (3). Of course many environmental influences are not mental in nature at all. Conversely, it is also conceivable that a psychological character trait, while being a contributing cause of a certain somatic disorder, is not due to environmental influences but belongs to the genetically determined constitution of the individual.

Concerning (4) (reasons versus causes), some philosophers and psychiatrists champion the idea that one should regard mental events and states as *reasons for actions*, rather than as *causes of behaviour*. There may be some truth in this idea (in certain contexts), but it cannot solve the basic theoretical problems of psychosomatic medicine. We have to find some way to accommodate the possibility that mental factors can actually *change* the course of somatic processes, that they are not *only* reasons, but actually causes. We want to discuss not only the eventuality that mental stress may give a person a *reason* to be ill, but also the possibility that mental stress (in combination with other factors) may *lead to* illness and disease.

Finally, one must reckon with the possibility that not all mental factors that influence the course of a disease are conscious. Hence one has to distinguish clearly between (3) and (5). To better see the relevance of this remark, let us dwell on the concept of consciousness for a while (for an alternative way of characterizing consciousness, compare Searle's perspective on the mind–body problem, which is essentially the same as mine although there are many differences of emphasis and of terminology).[8]

## The nature of consciousness

In English there are two terms—'conscious' and 'aware'—that correspond to only one term in German ('bewusst') and in Swedish ('medveten'). The use of these words and their immediate derivatives covers three different dimensions, which we may call the *cognitive*, the *experiential* (or *phenomenal*), and the *functional* dimensions.

### Cognitive awareness

If you say that someone is aware of a certain fact, for example, that they are aware that Fermat's last theorem has now been proved, you probably use the term in a purely cognitive sense. What you mean to say is that the person in question *knows* the fact in question and knowledge of a fact does not entail any kind of present experience. All the time, we have a lot of knowledge that is not reflected in present experience. For example, a minute ago you (the reader) knew that $2 + 2 = 4$, but did you then have a specific *experience* related to this mathematical knowledge? Most probably not. So, were you not *aware* of the fact that $2 + 2 = 4$? Yes, in the cognitive sense of 'aware', you were! (Try to say to yourself, 'no, I was not aware that $2 + 2 = 4$.') Similarly, we can say of a person who seems to be sleeping dreamlessly that because they have set the alarm, they are obviously *aware* that they have to get up early the next day.

In Swedish and German, the terms 'bewusst' and 'medveten' can be used in the purely cognitive sense. And as we have just seen, one may use the English 'aware' in this way. I do not know for sure, however, how the English word 'conscious' behaves in this respect. Is it correct to say that an hour ago, you were *conscious* of the fact that $2 + 2 = 4$ (just because you *knew* it then and even if you did not *think* of it)? I have to leave this question to the reader's linguistic intuition.

## Experiential or phenomenal consciousness

The experiential or phenomenal dimension of consciousness is exemplified by having an intense tooth pain or by hearing the sound of a trumpet. These events entail that you actually have specific experiences different from those that you had when not being in pain and before hearing the trumpet. Another pertinent set of examples is given by the recall of stored memories. At any point of time, most of our memories are *not* conscious in the experiential sense. Recall of an episodic memory means that one becomes *experientially* conscious of an earlier event that one otherwise only *knew* to have occurred.

The nature of experiential, or phenomenal, consciousness is a matter of intense philosophical controversy these days and my account of it has been deliberately simplified. A more careful analysis would probably reveal that it has several different components. For the purpose of this chapter the most important thing is that you understand that it is not the same thing as cognitive awareness.

## Functional consciousness

Consciousness may have yet another dimension, the functional one: consciousness as a set of *capabilities* or *dispositions* (to be in certain states). If you look at the psychiatric uses of the term 'consciousness', they nearly always refer to such capacities and dispositions. When a psychiatrist says that a delirious person suffers from a 'disturbance of consciousness', they refer not only to changes in the actual contents of his cognitive system or his experience, but also (and primarily) to changes in the patient's mental capabilities and dispositions. The delirious patient does not only lack certain knowledge (for example, of time and temporal relations) and does not only have unusual experiences, but it is also the case that these abnormal mental contents are due to the fact that their mental *capabilities* for knowing the environment and experiencing it in a proper way are disturbed. This is the functional level of consciousness (it is of interest to note that Freud used 'consciousness' in a similar, functional sense in his early writings, but in later writings prefers the term 'ego' for the set of mental functions that he previously referred to as 'consciousness in the systematic sense').[9] If you look at phenomenologically oriented European psychiatry, you can find broad functional uses of 'consciousness' with the consequence that, for example, depression and mania are classified as 'disturbances of consciousness'.[10]

## Mind, consciousness, and the unconscious

It is important to appreciate that in *none* of these senses of consciousness—except perhaps in some unusual global–functional sense that some phenomenological psychiatrists might have given to the term—does consciousness equal *mind*. A lot of terms both in psychology and in everyday language refer to mental states or traits, for example, to kindness, aggressiveness, and stubbornness, which are in themselves neither cognitive nor experiential, nor dispositions to certain cognitions or experiences. However, these states or traits are of course *causally relevant* to cognition and experience. Aggressiveness, for example, tends to give rise to experienced anger.

Then we must consider the Freudian unconscious, which is yet another thing. So far we have distinguished three aspects of consciousness: the cognitive, the experiential, and the functional aspects. To understand what one could mean by an *unconscious mental state*, we also have to note another kind of ambiguity in the expression, 'X is a conscious mental state'. This expression can refer to the fact that X is itself a state of consciousness, in any of the three possible senses. But it can also mean, and usually means, that the person who is in mental state X is also conscious *of* X, or of the fact that they are in X. Indeed, when Freud (in his later writings) speaks about *un*conscious mental states and processes, he is primarily referring to the absence of such 'meta-consciousness'. He discusses its nature at length but here I will only mention the simplest interpretation in which the meta-consciousness is taken in the cognitive sense, that is, an unconscious mental state is one that the owner does not *know* about (is not aware of). Not only Freudians but also several modern cognitive psychologists believe that there are many unconscious mental states in this sense.[11]

Hence, the concept of mind is in *several* ways wider than the concept of consciousness, which in turn is wider than the concept of *experiential* (phenomenal) consciousness. This means that the problem of how experiential consciousness relates to the brain is only a special case of the more general mind–body problem. But it is the most interesting and problematic case. How can pain, experienced anger, or the conscious hearing of a sound be caused by electrochemical processes in the brain and how can these experiences cause events in the body? We will now discuss the core mind–body problem in the abstract, without specifying which kind of 'mental' processes we are talking about. But to make the argument more concrete and easy to follow, you are of course allowed to think of the mental in terms of phenomenal consciousness.

## The core mind–body problem

The basic mind–body problem can be summarized as follows: if every event has a sufficient physical cause, then there is no room for intervening in the course of events by non-physical means. Here is a more complete formulation. Suppose, for the sake of the argument, that

(1) mental events and processes are not identical to any physical or chemical events or processes.

Most of us would probably agree that

(2) all bodily events obey the laws of physics and chemistry and are therefore completely determined by earlier physico-chemical events (quantum effects apart).

The last premiss can also be stated as follows:

(3) for every bodily occurrence there is a set of earlier physico-chemical events, which together act as its sufficient cause (again not counting quantum mechanical effects).

It seems to follow from (1) and (2) that

(4) mental events cannot change the predetermined course of physical events and hence cannot make any difference to the course of events in the body

and thus

(5) mental events cannot even be contributory causes to bodily events.

Summarizing the problem so far, how can the mind possibly contribute to the occurrence of bodily events, if the latter already have non-mental events as sufficient causes? However, the mind–body problem has an even wider scope because a very similar argument seems to entail that *mental events cannot even cause other mental events*. Let us add a postulate that is believed by most psychiatrists and psychologists today, usually called the *supervenience postulate* by philosophers of mind (Kim gives a very careful discussion of the concept of supervenience[12]):

(6) all mental events are completely determined by simultaneous physical and chemical events in the brain.

From (3) above it follows that

(7) all mental events are completely determined by earlier physicochemical events.

It now seems to follow that

(8) mental events cannot make any difference to the course of other mental events

and

(9) mental events cannot even be contributory causes, even to other mental events.

In short, if all mental events are completely determined by earlier non-mental factors, how can they even be partially caused by mental factors?

It seems that if we do not want to accept that there are no mental causes, then we are caught in a dilemma. Either we have to take recourse to quantum gaps in the physical system, or we have to regard the mental and the physical as in some sense *identical*, that is, we must deny premiss (1). However, both horns of the dilemma may seem unattractive. Personally, I find it difficult to take the quantum solution seriously (which does not mean that I do not take quantum physics seriously). So I will say no more about the first horn of the dilemma.

## A computer analogy

Do we then have to say that mental events are identical to bodily events? Is my experience of pain really the same as an excitatory pattern in my somatosensory cortex? To elucidate this question, the parallel between on the one hand *human body and mind* and on the other hand *computer hardware and software*, is very apt. Please do not take this to mean that the mind is to the body *exactly* as software is to hardware! But consider the following argument about computers and note the parallel with the body–mind issue above.

(a) Software states of a computer are not identical to hardware states.

(b) All hardware states in the computer obey the laws of physics.

Hence,

(c) every hardware state in the computer is completely determined by earlier hardware states of the computer and its input device (not counting quantum effects).

Hence,

(d) software events cannot make any difference to the course of hardware events in the computer.

If we then add the supervenience postulate for computers,

(e) which software state a computer is in at a certain time is completely determined by its simultaneous hardware state,

it seems to follow that

(f) software states in the computer cannot make any difference to later software states either.

Conclusions (d) and (f) correspond to our conclusions (6) and (9) concerning the mind–body problem, but are even more obviously false than these. How can the paradox be resolved in the case of the computer? Here it is quite clear that the quantum solution does not offer any hope of success. On the other hand it is perhaps not so intuitively implausible to suppose that software and hardware states are in some sense identical. Let us dwell upon the latter possibility for a while.

To describe a computer as following the routines of a certain programme is to give a *functional* description of it. It is to give a description of the computer from the perspective of the job that it presently does, such as *adding* (while doing a calculation) or *deleting a word* (while word processing). We surely all believe that the computer follows its programme by being in a certain electronic state, or sequence of states. However, saying that it follows its programme is *not* to give a description of such an electronic state or sequence. You may compare the description of a computer doing word processing with describing a household device as a vacuum cleaner. To describe it so is to say that it is a device that can clean your home using a vacuum pump. It does not say anything about the kind of motor or the specific design of the pump.

On the other hand, it is understood by everybody that a vacuum cleaner does its job according to physical principles, using *some* kind of motor and *some* kind of pump system. The physical make-up that makes a certain vacuum cleaner actually perform its function is called the *realization* of that function. Similarly, the hardware transition that makes a certain computer perform a certain software operation is called the *realization* of the software operation (in this computer at this time). Now, the same job on a functional level can be done in many different ways in hardware. This is called *multiple realizability*. Spell checking can be done in many different ways on the hardware level on an ordinary computer, just as *adding* can certainly be done by many different kinds of computers (which need not even be electronic in character) and just as vacuum cleaning can in principle be done using electric motors, combustion engines, hand-driven pumps or nuclear power.

From this account, it emerges clearly in which sense a software state is or is not identical with a hardware state. The operation of *adding* is identical with the underlying hardware process in the adding machine in the sense that the latter realizes the former—*the hardware process is the way this machine adds.* Adding is therefore *supervenient* on the hardware process, or in other words completely dependent on the latter. It is however not *conceptually* identical with the hardware process. In other words, saying 'the machine adds' does not have the same *meaning* as any description of the specific hardware process by means of which the present computer adds. Saying that it adds actually leaves the issue completely open as to whether it adds using the one process or the other, just like describing something as a vacuum cleaner leaves the issue open as to how the vacuum cleaning function is realized.

On the other hand, just like vacuum cleaning cannot be done by *any* machine, not *any* hardware state or process can realize a given software state or process. Software operations constrain the range of possible underlying hardware operations. For example, adding two numbers can only be done by means of hardware processes that are such that if their beginning state realizes a representation of the two numbers, then their end state realizes the representation of their sum.

## An integration

To sum up the last three sections: software is realized in hardware, it is multiply realized and it constrains the hardware, but software and hardware descriptions are conceptually independent. Now note that as a consequence of this conceptual independence, *we do not have to know how to describe the hardware in order to be able to recognize, manipulate, and make use of software states.* We can easily find out which software state a computer is in by hitting some keys, moving and clicking the mouse, and looking at the display or the printout. In this way we can know a lot about the workings of different programmes without having any idea of how they are realized on the hardware level. And when the software does not work as expected, we certainly do not immediately go to hardware diagnosis in order to fix the problem, but first do our best to find the cause in the software or our handling of it. Well, how can there be causes in the software, if physics is a closed system? *Because the software process has a physical, hardware realization.* Speaking of software causation is therefore a roundabout way of speaking about hardware causation—and it is a *necessary roundabout* when we do not know which the relevant hardware states are (as we usually do not).

There is a thesis in the philosophy of mind called 'functionalism' (not to be confused with functional concepts of consciousness as defined above). This is a philosophy that accepts a far-reaching parallelism between humans and computers and considers *all* mental states as similar to software states in the computer. There are strong arguments against functionalism, especially when we look at experiential states such as pain. Pain is not (or at least *not only*) a functional state; to say that a pain is sharp rather than dull is to describe it from a phenomenal, not a functional perspective. Yet the parallel between computers and humans is valid in the sense that just as software is supervenient on hardware and there is multiple realizability of software in hardware, mental states are most probably supervenient on brain states and multiply realized in the latter. In neither case is the one kind of description equivalent to the other kind; there is a *conceptual independence* between the *ontologically dependent* levels. And that is why we have to speak about mental causation. In one sense, the real causal processes go on at the physical level. But we can only describe these processes through the mental processes that they realize.

## First-, second-, and third-person perspectives

The existence of different conceptual systems to describe people is closely related to the fact that there are several different ways of knowing a person. In psychology, psychiatry, and medicine, as well as in everyday encounters with our fellow people, at least *three* different modes of knowledge are at play, which lead to at least *two* and maybe *three* distinct conceptual systems. First, there is direct self-knowledge or introspection, 'the first-person perspective', that is, when we study our own pain, after-images, or thinking. Second, there is objective knowledge about people, 'the third-person perspective'. This is when we look at magnetic resonance images of the human brain, for example. Third, there is another kind of knowledge that cannot be reduced to the other two categories, which is the knowledge we get from talking to people, looking at them, and assessing them in a personal encounter—I call this 'the second person perspective'.

These three modes of knowledge typically do not all provide information about the same state. For example, if you ask yourself what you are thinking of, you may come up with an answer like 'the number 3'. If you tell this to a friend, they will know from your testimony which cognitive state you are in. So it seems that the first- and second-person perspectives can lead to knowledge about the same cognitive state. In contrast, this state—thinking of the number 3—cannot be singled out by means of investigations using *only* the third-person perspective—not today, not in a thousand years. Of course you may one day be able to gather the content of a person's thought by using some future form of brain scanning. But it is important to understand that using the brain scanner *alone* will never suffice. To know that a certain signal from the future brain scanner means thinking of 3, you must first have sought a correlation between what the scanner says *and what the patient says* (or do you expect the output screen from the scanner suddenly to show a big '3' instead of the usual brain tissue?). So, the element of self-report is essential after all, which shows that first-person descriptions cannot be reduced to third-person descriptions.

## Are the first- and second-person perspectives the same?

The question whether the first- and second-person perspectives generate the same conceptual systems is an interesting one, which I would like to tentatively answer in the negative. One case in point is observing unconscious intentions. To take a less controversial example, it happens that you interview a patient and come to a distinct conclusion that this individual is depressed, although the patient him- or herself does not feel depressed. The more-or-less permanent tendency to lowered mood that we call depression is not always introspectively accessible (compare 'your friends always know you better than you yourself do'). However, I do not want to press home this point because the important message of this chapter is that you cannot know from the unaided *third-person* perspective that a person has a depression or that they feel depressed right now.

## Do we need the first- and second-person perspectives?

You may object that even if my argument shows that several independent conceptual systems to describe people are available to us, it does not show that we cannot do without all except one of them. Specifically, you may say, I have not shown that medicine and psychosomatics cannot do without the first- and second-person perspectives. To counter this I want to revert to the computer parallel once more. There are two reasons why we use functional descriptions of the computer and not only physical ones. First, we have computers because they fulfil certain functions, not because they have an interesting interior. Hence, without functional descriptions we could not even *talk* about the things that make us build and buy computers (such as adding or word processing). Similarly, without the psychological vocabulary we could not even speak about the primary concern of all of medicine: the patient's well-being (how does subjective quality of life look on the screen of the future brain scanner?).

Second, and equally important, is the fact that without using the software approach we could not predict and manipulate the behaviour of the computer nearly as well as we can. I challenge any computer expert, next time their computer is attacked by a virus, to find out by looking with physical methods at the electronic processes of the computer and *not using any software tool whatsoever* what the virus has done to their machine and how to best avoid damaging consequences of it. In the same vein, to make reliable predictions about human behaviour we need to access the human being from the psychological side. It is obvious to me that a neuroscientist skilled in brain imaging and biochemistry but ignorant of human communication will not be able to tell whether a certain patient will take their medications or not.

It is also quite probable that many other kinds of predictions—not about behaviour—are better made from a psychological standpoint than from a physical one. For example, the mechanisms which in combination with a *Helicobacter* infection lead to peptic ulcer may not be easily accessible for the physiologist, but more easily so for the psychologist or epidemiologist. This is no more mysterious than the fact that the computer hardware specialist sometimes has to cooperate with the software specialist to find out why the machine broke down. Perhaps they can find out by their own methods that the immediate cause of breakdown was that the fan stopped well before the processor did, but the cause of *this* may lay in a faulty algorithm for shutting down the computer—clearly a matter of software.

## Do I advance dualism?

It might be thought that my argument reintroduces Cartesian dualism. However, it does not, because Descartes' version of psychophysical inter-actionism presupposes both that the mental does *not* supervene on the physical and that the system of physical laws is *not* closed. But I am quite willing to call my position a kind of *conceptual dualism*. Indeed, different versions of conceptual dualism are today advanced by many philosophers, while the radical materialist position that mental concepts can be dispensed with is nowadays defended by few.

## A final consideration

There is one final detail that must be borne in mind when discussing these issues; it may not be very relevant for today's scientists, but will become more important as more and more is discovered about the neural basis of mind. The point is this: if you want to talk about *joint effects* of two factors, one mental and one physical, you have to take care that the one is not supervenient on the other. Because if they *are* so related, then you are in a sense talking about the same process twice. For example, you may say that a brain contusion together with a premorbid-sensitive disposition has led to paranoid decompensation. If you were a future brain scientist, you could possibly also describe this effect as a joint effect of the contusion and a certain neural process X (which, indeed, happens to be the process which realizes the sensitive disposition in this patient). The contusion and the disposition are independent entities; so are the contusion and process X. Similarly you can consistently say (although what you say may of course be false) that a chronic experience of stress together with a *H. pylori* infection has led to peptic ulcer in a certain case. The *H. pylori* infection is certainly not the neural realization of the chronic experience of stress; these are two independent factors that can interact. But now suppose, however implausibly, that the experience of stress has been found by a future neuroendocrinologist to be supervenient on the neurohormonal response Y to environmental stressors. Then you should *not* say that the bacterial infection, the neurohormonal response Y, *and* the experience of stress have *together* led to a peptic ulcer. Why? Because it would in effect be to count one thing for two in the explanation—just as if I said 'Lena, Helge, and I wrote this lecture together' without mentioning that I am Helge. The mistake we have made is that we have treated an experience and its physical realization as two ontologically independent factors.

## Conclusions

With these comments and examples I hope I have succeeded in making sense of causal talk in medicine and psychosomatics. The mystery surrounding mental causes in a closed physical universe disappears when we understand that although *realized* by physical processes, mental events and processes are *known* in a unique way. The concepts we have created to name these events and processes are therefore indispensable in our descriptions of the human being, including our *causal* descriptions.

The original model by Engel should be updated to include recent insights into the nature of mind–body relations and the possibilities of mind–body interactions. It should also be freed from its ties to general systems theory, which is not a bad theory, but does not add any power to the model. With these changes, the biopsychosocial model is philosophically uncontroversial. We can use different conceptual systems to describe our patient and we can mix factors from the different conceptual systems without giving up our belief that the brain is a biochemical and physical system and that the mind is determined solely by processes in the brain. Because the first-, second-, and third-person perspectives offer three distinct ways of decomposing reality and include the unique perspective of the patient, such an updated biopsychosocial model is of vital importance for the proper understanding, practice, and theoretical approaches to psychiatry, psychosomatics, and medicine in general.

## References

1. Engel GL. A unified concept of health and disease. *Perspect Biol Med* 1960; 3: 459–85.
2. Engel GL. The need for a new medical model: a challenge for biomedicine. *Science* 1977; 196: 129–36.
3. Engel GL. The clinical application of the biopsychosocial model. *Am J Psychiat* 1982; 137: 535–44.
4. Bertalanffy L. *General system theory.* New York: George Braziller; 1968.
5. Bernard C. *Introduction à l'étude de la médecine expérimentale.* Paris and New York: Baillière; 1865.
6. McLaren N. A critical review of the biopsychosocial model. *Austr NZ J Psychiat* 1998; 32: 86–92.
7. Levenstein S. The very model of a modern etiology: a biopsychosocial view of peptic ulcer. *Psychosom Med* 2000; 62: 176–85.
8. Searle JR. Consciousness. *Ann Rev Neurosci* 2000; 23: 557–78.
9. Freud S. The unconscious. In: *Collected papers, volume IV: papers on metapsychology.* London: Hogarth Press and Toronto: Clarke, Irwin & Co; 1925. pp. 98–136 (German original, Das unbewusste. *Int Zeitschr Ärtzliche Psychoanalyse* 1915; III).
10. Ey H. *La conscience.* 2nd edn. Paris: Desclée de Brouwer; 1968.

11. Kihlstrom J. The psychological unconscious and the self. In: Bock GL and Marsh J, eds. *Experimental and theoretical studies of consciousness (CIBA Foundation Symposium 174)*. Chichester: Wiley; 1993, pp. 147–55.

12. Kim J. *Philosophy of mind*. Boulder, Colorado: Westview Press; 1998.

## Discussion

*Wessely*: At the beginning of your paper you stated that a 'common sense' intuition is that mental factors matter. My impression was that all you thought of Engel's work is that this is simply another version of common sense intuition and that it lacked any methodological rigour or clarity. Is that right?

*Malmgren*: I didn't use 'common sense' in a pejorative way. George Edward Moore at Cambridge raised common sense to the standard of philosophy. If something is a common sense opinion and you can't come up with any good counter arguments, then it is probably true. And I haven't found any powerful arguments against the biopsychosocial (BPS) model in its crude formulation that mental and social events influence and interact with biological events. But Engel's ideas are not philosophically very deep. Specifically, he does not explain how such an interaction can take place, taking into account the laws of physics and chemistry. What was new in his approach compared with the common sense perspective is the systems theory approach, which does not solve the just-mentioned problem.

*Main*: One of the interesting themes raised in your talk has to do with the nature of explanations. If we think about what we are doing, in talking about the BPS model, we run into two problems. One concerns the nature of disease and illness. Historically the shift from disease to illness, from illness to aspects of illness, and then to coping with illness and disability has led to very different types of models being constructed. In terms of the nature of explanations, one of the difficulties that you highlighted is what are the rules by which we count an explanation as satisfactory? It is clear that quite often what happens is that people haven't articulated the rules. The philosophy of common sense actually precedes Moore and can be traced back ultimately to Arisotelian and Scholastic philosophy, and more recently to the nineteenth-century Scottish philosophy of common sense. Indeed common sense was not pejorative—it was to do with recognizing the primacy of experience, as opposed to the Kantian pre-ordained structures. Where I think we are getting into a bit of a muddle with the BPS model is that we have actually constructed several different BPS models. This is partly because a lot of the ideas were derived from models of illness that weren't working too well. We had physical disease models and we had psychiatric and mental disease models. Then we started to talk about illness in a sociological sense and we talked about managing it. Later, we began to look empirically at what things fitted together to make 'illness' as opposed to disease. In a sense, a lot of the problems that have emerged have been because of the use of different forms of explanation and different focus.

*Malmgren*: I agree. These shifts of focus complicate things. But I would like to emphasize that the BPS model should not be limited to explaining illness, as opposed to disease. We are talking about the possibility of mental factors causing real peptic ulcers and high blood pressures, not 'only' pain, suffering, and a lowered quality of life.

*Stansfeld*: Could you say more about the interactions between different levels? To me, this seems to be the crux of the problem. Presumably for stressors to be having an effect on biological processes in the brain, for example, you are suggesting that there is some external stimulus, or perhaps that one bit of the brain is influencing other bits of the brain. This could be the way that physical and chemical processes within the brain can be altered.

*Malmgren*: There are several different possibilities. But first note that I don't speak about an interaction between 'levels'. That was Engel's term, based on a hierarchy. I would describe what happens as interactions between differently conceptualized systems. Compare when you ask someone, 'Why isn't the floor clean?' One answer could be, 'I tried to clean it with the vacuum cleaner but there was a power cut.' This is a mix of explanatory 'levels' in Engel's sense. I wouldn't call these levels, though: is a vacuum cleaner at a higher level than electricity? The functional and the physical descriptions are simply conceptually independent.

To return to the substantive issue that you raise, I don't see any real problem because there are so many different possibilities for the brain to be affected by the environment. First of all, think of the ordinary sensory processes. Sensory experiences supervene on afferent neural processes and higher-order perceptual processing in the brain. Here we have one obvious basis for the influence of mental factors on the brain: the brain process on which experience supervenes. For example, suppose a memory is formed of an experience. Psychologists usually describe this as a psychological process: the modulation of memory by experience. But you could equally describe it as the modulation of memory by sensory processes, or as a modulation of the brain by experience. These descriptions are all correct.

*Marmot*: You mentioned that psychological processes and genetic predisposition could interact without one being supervenient to the other. When you gave the example of an infection (*Helicobacter pylori*) and psychological processes, you then said that it doesn't make sense to talk about them together. Could you clarify what you meant?

*Malmgren*: I said it doesn't make sense to talk about a psychological process and its underlying substrate interacting, because then you are in a sense talking about the same thing twice (although in different ways). It is like saying that the floor is clean because I have used a vacuum cleaner *and* have used an electric machine that works by sucking air. You cannot look at these as partial causes, because the vacuum cleaning process is supervenient on the workings of the electric machine and suction pump. One could express the same point by saying that since the electric machine is the physical realization of a vacuum cleaner, they are not really two things.

*Marmot:* I still don't follow this. You gave the example of gene–environment interaction. Let's assume that our brains got to be the way they are by the long-term impact of the environment on evolution. We then have these structures in our heads and this is the substrate. But doesn't it still make sense to talk about the impact of the psychological or social on that substrate.

*Malmgren:* You are using the word 'substrate' in a more general sense here. When I say 'substrate' I mean the underlying neural substrate or realization of the very psychological process which we want to talk about as having an impact. Think of the following shocking experience: you come home and see your house on fire. Suppose that you know a neurophysiologist who has studied the brain physiology of shocking experiences and that you discuss the event with them afterwards. They tell you exactly what state $S$ of your brain was the underlying substrate or realization of this shocking experience (this is science fiction, of course). Also suppose that your shocking experience *together* with your pre-existing knowledge that you had no insurance were bad for your mood. You can alternatively frame this in terms of physiology and say that the state $S$, which the neurophysiologist specifies as the substrate of your shocking experience, together with the substrate $S'$ of your earlier knowledge about your lack of insurance, gave rise to a new process $S''$ in the brain on which the mood change supervenes. But what you should *not* say is that the shocking experience *together* with the neurophysiological process $S$ underlying the same experience produced a certain response. Then you would again be considering a factor together with itself.

*Wessely:* I don't know if it is possible to sum up what we have discussed so far, but I'll try. We began by seeing Engel in his appropriate historical perspective, from within the problems in psychiatry and the crisis in confidence in medicine. Yet it remains a source of some contention within psychiatry. In a little aside, that we will come back to, we have heard how little influence this has in medicine. We have also heard the philosophical rationale for mind–body interactions and that there are no serious philosophical objections to the BPS model, if properly updated.

# 3 Remediable or preventable social factors in the aetiology and prognosis of medical disorders

## Michael Marmot

## Summary

This chapter will review the role of social factors in disease incidence. I will show data suggesting that social gradients affect differences in morbidity and mortality and that these change with time. I will argue that this relationship is not due to confounding factors or other methodological errors. Although consequent health risk behaviours, such as smoking, help to mediate this effect, work-related stressors have an independent effect. Non-human primate studies suggest that the relationship between social position and health may be causal in different ways in both sexes.

## Introduction

Inquiries into social and psychological influences on medical disorders have attracted their share of controversy. In particular, the field of health inequalities has been marked by turf wars. Some, but not all, of this controversy can be attributed to differences in disciplinary perspectives. When I started tentative wanderings beyond my discipline of epidemiology, psychologists would commonly introduce themselves by explaining that their core concern was with individual differences. This jarred with the approach that I thought I was taking. By investigating social factors in the aetiology of medical disorders, I am interested in differences that arise from the social environment and which by their very nature are likely to play out as group differences. A perspective that focuses solely on individual differences may well miss these important differences.

This contrast between individual and group differences raises tension with other parts of medicine. For instance, a geneticist might be interested in knowing whether an individual with a particular genetic profile will live longer than an individual with a different profile; interesting question. A different question is why Russian men have had a recent decline in life expectancy of some 7 years.[1] The point is that the question of individual differences, which relates to genetic profile, is quite different to the social one. The answer to the first question of individual differences may shed little light on why Russian mortality rates increased when those in Western Europe decreased.

Continuing my cross-disciplinary wanderings, I talked to economists. Not only are economists interested in individual difference but, for many, their real interest is how people's robustness—their level of health—determines their economic fortunes. For many economists, health is an input into economic status and robust people end up higher up in the hierarchy. This is endogeneity; health determines social position, so there is no problem of social causation of illness to sort out. The first thing to understand in talking to people from these different disciplines is that they are looking at the same data with different mindsets—different language, concepts, and causal structures. Until this is sorted out, you cannot have a conversation.

That there is a social gradient in health and disease is beyond dispute from any perspective. From the original Whitehall study of coronary heart disease (CHD) mortality of civil servants, we did a 25-year follow-up of men according to their level in the hierarchy: administrators, professionals/executives, clerical officers, and office support grades. The lower the status in the hierarchy, the higher the mortality.[2] This is a social gradient. We do not have the poorest people in this study, because we are looking at people in stable employment, so it is not just that the poorest have worse health status than the rich. We do not have the richest people in this study either, because these are civil servants. If we adjust for age, smoking, systolic blood pressure, plasma cholesterol concentration, height, and blood sugar, we still see this social gradient.

## Social gradients can and do change

In searching for causes of the social gradient, the first thing we must note is that social gradients in health can change. If the effects of the social gradient we see in the Whitehall study were all to be caused by genetic profile—if high-grade civil servants are genetically predisposed to both good health and achieving high social position and clerical officers are predisposed to be clerical officers and in worse health—then the social gradient would be fixed. But it is not; it can change. Data on life expectancy in England and Wales from the period 1972–1976 show that for men in the top and bottom social classes (I and V) the gap in mortality was 5.5 years. In contrast, from 1992 to 1996, while life expectancy has increased for social class I by 5.7 years, in this same

**Table 3.1** Life expectancy by social class and the difference between social classes I and V in England and Wales

| | Men | | | Women | | |
|---|---|---|---|---|---|---|
| | Social class I | Social class V | Difference (years) | Social class I | Social class V | Difference (years) |
| 1972–1975 | 72 | 66.5 | 5.5 | 79.2 | 73.9 | 5.3 |
| 1992–1996 | 77.7 | 68.2 | 9.5 | 83.4 | 77 | 6.4 |

Data from the Office for National Statistics (ONS) Longitudinal Study.

period it only increased by 1.7 years for social class V. So the gap is now 9.5 years (see Table 3.1).[3] This is quite a difference; if we abolished heart disease we would add somewhat less than 4 years to life expectancy. There are recent data from the Office for National Statistics Longitudinal Study which suggest that this gap may be narrowing slightly again.[4] For women the gap has also widened, although not as much as for men.

## Is the relation of social position to mortality general or specific?

One of the questions debated in this field is whether the relation between where you are in the hierarchy and disease is general or specific.[5] The answer is, of course, that it is both. It is a remarkably general finding that people in low social positions have higher mortality rates than people in higher positions. The specific diseases that contribute to that excess are, to some extent,

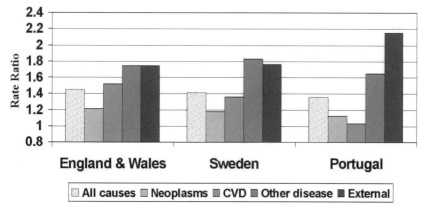

**Fig. 3.1** Mortality rate ratio comparing manual classes with non-manual classes for all causes and specific causes of death in men aged 45–59. Adapted from Reference 6. CVD, cardiovascular disease.

contingent on the prevailing major causes of death. For example, Kunst and colleagues have compared manual versus non-manual workers in England and Wales and other countries (Fig. 3.1). For men aged 45–59, all-cause mortality is 40 per cent higher in the manual than the non-manual workers.[6] The excess mortality applies to a whole range of causes. The magnitude of that excess differs by cause and by country. In England and Wales the excess mortality among manual workers for neoplasms is less than average, the excess for 'other' diseases and external causes of death is higher, and the excess for cardiovascular disease is rather similar to that for all causes.

The picture in Sweden is similar to that in England and Wales. It differs in Portugal. Interestingly, there is no excess in cardiovascular disease in manual workers. Going back to England and Wales earlier in the twentieth century we see a similar picture. Osler described heart disease as being more common in his rich patients[7] and the data bear this out. One way we can understand what is happening here is by looking at age (Fig. 3.2). Comparisons of ischaemic heart disease mortality in Italy and Portugal show that among older people, rates are highest in the non-manual categories.[8] By contrast, in the youngest age group manual workers have a higher rate of heart disease than non-manual workers. Data from southern Italy show that higher-status people have higher rates of heart disease than lower-status people; a picture reversed in northern Italy.[9] This is consistent with a cohort effect: in the older cohort, the spectrum of causes responsible for population rates of heart disease is more common in higher-status people; the younger people are in the cohort where

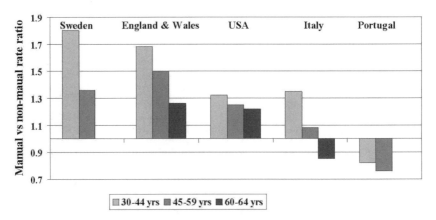

**Fig. 3.2** Ischaemic heart disease mortality rate ratios comparing manual classes with non-manual classes among men aged 30–44, 45–59, and 60–64 years at death. Adapted from Reference 8. E&W, England and Wales.

it is more common in lower-status individuals, as it is in the USA, England and Wales, and Sweden.

Where does that leave us? Is the relationship between social position and disease general or specific? Of course, we have to look for specific factors. Why does the social distribution of heart disease change? It changes because of change in specific factors. Lung cancer is caused overwhelmingly by smoking. Its social distribution will be importantly driven by whether smoking is closely related to social position. In most northern European countries this is the case, but in southern European countries smoking is less closely related to social position. One would therefore predict that the social distribution of lung cancer would be different in northern Europe than in southern Europe if smoking is the major driver. It follows that specific causes do matter. But this begs the question, why is it that accidents, violence, cardiovascular diseases, and neoplasms all show this social gradient? You could look for specific factors for each, or alternatively, ask is there something more general about being in a lower social position that puts people at higher risk of all these different causes? It is an important question.

## Causation or confounding?

I have been pursuing the hypothesis that psychosocial factors play an important role in generating inequalities in health among social groups. Given how many factors vary among social groups, how can I pick on one set and argue for those? Is there not a danger of mistaking causation for confounding? In other words, is it the factors that we think are related to a particular social position that are somehow driving the whole process, or is something else going on? Coming back to the Whitehall study, people had the idea that if we could explain the gradient in CHD mortality by cholesterol, then social class would not be causal. I think this is too simplistic, because social class can determine the cholesterol level. In fact, mean plasma cholesterol in the first Whitehall study was marginally higher in the top grades and in the Whitehall II study there was essentially no difference by grade of employment.[2] In both studies there was a very clear social gradient in smoking.

This comes back to asking the question of why do we need a biopsychosocial model if we have smoking? An important psychosocial question is why is there a social gradient in smoking? It is not enough to know that smoking causes disease. We need to know why it is that in the UK as a whole, close to 100% of women and 80% of men in the most deprived category are smokers. Smoking is an important cause of disease and this then leads to a consideration of the factors responsible for such a marked social distribution of smoking.[10] Interestingly, when we look at obesity, another important cause of disease,

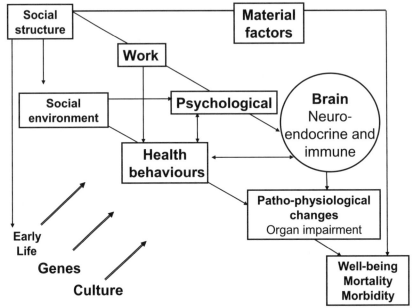

**Fig. 3.3** Social determinants of health. The model links social structure to health and disease via material, psychosocial, and behavioural pathways. Early life, genes, and culture are further important influences on population health. Marmot M. Multilevel approaches to understanding social determinants. In: Berkman LF, Kawachi I, eds. *Social Epidemiology*. New York: Oxford University Press; 2000. Reprinted by permission of Oxford University Press.

most data sets do not show much of a gradient of obesity in men, but they show a steeper gradient in women.[11] This could be part of the story.

In thinking about this question of causation and confounding, about how to sort through a mass of inter-correlated variables, we need a model. The model with which my colleagues and I have been working is shown in Fig. 3.3. I start with the social structure, the social environment, and the work environment. What happens throughout life is also of vital importance: people are not randomly allocated to social positions, but where they end up socially is affected by earlier life experiences. Where they end up affects psychological processes and this is the topic of the biopsychosocial model. This plays out on a substrate of genes and cultural differences. In asking about the role of a particular factor, the question is not so much whether this is confounded, but rather how it fits into this model. In other words, asking whether smoking could account for the whole gradient does not get away from the question of what the psychological links with smoking are.

While smoking is an important factor, the data show that smoking, by itself, does not account for the social gradient in disease. For example, in the first

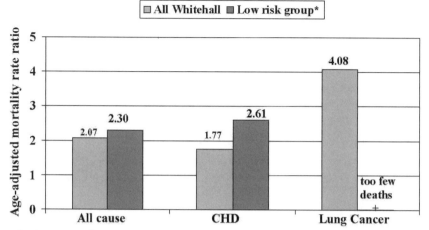

**Fig. 3.4** Twenty-five year mortality for 'other' versus administrative grades (by age at death). *Non-smokers, low cholesterol, and low systolic blood pressure. CHD, coronary heart disease. Whitehall study. Adapted from Reference 12.

Whitehall study, after 25 years of mortality follow-up, neoplasms not related to smoking showed about the same social gradient in mortality as was observed for 'all causes'.[12] We also looked at the social gradient in mortality for all causes, CHD, and lung cancer in a low-risk group of non-smokers with low cholesterol and systolic blood pressure. There were too few lung cancer deaths in this non-smoking group to assess the magnitude of the social gradient (Fig. 3.4). However, when we look at heart disease in this low-risk group, the social status effect is more pronounced than in the whole population.

These coronary risk factors are important for mortality but as explanations of the social gradient, they are not the whole story. Among the important elements are psychosocial factors in the workplace. We have examined self-reported job control (the degree to which an employee feels they can control their work ) and risk of CHD (Fig. 3.5).[13] We also adjusted these data for effort–reward imbalance (when a worker puts in high effort without receiving appropriate reward in terms of esteem, career opportunities, and financial remuneration), employment grade (a rather severe adjustment because low control is related to employment grade), the standard coronary risk factors, and a measure of negative affect (this is a measure of reporting bias). In these adjusted models, low control was associated with increased risk of incident CHD. Interestingly, a Finnish study was recently published showing that low control is related to coronary mortality.[14] Both our study and this recent Finnish one show that effort–reward imbalance is related to coronary mortality (Fig. 3.6). The association survives these confounders.

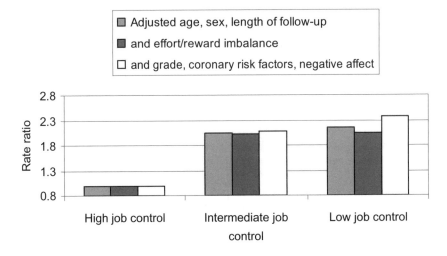

**Fig. 3.5** Self-reported job control and coronary heart disease incidence (men and women). Whitehall II study.[13]

Among the coronary risk factors we also included height, which is a marker of genes and environment from early life. This did not change this relationship between psychosocial factors at work and CHD. We also looked at parents' social

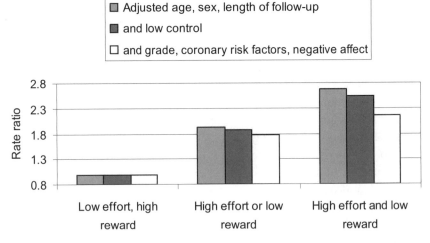

**Fig. 3.6** Effort–reward imbalance and coronary heart disease incidence (men and women). Whitehall II study.[13]

class and this did not change the relationship either. The social environment from which people come does not account for the relationship between the psychosocial work environment and CHD. The work factors explained about half the social gradient in CHD.[15] In recent work we have turned attention to control outside the work environment. Low control at home, for women in particular, predicts CHD incidence.[16] Is this somehow confounded by low status? As I have indicated, this is the wrong question: low status could actually be related to coronary disease because of its association with low control. Thus low status is not a confounder, but low control may be a mediator in relation to low status and disease. Hallqvist and colleagues in Sweden looked at this in a slightly different way, showing an interaction between low control (decision latitude) and low demand/high demand.[17] People with high-demand and low-decision latitude had a high risk of myocardial infarction. In the same study, with respect to the relationship between high demand/low control and myocardial infarction, the odds ratio was 3.4 in the non-manual workers and 11 in the manual workers. It was not so much that there was confounding by low social position, but that the risk was higher in blue-collar workers than in white-collar workers.

## Is a reporting bias important?

The question of reporting bias in epidemiological and other investigations has a long history. The founders of modern epidemiology were concerned with this issue. Doll and Hill considered it, in the 1950s, in their early case–control study of smoking and lung cancer.[18] Lilienfeld tussled with it in his early studies of sexual relations and cancer of the cervix. It has surfaced again recently as a criticism of studies that use self-report measures, as any questionnaire-based epidemiological study does, be it of diet, smoking, social class, occupational history, or anything else.[19] Could all the relationships described above be due to reporting bias? This is unlikely. While there could be a reporting bias in measuring psychosocial work characteristics, it is most unlikely that there could be one when assessing mortality. The Finnish study I referred to earlier showed that low control at work was related to mortality.[14] We conducted a systematic review of psychosocial factors and CHD, including only studies that passed a quality filter. Of 13 cohort studies, 10 showed clear evidence that work characteristics were related to CHD with validated end-points.[20] Low social supports predicted CHD as did depression. Type A personality and hostility were less consistently related to CHD incidence.

## Early life or current circumstances?

Life-course epidemiology has suggested that we look not only at where people end up socially as a determinant of their health, but also what happened to them earlier in life.[21] Three models have been proposed in relation to early life influences. There is the Barker-type model, where conditions *in utero* programme the fetus and affect risk of disease in adult life.[22] The second is the idea of the accumulation of advantage or disadvantage, that exposure at various points in the life course could accumulate to change disease risk.[23] This is consistent with a chronic stress model.[24] The third is a pathway model. It suggests that what is important about early life is that it determines where you end up; it is this that matters for disease risk.

There may be elements of all these models that are important. For example, the Whitehall II study has shown that height is related to employment grade.[2] In the UK Civil Service, the taller the man, the higher his employment grade is likely to be—the relationship is weaker in women. This is a measure of the influence of genes and environment and it is clearly related to where you end up. The question is, when we look at where you end up and its relationship to disease, are we missing out what happened earlier? One of Barker's recent studies in a Finnish cohort looked at the incidence of CHD by adult social class and thinness at birth.[25] In this study, men of low social class (labourers) had increased rates of CHD compared to men of high social class, but labourers who were thin at birth had increased rates of CHD with respect to labourers who were not thin at birth. Barker and I describe these findings slightly differently. I would say that they show that thinness at birth only matters for CHD if you have a low social class in adulthood. He describes the findings as showing that adult social class only matters if you are thin at birth. We agree that there is an interaction here. In this study they looked at income, which had no predictive power. They also looked at education, which of course does relate to adult social position, but drops out of the model when you look at adult social position.

## Biological plausibility

In considering whether there is a causal connection between social position and psychosocial factors and disease, we have dealt with specificity, confounding, reporting bias, and the importance of the life course. Is an effect of psychosocial factors on mortality biologically plausible? After all, epidemiology can only take us so far. It is instructive, in our search for a mechanism that links low-status position to increased risk of cardiovascular disease, to broaden our perspective from human to non-human primates. The model is appropriate because, as in humans, the health and survival of non-human primates is dependent to some extent on their position in the social hierarchy in which they live. Sapolsky's studies of baboons living in the wild have shown that, as in the case of UK civil servants, there is a social gradient in the risk of cardiovascular disease; dominant baboons are less at risk from cardiovascular disease and have less atherosclerosis than subordinate baboons.[26] There are measurable physiological differences between baboons at different levels in the hierarchy. Dominant baboons have higher high-density lipoprotein cholesterol levels than the subordinates. There are parallels within the hierarchy of UK civil servants: high-grade civil servants have higher high-density lipoprotein cholesterol levels than low-grade civil servants.[27]

Studies by Shively on rhesus macaque monkeys, which looked at the response of coronary arteries to acetylcholine,[28] are also interesting in terms of better understanding the biological effects of social status. In dominant monkeys, acetylcholine dilates coronary arteries, whereas in subordinate monkeys it constricts the arteries. There is evidence that putting monkeys under stress changes the response of coronary arteries to acetylcholine from dilatation to constriction. Shively has carried out extensive studies on atherosclerosis in communities of captive macaque monkeys. As you might expect, male monkeys had more atherosclerosis than female monkeys. Removing the ovaries of a female monkey removed her protection from atherosclerosis, compared to a male. However, subordinate monkeys had a higher risk of atherosclerosis than dominant monkeys. A subordinate female monkey had nearly the same level of risk as one whose ovaries had been removed.

One obvious question is whether there is some sort of stable characteristic of monkeys to be subordinate or dominant and this tendency is also related to risk of atherosclerosis. This is akin to the endogeneity question of the economists that I touched on at the beginning of this chapter. This does not appear to be the explanation. Experiments have been carried out to change monkeys' position in the hierarchy. This changed their risk of atherosclerosis. In

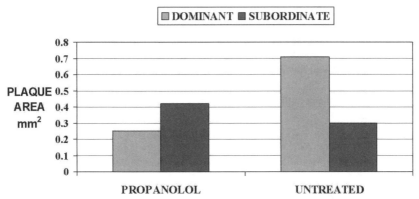

**Fig. 3.7** Atherosclerosis in male cynomolgous monkeys in unstable hierarchies. Adapted from Reference 29.

these 'unstable' experiments, researchers took subordinate monkeys from different troops and put them together; they took dominant monkeys from different troops and put these dominant monkeys together. They formed into new hierarchies, so that some monkeys that were previously subordinate became dominant in the new hierarchy and vice versa. Under this unstable condition, the subordinate females still had more atherosclerosis than the dominant females. It was different for males. If you subjected the males to this experiment, this was very threatening. Under these circumstances the dominant monkeys got more atherosclerosis than under the stable conditions. If you pretreated them with a beta-blocker before the experiment, this effect was abolished (Fig. 3.7).[29] The effects seen in Shively's studies are the result of stress related to position in the social hierarchy.

## Proof?

In this quick tour through the idea that the social environment is crucial as a determinant of health, we have looked at some epidemiological evidence for the importance of psychosocial factors in generating differences in disease among people in different socio-economic groups. We have touched on some of the criticisms that have been made against this type of evidence. Looking to non-human primates does not settle the issue, but such studies do suggest the biological plausibility of the relationship. This is borne out by possible biological links in human studies.[30]

My own view is that people's social situation has a profound effect on their well-being. The idea that this may affect physical disease is borne out by the evidence. It is important and it is something that we could do something about, given the way these gradients have changed over time.

## References

1. Marmot M, Bobak M. International comparators and poverty and health in Europe. *BMJ* 2000; **321**: 1124–8.

2. Marmot MG, Shipley MJ. Do socioeconomic differences in mortality persist after retirement? 25 year follow up of civil servants from the first Whitehall study. *BMJ* 1996; **313**: 1117–80.

3. Hattersley L. Trends in life expectancy by social class—an update. *Health Stat Quart* 1999; **2**: 16–24.

4. Donkin A, Goldblatt P, Lynch K. Inequalities in life expectancy by social class. *Health Stat Quart* 2002; **15**: 5–15.

5. Davey Smith G. The uses of 'Uses of Epidemiology'. *Int J Epidemiol* 2001; **30**: 1146–55.

6. Kunst AE, Groenhof F, Mackenbach JP. The EU working group on socioeconomic inequalities in health. Occupational class and cause specific mortality in middle aged men in 11 European countries: comparison of population based studies. *BMJ* 1998; **316**: 1636–8.

7. Osler W. The Lumleian Lectures on angina pectoris. *Lancet* 1910; **i**: 839–44.

8. Kunst AE, Groenhof F, Andersen O, Borgan J-K, Costa G, Desplanques G *et al.* Occupational class and ischemic heart disease mortality in the United States and 11 European countries. *Am J Pub Health* 1999; **89**: 47–53.

9. Costa G, Cadum E, Faggiano F, Cardano M, Demaria M. Social inequalities in the mortality due to cardiovascular disease in Italy. *G Ital Cardiol* 1999; **29**: 684–91.

10. Jarvis MJ, Wardle J. Social patterning of individual health behaviours: the case of cigarette smoking. In: Marmot MG, Wilkinson RG, ed. *The social determinants of health.* Oxford: Oxford University Press; 1999. pp. 240–55.

11. Erens B, Primatesta P. *The health survey for England 1998. Cardiovascular disease.* London: The Stationery Office; 1998.

12. van Rossum CTM, Shipley MJ, Van de Mheen H, Grobbee DE, Marmot MG. Employment grade differences in cause specific mortality. A 25 year follow up of civil servants from the first Whitehall study. *J Epidemiol Comm Health* 2000; **54**: 178–84.

13. Bosma H, Peter R, Siegrist J, Marmot MG. Two alternative job stress models and the risk of coronary heart disease. *Am J Pub Health* 1998; **88**: 68–74.

14. Kivimaki M, Leino-Arjas P, Luukkonen R, Riihimaki H, Vahtera J, Kirjonen J. Work stress and risk of cardiovascular mortality: prospective cohort study of industrial employees. *BMJ* 2002; **325**: 857–60.

15. Marmot MG, Bosma H, Hemingway H, Brunner E, Stansfeld S. Contribution of job control and other risk factors to social variations in coronary heart disease. *Lancet* 1997; **350**: 235–40.

16. Chandola T, Kuper H, Sing Manoux A, Bartley M, Marmot M. The effect of control at home on CHD events in the Whitehall II study: gender differences in psychosocial domestic conditions. *Soc Sci Med* 2004; **58**: 1501–9.

17. Hallqvist J, Diderichsen F, Theorell T, Reuterwall C, Ahlbom A and the Stockholm Heart Epidemiology Program study group. Is the effect of job strain on myocardial infarction due to interaction between high psychological demands and low decision latitude. Results from the Stockholm Heart Epidemiology Program (SHEEP). *Soc Sci Med* 1998; **46**: 1405–15.

18. Doll R, Hill B. Smoking and carcinoma of the lung. *BMJ* 1950; **ii**: 739–48.

19. Macleod J, Davey Smith G, Heslop P, Metcalfe C, Carroll D, Hart C. Limitations of adjustment for reporting tendency in observational studies of stress and self reported coronary heart disease. *J Epidemiol Comm Health* 2002; **56**: 76–7.

20. Kuper H, Marmot M, Hemingway H. Psychosocial factors in the aetiology and prognosis of coronary disease: a systematic review. *Sem Vasc Med* 2002; **2**: 267–314.

21. Kuh D, Hardy R. *A lifecourse approach to women's health.* Oxford: Oxford University Press; 2002.

22. Barker DJP. *Mothers, babies and health in later life.* Edinburgh: Churchill Livingstone; 1998.

23. Power C, Hertzman C. Social and biological pathways linking early life and adult disease. *Br Med Bull* 1997; **53**: 210–21.

24. McEwen BS. Protective and damaging effects of stress mediators. *N Engl J Med* 1998; **338**: 171–9.

25. Barker DJP, Forsen T, Uutela A, Osmond C, Eriksson JG. Size at birth and resilience to effects of poor living conditions in adult life: longitudinal study. *BMJ* 2001; **323**: 1273–6.

26. Sapolsky RM. *Why zebras don't get ulcers: an updated guide to stress, stress-related diseases, and coping.* New York: Freeman; 1998.

27. Brunner EJ, Marmot MG, Nanchahal K, Shipley MJ, Stansfeld SA, Juneja M *et al.* Social inequality in coronary risk: central obesity and the metabolic syndrome. Evidence from the WII study. *Diabetologia* 1997; **40:** 1341–9.

28. Shively CA. Social status, stress and health in female monkeys. In: Tarlov AR, St. Peter RF, ed. *The society and population health reader—a state and community perspective.* New York: New Press; 2000. pp. 278–9.

29. Kaplan JR, Manuck SB, Adams MR, Weingand KW, Clarkson TB. Inhibition of coronary atherosclerosis by propranolol in behaviorally predisposed monkeys fed an atherogenic diet. *Circulation* 1987; **76:** 1364–72.

30. Steptoe A, Marmot M. The role of psychobiological pathways in socio-economic inequalities in cardiovascular disease risk. *Eur Heart J* 2002; **23:** 13–15.

## Discussion

*Waddell*: As a clinician, the model that you proposed seems odd. From my perspective it looks very much like a social medicine model. Although it allows for social factors, it is a biomedical model, because while you have a lot of factors and a lot of links, it is entirely linear. It assumes that everything starts with the social element and then always goes through a biological mechanism. This may be true with respect to disease, but I don't think it is true for illness, well-being and morbidity. As a clinician, I would suggest there should be some two-way links. For example, behaviour can certainly influence one's social position and many of the factors might end up affecting well-being without necessarily going through a pathophysiological mechanism.

*Marmot*: Those are important points and I don't disagree. The way I use this model is as an abstraction to guide us in our thinking. The way my colleagues and I have used this model is that we have been busy trying to put pieces of it together, so we can look at the relation between social structure and work, for example, or the relationship between work and psychological processes. Some of my economist colleagues would like to drive it the other way, with the arrows going in the other direction: health causing social position. One could make it impossibly complicated with arrows going everywhere. It is an abstraction: it is not supposed to represent reality but to guide us in the research we are doing. Of course, as you say, some factors could directly link to well-being without going through a pathological mechanism, but in relation to the discussion we had about Engel, it is a question of whether you think that well-being drives the molecules or the other way round. At some point there has to be a process involved at the molecular level.

*Waddell*: The problem is that not only do models guide us, but they also constrain our thinking.

*Marmot*: I take your point completely. But as a scientist who looks at relationships between variables A and B, I do need to constrain my thinking. Otherwise I cannot move: I am just paralysed by complexity.

*Chalder*: An epidemiologist/psychiatrist colleague of mine, Jan Neeleman, in the Netherlands, has done some interesting work looking at common risk factors for various outcomes including death through ill health, accidental death, suicide, and other mental health outcomes.[1] He found that the risk factors are indeed common and don't hugely differentiate between conventional psychiatric disorders, illness, or disease.

*Marmot*: Something has to determine whether you go under a bus, take your own life, get lung cancer, or have a heart attack. Something has to influence why one thing happens and not another. At some level there have to be some unique risk factors for those different conditions. What you are saying is that there may also be common factors, and I am comfortable with this. We can think about these common factors. For example, Stephen Stansfeld and I have discussed at great length the various models of how depression and myocardial infarction might be linked.[2] One plausible model is that mechanisms mediated by the hypothalamic–pituitary–adrenal (HPA) axis are related both to depression and to the processes that lead on to coronary heart disease. There is, therefore, a plausible biological reason why 'diseases' as different as depression and myocardial infarction may have a common predisposition. A common predisposition may lead to very different diseases! The fact that psychiatrists treat depression and cardiologists treat heart attacks is an artefact of how we organize our medical care system and train medical students. It doesn't mean that they are conceptually totally distinct from the point of view of causation. They may be totally distinct from the point of view of treatment. Putting someone who is depressed in a coronary care unit is probably not what most people in this room would recommend. But a coronary care unit is quite a good place to be if you have had a heart attack.

*Chalder*: Of course, what we are talking about is people's behaviour. If they are engaged in self-destructive behaviour, this will affect health outcomes generally.

*Marmot*: We have been interested in mortality in Russia. If you want to see self-destructive behaviour, look at the drinking patterns of Russian men. This is likely to have a certain set of effects. What our data show is that they have huge excess risks of violent deaths, no doubt related to intoxication. This particular form of self-destructive behaviour is going to relate to the things that acute binge drinking causes. Fragmentation of society may link to other forms of self-destructive behaviour, as evidenced by high rates of drug abuse and HIV infection. We wouldn't want to confuse HIV infection with a traffic accident. They are quite different conditions, although they both may have their origins in the total fragmentation of society and the destructive behaviour that then ensues.

*Sharpe*: Let us accept that social factors determine health not only as common sense, but also as empirical sense. This meeting is about the biopsychosocial (BPS) model of practising medicine and we heard from Ned Shorter that one of the obstacles to the implementation of the BPS approach in medicine has been politics within psychiatry. Acceptance of the BPS model, both in general and the role of social factors in health in particular, is potentially political dynamite. Because if we are going to practise BPS medicine fully we would need to change society. Presumably you are faced with this question frequently: how do you respond?

*Marmot*: As Leonard Syme, my former teacher at Berkeley said, changing individuals is too difficult, so I am going to do something easy: change society!

People used to ask how we could ever get anyone to give up smoking. You are old enough to remember when doctors used to say there was no point in knowing about the ill effects of smoking because it would never be possible to get people to give up smoking. Yet the rates of smoking in this country have halved. Unfortunately, what has become more apparent is the social gradient of smoking. How did the rates halve? It wasn't simply because individual doctors told individual patients that this is bad for them. The rates halved because the medical profession said that smoking is bad for all of us and we, the doctors, gave up first. Remarkably, the doctors are still agitating about reducing the health toll of smoking. That radical left-wing organization, the British Medical Association, has been in the vanguard of trying to change society! They have been campaigning about smoking. They urged the chancellor to raise the tax on tobacco and for a ban on tobacco advertising. This changes individual behaviour. There is no way we can get individuals to reduce their saturated fat intake one at a time, but in the population the amount of saturated fat in the diet has fallen from 18% of calories to about 14%. What can we do about other factors intimately linked to the nature of society? I have spent a good part of the last 5 years working on this, starting with the independent inquiry into inequalities in health (the Acheson Report).[3] Most recently I was the academic adviser on a Treasury cross-cutting spending review on what to do about health inequalities. This involved 17 government departments sitting round a table discussing policies that would reduce health inequalities. The medical profession actually has quite a good record of changing society.

*Sharpe*: If the BPS approach is so self-evident and empirically supported, why is a BPS approach not more universally embraced? Is it unsettling for a lot of vested interests? Isn't it easier to say that we'll send patients to hospital and give them drugs than to set out to change society?

*Marmot*: A lot of people would take that view. Look at the arguments about whether salt is bad for blood pressure or not. Some people would take the argument that it is easier just to take anti-hypertensive medication than to cut out dietary salt. Or, why bother reducing saturated fat consumption when we can all be on statins? Give everyone over 50 a cocktail of statins and anti-hypertensives and forget society: why bother about all this social rubbish? I don't agree, by the way.

*Fitzpatrick*: I was interested in the case you made about smoking and changes in people's behaviour. Shouldn't you apply the same sort of epidemiological rigour to that association? In other words, is the association between the medical campaign against smoking and the decline in public smoking a causative one? The correlation is rather complicated. Looking back, the key event in the decline in smoking was the issue of passive smoking and the definition of smoking not as something that is damaging to the individual but as damaging to other people. Epidemiologically this is a more dodgy area than the link between smoking and lung cancer. In some way, I doubt that the medical campaign had that great an influence, but the passive smoking issue came up at a time when there was a greater climate of social receptivity to campaigns about changing behaviour and campaigns of a more intolerant character. The smoker became a pariah, which is a wider social trend that came to the UK via the USA and has that social class gradient that you describe. I would be careful about attributing a direct causative role to the medical campaign.

*Marmot*: I agree about applying the same rigour to these proposed causal associations. There are data that show acute effects on smoking after the 1957 and 1963 reports of the Royal College of Physicians on smoking; you can actually see acute impacts on smoking patterns immediately following the release of these reports. There is some evidence of association. I think the concern about passive smoking was rather more recent.

*Creed:* Is it only by chance that you are looking at heart disease? Looking at your social gradients, is the social gradient similar across different diseases, or do the gradients differ? If they differ, does this allow a model that has different degrees of influence on causation and mortality? Going on from this, how does the BPS model become incorporated into different parts of medicine according to different diagnoses?

*Marmot*: This is one of those 'is the glass half empty or half full?' phenomena. When you look at the different diagnoses, the magnitiude of the gradient differs. The gradient does cut across most of the major causes of death, but the slope is not identical. This is why I said we have to think in terms of why someone gets lung cancer and not coronary disease, but we also have to consider why someone gets sick and whether there are some common factors that underlie these different diseases. I think there are.

*Creed:* One of the issues that Peter White wants us to consider is why is the BPS model not taken up? From your data you would think that cardiologists would be more psychosocially oriented than cancer physicians, but in fact it is the other way round.

*Marmot*: I find it curious that most cardiologists that I have encountered say that when they deal with their patients, as any good clinician would, they talk about what is going on in their patients' lives. But when they get a scientific hat on, their only question is how far up can they push the catheter, or how far down statins can push the cholesterol; they consider what is going on in the patients' lives to be irrelevant.

# References

1. Neeleman J, Wessely S, Wadsworth M. Predictors of suicide, accidental death and natural death in a general population birth cohort. *Lancet* 1998; **351**: 93–7.

2. Stansfeld SA, Fuhrer R. Depression and coronary heart disease. In: Stansfeld SA, Marmot MG, ed. *Stress and the heart: psychosocial pathways to heart disease.* London: BMJ Books; 2001. pp. 101–23.

3. Acheson D. *Inequalities in Health: Report of an Independent Inquiry.* London, HMSO, 1998.

# 4 Remediable or preventable psychological factors in the aetiology and prognosis of medical disorders

Andrew Steptoe

## Summary

This chapter outlines some recent developments in understanding how psychological factors contribute to medical disorders. Traditional clinical and epidemiological studies in which psychological constructs are measured in population samples or diagnosed patient groups have been supplemented by more direct investigations of the effects of psychological stimulation on pathophysiology. For example, it has been found that psychological stress induces transient vascular endothelial dysfunction and causes the release of proinflammatory cytokines, processes that are central to atherogenesis. The pathways through which psychophysiological responses affect disease development and progression have also been clarified. There is evidence that psychobiological responses may have a direct causal role in some illnesses, may act through inhibiting host resistance in other cases, or may aggravate the course of existing disease. The links between psychological factors and biological responses are two way and recent animal and human studies have shown that peripherally released inflammatory cytokines can induce depression-like syndromes. Findings of this type call for a genuine integration of psychological, social, and biological perspectives.

## Introduction

A wide range of remediable or preventable psychological factors have been investigated over the last 40 years as being potentially relevant to the aetiology and prognosis of medical disorders. Space prohibits a detailed discussion of this field and the literature has been extensively reviewed elsewhere.[1–4] As a psychologist interested in the processes through which behaviour and emotion affect physical systems and medical disorders, I will focus this presentation on current research at the interface between biology and psychology. In the first section, I will give a brief overview of psychological factors relevant to the aetiology and prognosis of medical disorders, focusing particularly on the methodological issues that have handicapped this field. The second section discusses the impact of psychological factors on basic pathophysiological and biological responses, because an understanding of these effects is fundamental to appreciating the role of psychosocial processes in disease. In the third section, I summarize the pathways through which these factors influence medical disorders, emphasizing that several quite distinct processes are relevant to different disorders. Finally, the two-way interplay between psychosocial and biological factors is illustrated by the case of depression and its biological concomitants, to bring home the point that psychological experiences are affected by the bodily manifestations of illness, as well as the reverse.

## Psychological factors in medical disorders

Three types of psychological and social factors relevant to medical disorders can broadly be distinguished: adverse life experiences, such as life events and chronic stressors, psychological dispositions or traits, which are either protective or increase vulnerability to stress, and factors in the social environment, like social support and social isolation. It is widely acknowledged that there is an interplay between exposure to adversity and psychosocial protective factors, such that the impact of negative experiences may be offset by adequate coping resources.[5] This means that studies ideally need to evaluate several different factors simultaneously, instead of focusing exclusively on stressors, psychological traits, or social factors alone. Some of the inconsistency in results in the biopsychosocial field arises from failure to take a multidimensional approach to the measurement of people's experiences.

There have also been substantial problems in measurement, design, and analysis of studies, which have contributed to variability in research results. Take, for example, research on psychological traits. It has been common for researchers to group constellations of psychological characteristics into syndromes. Two syndromes that are very familiar are Type A behaviour (supposedly predisposing to coronary heart disease) and Type C personality (thought to predispose to cancer). More recently, the term type D personality has been coined to describe a combination of negative affectivity and emotional inhibition that might be relevant to heart disease.[6] Some investigators have gone further and developed the notion of a 'disease-prone' personality. Friedman and Booth-Kewley[7] even carried out a meta-analysis in which a range of negative psychological traits such as high anxiety, high depression, and high hostility were found to be associated with a wide range of different health outcomes, including coronary heart disease, asthma, arthritis, and headache.

This approach to examining psychological factors is problematic in several ways.[8] First, these constructs involve binary classifications of psychological features that are continuously distributed; they give the false impression that the population can be divided into categories of people who either have or do not have the relevant characteristics. Second, much of the evidence has been cross-sectional—comparing people who already have heart disease or rheumatoid arthritis with controls. This ignores the psychological changes that can take place with the onset of a medical condition. Third, many studies are carried out with people who have consulted and been diagnosed with the disorder in question, rather than using population sampling. For many chronic disorders there is a clinical iceberg and a substantial number of people in the population have conditions like hypertension, coronary heart disease, asthma, and arthritis without ever being diagnosed. People who are aware of their medical condition may differ from those who are not aware.[9] Another difficulty that has been alluded to elsewhere (see Chapters 3 and 5) is the problem of negative affectivity and reporting bias. Negative affect can influence reporting of life events, symptoms, social support, and mood ratings.[10] Studies that rely on self-report of illness outcomes potentially suffer from biases that underlie both illness measures and psychosocial factors.

The illnesses with which I am most involved are the cardiovascular diseases. Here, contemporary research on psychological factors has focused on traits such as depression and hostility and also to a lesser extent on potentially protective factors such as optimism.[11] These characteristics are best seen as co-factors in aetiology and not as sole causes of coronary heart disease. Perhaps the most interesting of these factors from the biopsychosocial perspective is depression. Hemingway and Marmot's[12] systematic review of population-based studies concluded that even when known risk factors are controlled, measures of depression and some other types of psychiatric morbidity consistently predict the development of coronary heart disease. Recent prospective longitudinal studies have confirmed this pattern.[13,14] Depressive illness and symptoms are also thought to be important in the period following admission for an acute cardiac event.[15] One study from Montreal followed up nearly 900 patients after acute myocardial infarction and found that survival was diminished not only among patients with severe depression, but also among those with elevated depressive symptoms within the normal range, after controlling for multiple markers of clinical disease severity.[16] Recent research on depression has largely overcome the methodological limitations alluded to earlier, by using prospective designs with objective disease indicators and measuring the construct of depression as a continuous rather than categorical variable.

## Psychological factors and pathophysiological processes

The second issue I would like to discuss is the impact of psychological factors on pathophysiological processes. This is an exciting topic because there have been major advances over the last 10 years in understanding exactly how biological responses that underlie disease pathology can be affected by stress and other factors. Previously, studies were limited to measurement of variables like blood pressure, heart rate, or muscle tension. Although it was repeatedly shown that acute stress elicited changes in these measures and that responses were modulated by psychological characteristics such as hostility and social factors such as support, critics rightly questioned whether the changes observed were relevant to pathology. But advances in medical technology and the growth in the understanding of basic disease mechanisms has transformed research, so that the impact of psychological factors on fundamental pathophysiological processes is now being explored more directly.

I can illustrate this by research on coronary heart disease. It is now believed that the early stages in atherogenesis are inflammatory in nature and involve

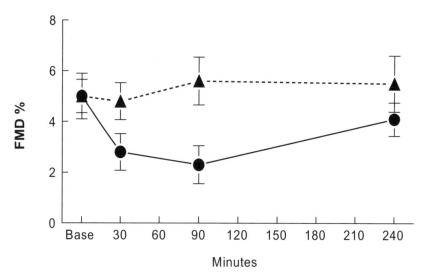

**Fig. 4.1** Mean levels of flow-mediated dilatation (FMD %) in healthy men during stress (solid line) and control (dashed line) sessions. The 3-minute stressor was administered directly after the baseline assessment of FMD. Compared with control, FMD was reduced at 30 and 90 minutes post stress. Error bars are standard errors of the mean. For details see Ref. 20.

disturbances of vascular endothelial function.[17,18] Endothelial dysfunction facilitates the adhesion of different types of circulating blood cells to the vessel wall surface and then the migration of cells through the endothelium, initiating inflammatory responses within the wall. Endothelial dysfunction, which is related to nitric oxide signalling at the biochemical level, can be assessed non-invasively using flow-mediated dilatation (FMD).[19] We used this method in a recent study, assessing endothelial function before and after mental stress in a group of healthy men.[20] Figure 4.1 summarizes results for stress and control sessions. The stressor in this study was a 3-minute simulated public speech. Stress induced a temporary impairment in endothelial function (reduced FMD), which evolved over quite an extended period. Blood pressure had returned to baseline after 20 minutes and cortisol also normalized quite quickly. But even this very brief acute psychological challenge stimulated a long-term disturbance in vascular endothelial function. Non-endothelial dependent dilation was unchanged during the experiment, indicating that the stress-induced response was a nitric oxide-related phenomenon. These results have now been replicated[21] and it has also been shown that clinically depressed patients without signs of coronary heart disease have similar disturbances of endothelial function.[22]

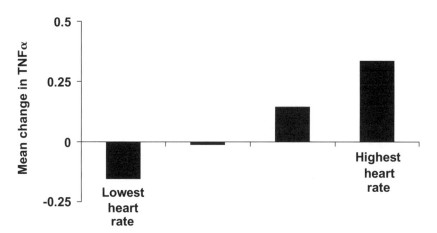

**Fig. 4.2** Mean changes in plasma TNF (pg/ml) following stress in a sample of 211 middle-aged men and women, showing the relationship between cytokine response and heart rate following stress. The sample was divided into quartiles of post-stress heart rate. The association was significant after controlling for age, sex, socioeconomic position, change in hematocrit, and baseline heart rate post stress. For details, see Ref. 27.

As atherogenesis progresses, foam cells are formed and smooth muscle cells migrate into the intima of the vessel wall. These processes are driven in part by the activation of T cells, which contribute to the release of chemical mediators known as pro-inflammatory cytokines, which organize the inflammatory process. It appears that interleukin (IL)-6, IL-1 , and tumour necrosis factor (TNF ) are all involved.[23] Some of these cytokines have been shown to respond to stress in animals.[24] Results in humans have been less consistent, with some investigators reporting increases in circulating levels, while others have seen no change following stress. However, in two recent studies we have sampled blood 45 minutes and 2 hours following acute stress and have recorded increases in IL-6, TNF , and IL-1 receptor antagonist concentrations.[25,26] We believe that changes in these mediators of the inflammatory response take some time to emerge, so may not be measurable in blood samples taken immediately after stress. Interestingly, the magnitude of the inflammatory cytokine responses to stress varies between individuals in a systematic fashion. We have recently found that individuals who are more reactive to standard stressors in terms of heart rate (an indicator of autonomic cardiovascular activation) also show greater stress-induced increases in IL-6 and TNF . Figure 4.2 illustrates this pattern, showing stress-induced increases in TNF plotted against heart rate. Participants with lower heart rate after stress showed reductions in TNF , while marked increases were recorded from individuals with higher heart rates.[27] This is an important relationship, because it helps us to understand how individual differences in stress responsivity might translate into cardiovascular disease risk.

These are just a few examples of how the investigation of biological stress responses has become more detailed and sophisticated over recent years. In addition to the changes in endothelial function and inflammatory cytokines described here, the impact of stress has been demonstrated on lipid levels, fibrinogen, homocysteine, haemostatic factors such as Factor VIII and plasma viscosity, and on a range of immunological responses.[28,29] Research of this type provides an insight into the precise ways in which psychological factors influence biological processes involved in disease and provides fresh possibilities for modifying stress-related responses.

## Pathways to disease

A critical issue in the elaboration of the biopsychosocial model is to understand the pathways through which psychological factors influence medical disorders. We know that various biological responses are sensitive to psychological factors, but how are these responses translated into disease risk? Two broad pathways link ill-health with psychosocial factors: the behavioural

**Table 4.1** Psychophysiological processes and illness

| *Psychophysiological responses may act as* |
| --- |
| (1) Causal factors in disease |
| (2) Inhibitors of host resistance |
| (3) Modulators of disease course |

and the physiological. At the behavioural level, psychosocial factors such as job stress, depression, and lack of social support may encourage unhealthy lifestyle choices, including smoking, excessive alcohol consumption, physical inactivity, poor diet, risky sexual practices, and lack of treatment adherence.[30,31] It is conceivable that psychosocial factors influence medical disorders through changes in habitual behaviours of this type, without any stress-induced biological responses being involved at all. However, behaviour changes are unlikely to account completely for associations between psychosocial factors and medical disorders, because relationships persist even after health behaviours are measured and taken into account.[32,33] Direct influences on physiological responses such as the ones described in the previous section constitute the alternative pathway through which psychosocial factors impact on medical disorders.[34] One of the major gaps in our present knowledge is that we are not in a position to quantify the relative importance of behavioural and physiological pathways. It is likely that the balance varies considerably between disease endpoints and between individuals. The precise way in which physiological pathways operate also differs across medical disorders. I would argue that distinctions can usefully be made between at least three broad processes (summarized in Table 4.1).

## Psychophysiology as a cause

The first process is perhaps the most familiar and is based on the notion that psychophysiological responses are causal factors in disease.[34] The argument is that certain individuals are either more responsive than others, or they are exposed more frequently to stimuli that provoke relevant biological responses. Over time, these disturbances of physiological function will, in the presence of genetic and biological predispositions, accelerate the development of disease.[35] The strongest tests of this process involve longitudinal studies in which psychophysiological responsivity is assessed in healthy samples and participants are followed up to record disease progression. This strategy has been used most extensively so far in the investigation of hypertension, to test the hypothesis that heightened stress reactors are more likely to develop the disorder than low stress reactors. Current evidence suggests that the likelihood of disease development depends not only on heightened stress reactivity, but also on exposure to conditions in everyday life that provoke these responses. For example, Light and colleagues[36] followed up men whose blood pressure and heart rate responses to standard mental stress tests had been tested 10 years previously. They found that men who had originally been high stress responders and who also reported high stress levels in their lives were at increased risk for developing hypertension. Another longitudinal study of men in Finland assessed carotid plaque as an index of atherosclerosis.[37] Over a 4-year period, it was found that the combination of high blood pressure stress responsivity and high job demands predicted rapid progression of carotid plaque, after controlling for covariates and health behaviours. Neither high stress reactivity nor high job demands in isolation were associated with progression.

## Psychophysiology as an inhibitor of the host response

The second possibility is that psychophysiological responses do not act in a direct causal fashion, but inhibit host resistance to disease (see Table 4.1). This process may underlie links between psychosocial factors and infectious illness. When exposed to an infectious agent, such as a bacterium or virus, the host mounts an immune response that is often sufficient to destroy the infection, so no illness arises. However, it is possible that stress leads to an impairment of the immune response and under those circumstances the same agent will provoke illness. There is extensive evidence that chronic stress, depression, and other psychosocial factors are associated with down-regulation of immune responses.[3] Some studies have shown that individuals under severe long-term stress, such as familial carers for relatives with dementia, show impairments of immune responses to vaccines.[38] This process may underlie the observation in studies of experimentally administered rhinoviruses that the likelihood of developing symptoms of the common cold is increased by high levels of life stress or social isolation.[39,40]

## Psychophysiology as a disease modulator

The third way in which psychophysiological responses may affect medical disorders is through modulating disease course (see Table 4.1). In this scenario, psychophysiological responses are not acting causally, but impact on the progression of disease. Such patterns may be common in autoimmune diseases, in which covariation of life stress with disease severity has been well documented.[2,41] Stress-induced physiological responses may also provoke serious and even life-threatening episodes of illness in patients who have established disease. Perhaps the best studied phenomenon of this kind occurs in coronary heart disease, where a substantial proportion of patients show transient 'silent' myocardial ischaemia when exposed to emotional stress.[42] Over the last few years, it has been demonstrated that people who experience stress-induced ischaemia to standardized mental stress tests more frequently fall victim to adverse cardiac events in subsequent years compared with those who are not reactive. This may be the process underlying the link between highly stressful events or sudden outbursts of anger and acute cardiac events that has been documented in clinical studies.[43,44]

## Influence of biological responses on psychological experience

The last point I would like to discuss in relation to the biopsychosocial model is that we should not lose sight of the fact that the interplay between psychosocial and biological phenomena is two way. The focus of interest of much research on medical disorders is on the evidence that psychosocial factors influence biological processes. But biological processes themselves affect central nervous system activity and may contribute to many of the psychological experiences associated with illness. An exciting programme of research into sickness behaviour has emerged over recent years. Sickness behaviour describes the constellation of behavioural responses, including reduced activity levels, reduced social interaction, suppression of appetite, reduced sexual behaviour, altered sleep pattern, and impaired learning ability, that accompanies many infectious illnesses.[45] Animal studies indicate that sickness behaviour is mediated by peripherally released cytokines, in particular IL-1.[46] If these cytokines are injected peripherally, the pattern of sickness behaviour can be duplicated.[47] Cytokine levels are also substantially increased during acute cardiac events in patients with coronary artery disease.[48]

It is interesting that depression has also been associated with many of these same responses, including raised plasma IL-6, IL-1, and TNF .[49] Cancer treatments that induce immune activation can also provoke depressive symptoms,[50] while impaired mood has been reported in people experimentally administered endotoxins such as *Salmonella abortus equi*.[51] These observations raise the possibility that some of the depressive symptoms associated with acute coronary events and other disorders may be a product of the inflammatory components of the illness. Large increases in IL6 and TNF in the first 24 hours following admission for acute coronary syndromes are predictors of poor prognosis.[52] It is therefore conceivable that part of the adverse prognosis for coronary heart disease associated with depression is due to biological responses that are common to cardiac inflammation and altered mood.

I hope that it is apparent from this brief review that research into psychological factors in the aetiology and prognosis of medical disorders is in an exciting phase. These developments may help to achieve a genuine integration of psychological, social, and biological processes and establish this field more firmly within medicine.

## Acknowledgements

This research was supported by the Medical Research Council and the British Heart Foundation.

## References

1. Rozanski A, Blumenthal JA, Kaplan J. Impact of psychological factors on the pathogenesis of cardiovascular disease and implications for therapy. *Circulation* 1999; **99**: 2195–217.

2. Herrmann M, Scholmerich J, Straub RH. Stress and rheumatic diseases. *Rheum Dis Clin North Am* 2000; **26**: 737–63.

3. Kiecolt-Glaser JK, McGuire L, Robles TF *et al.* Emotions, morbidity, and mortality: new perspectives from psychoneuroimmunology. *Annu Rev Psychol* 2002; **53**: 83–107.

4. Penley JA, Tomaka J, Wiebe JS. The association of coping to physical and psychological health outcomes: a meta-analytic review. *J Behav Med* 2002; **25**: 551–603.

5. Lazarus RS, Folkman S. *Stress, appraisal and coping.* New York: Springer; 1984.

6. Denollet J. Personality and coronary heart disease: the type-D scale-16 (DS16). *Ann Behav Med* 1998; **20**: 209–15.

7. Friedman HS, Booth-Kewley S. The 'disease-prone personality': A meta-analytic view of the construct. *Am Psychol* 1987; **42**: 539–55.

8. Steptoe A. Psychophysiological processes in disease. In: Steptoe A, Mathews A, ed. *Health care and human behaviour.* London: Academic; 1984. pp. 77–112.

9. Rostrup M, Mundall HH, Westheim A *et al.* Awareness of high blood pressure increases arterial plasma catecholamines, platelet noradrenaline and adrenergic responses to mental stress. *J Hypertens* 1991; **9**: 159–66.

10. Watson D, Pennebaker JW. Health complaints, stress, and distress: Exploring the central role of negative affectivity. *Psychol Rev* 1989; **96**: 234–54.

11. Smith TW, Ruiz JM. Psychosocial influences on the development and course of coronary heart disease: current status and implications for research and practice. *J Consult Clin Psychol* 2002; **70**: 548–68.

12. Hemingway H, Marmot M. Evidence based cardiology: psychosocial factors in the aetiology and prognosis of coronary heart disease: systematic review of prospective cohort studies. *BMJ* 1999; **318**: 1460–7.

13. Penninx BW, Beekman AT, Honig A *et al.* Depression and cardiac mortality: results from a community-based longitudinal study. *Arch Gen Psychiat* 2001; **58**: 221–7.

14. Ferketich AK, Schwartzbaum JA, Frid DJ *et al.* Depression as an antecedent to heart disease among women and men in the NHANES I study. National Health and Nutrition Examination Survey. *Arch Intern Med* 2000; **160**: 1261–8.

15. Ziegelstein RC. Depression in patients recovering from a myocardial infarction. *JAMA* 2001; **286**: 1621–7.

16. Lesperance F, Frasure-Smith N, Talajic M *et al*. Five-year risk of cardiac mortality in relation to initial severity and one-year changes in depression symptoms after myocardial infarction. *Circulation* 2002; **105**: 1049–53.

17. Libby P, Ridker PM, Maseri A. Inflammation and atherosclerosis. *Circulation* 2002; **105**: 1135–43.

18. Ross R. Atherosclerosis—an inflammatory disease. *New Engl J Med* 1999; **340**: 115–26.

19. Celermajer DS, Sorenson KE, Gooch VM *et al*. Non-invasive detection of endothelial dysfunction in children and adults at risk of atherosclerosis. *Lancet* 1992; **340**: 1111–15.

20. Ghiadoni L, Donald A, Cropley M *et al*. Mental stress induces transient endothelial dysfunction in humans. *Circulation* 2000; **102**: 2473–8.

21. Spieker LE, Hurlimann D, Ruschitzka F *et al*. Mental stress induces prolonged endothelial dysfunction via endothelin-A receptors. *Circulation* 2002; **105**: 2817–20.

22. Broadley AJ, Korszun A, Jones CJ *et al*. Arterial endothelial function is impaired in treated depression. *Heart* 2002; **88**: 521–3.

23. Black PH, Garbutt LD. Stress, inflammation and cardiovascular disease. *J Psychosom Res* 2002; **52**: 1–23.

24. Zhou D, Kusnecov AW, Shurin MR, DePaoli M, Rabin BS. Exposure to physical and psychological stressors elevates plasma interleukin 6: relationship to the activation of hypothalamic-pituitary-adrenal axis. *Endocrinology* 1993; **133**: 2523–30.

25. Steptoe A, Willemsen G, Owen N, Flower L, Mohamed-Ali V. Acute mental stress elicits delayed increases in circulating inflammatory cytokine levels. *Clin Sci* 2001; **101**: 185–92.

26. Steptoe A, Owen N, Kunz-Ebrecht S, Mohamed-Ali V. Inflammatory cytokines, socioeconomic status, and acute stress responsivity. *Brain Behav Immun* 2002; **16**: 774–84.

27. Owen N, Steptoe A. Natural killer cell and proinflammatory cytokine responses to mental stress: associations with heart rate and heart rate variability. *Biol Psychol* 2003; **63**: 101–15

28. von Kanel R, Mills PJ, Fainman C, Dimsdale JE. Effects of psychological stress and psychiatric disorders on blood coagulation and fibrinolysis: a biobehavioral pathway to coronary artery disease? *Psychosom Med* 2001; **63**: 531–44.

29. Zorrilla EP, Luborsky L, McKay JR *et al*. The relationship of depression and stressors to immunological assays: a meta-analytic review. *Brain Behav Immun* 2001; **15**: 199–226.

30. Wing RR, Phelan S, Tate D. The role of adherence in mediating the relationship between depression and health outcomes. *J Psychosom Res* 2002; **53**: 877–81.

31. Steptoe A. Health behaviors and stress. In: Fink G, ed. *Encyclopedia of stress*. San Diego: Academic Press; 2000 vol. 2, pp. 322–6.

32. Bosma H, Marmot MG, Hemingway H *et al*. Low job control and risk of coronary heart disease in Whitehall II (prospective cohort) study. *BMJ* 1997; **314**: 558–65.

33. Carney RM, Freedland KE, Miller GE *et al*. Depression as a risk factor for cardiac mortality and morbidity: a review of potential mechanisms. *J Psychosom Res* 2002; **53**: 897–902.

34. Steptoe A. Psychophysiological bases of disease. In: Johnston M, Johnston D, ed. *Comprehensive clinical psychology volume 8: health psychology.* New York: Elsevier Science; 1998. pp. 39–78.

35. Weiner H. *Perturbing the organism: the biology of stressful experience.* Chicago: University of Chicago Press; 1992.

36. Light KC, Girdler SS, Sherwood A *et al.* High stress responsivity predicts later blood pressure only in combination with positive family history and high life stress. *Hypertension* 1999; **33**: 1458–64.

37. Everson SA, Lynch JW, Chesney MA *et al.* Interaction of workplace demands and cardiovascular reactivity in progression of carotid atherosclerosis: population based study. *BMJ* 1997; **314**: 553–8.

38. Kiecolt-Glaser JK, Glaser R, Gravenstein S *et al.* Chronic stress alters the immune response to influenza virus vaccine in older adults. *Proc Nat Acad Sci* 1996; **93**: 3043–7.

39. Cohen S, Tyrrell DAJ, Smith AP. Psychosocial stress and susceptibility to the common cold. *New Engl J Med* 1991; **325**: 606–12.

40. Cohen S, Doyle WJ, Skoner DP *et al.* Social ties and susceptibility to the common cold. *JAMA* 1997; **277**: 1940–4.

41. Zautra AJ, Hamilton NA, Potter P. Field research on the relationship between stress and disease activity in rheumatoid arthritis. *Ann NY Acad Sci* 1999; **876**: 397–412.

42. Strike PC, Steptoe A. Systematic review of mental stress-induced myocardial ischaemia. *Eur Heart J* 2003; **24**: 690–703.

43. Kloner RA, Leor J, Poole WK *et al.* Population-based analysis of the effect of the Northridge Earthquake on cardiac death in Los Angeles County, California. *J Am Coll Cardiol* 1997; **30**: 1174–80.

44. Mittleman MA, Maclure M, Sherwood JB *et al.* Triggering of acute myocardial infarction onset by episodes of anger. *Circulation* 1995; **92**: 1720–5.

45. Dantzer R. Cytokine-induced sickness behavior: where do we stand? *Brain Behav Immun* 2001; **15**: 7–24.

46. Rothwell NJ, Luheshi GN. Interleukin 1 in the brain: biology, pathology and therapeutic target. *Trends Neurosci* 2000; **23**: 618–25.

47. Larson SJ, Dunn AJ. Behavioral effects of cytokines. *Brain Behav Immun* 2001; **15**: 371–87.

48. Liuzzo G, Baisucci LM, Gallimore JR *et al.* Enhanced inflammatory response in patients with preinfarction unstable angina. *J Am Coll Cardiol* 1999; **34**: 1696–703.

49. Maes M. Major depression and activation of the inflammatory response system. *Adv Exp Med Biol* 1999; **461**: 25–46.

50. Capuron L, Ravaud A, Gualde N *et al.* Association between immune activation and early depressive symptoms in cancer patients treated with interleukin-2-based therapy. *Psychoneuroendocrinology* 2001; **26**: 797–808.

51. Reichenberg A, Yirmiya R, Schuld A *et al.* Cytokine-associated emotional and cognitive disturbances in humans. *Arch Gen Psychiat* 2001; **58**: 445–52.

52. Biasucci LM, Liuzzo G, Fantuzzi G *et al.* Increasing levels of interleukin (IL)-1Ra and IL-6 during the first 2 days of hospitalization in unstable angina are associated with increased risk of in-hospital coronary events. *Circulation* 1999; **99**: 2079–84.

# Discussion

*Drossman*: One of the advantages of this sort of meeting is that people from different disciplines see the analogies with their own field. This could be replicated in chronic gastrointestinal illness as well, including the transmigration of macromolecules and the penetration of bacteria in stress models in animals, leading to the development of inflammatory bowel disease in genetically susceptible hosts.

*Steptoe*: It is interesting that the same sort of thing is happening there.

*Furnham*: Andrew, why don't you measure individual differences in your experimental studies? You seem to dismiss all the trait work and I can understand why. But if you simply measured neuroticism (negative affectivity), surely you would account for interesting variance. Why not combine correlational and experimental psychology?

*Steptoe*: I do that; I just wasn't describing it here. The question is whether individual psychological differences help to predict these biological responses. To some extent they do, but really only under conditions where you are tapping into environments that particularly address the characteristic in question. An example of this is work on hostility. If you just compare people measured on a hostility measure, you don't tend to find very much association. If you have tasks which are particularly designed to provoke hostile responses, then you do see changes. The sort of study that is done is to ask people to do a task ordinarily. Then in an alternative hostility provocation condition the experimenter comes in and is rude about them and what they are doing. These types of manipulations are meant to make people irritable and hostile towards the experimenter and under these circumstances hostile individuals do show much bigger responses.[1]

*Aylward*: Do you have any subjects who are smokers as well? What happens to them?

*Steptoe*: We see two things. Firstly, we see an overall difference. For example, smokers have a worse endothelial function than non-smokers.[2] Secondly, we see an acute effect of smoking on biological stress responses, so that when the effects of mental stress are measured after someone has been smoking, the changes are greater than with either stress or smoking on its own.[3] But there's less evidence for a real synergism.

*Aylward*: Have you looked at the cytokine profiles in smokers? Do they have higher concentrations?

*Steptoe*: With some cytokines, such as interleukin 6, they do.[4] Most of the data that I showed controlled for smoking because this is an influential factor.

*Davey Smith:* If you were giving this talk 15 years ago and you were talking about psychophysiological mechanisms linking external stressors and coronary heart disease (CHD), what mechanisms would you have talked most about? What has been the fate of research into those mechanisms? I'll add here that I did actually hear you talk about this subject 15 years ago and I have total recall!

*Steptoe*: That is a fair point. As you know, at that time we were much more limited in our ability to use biological measures. We could measure blood pressure and heart rate, but not much more. Fifteen years ago, I was certainly much more involved with studying individual psychological differences in relation to physiological responses, rather than broader exposure factors. I also think our understanding of how these pathways might operate has improved since that earlier time, because of new knowledge from biomedicine about the mechanisms of disease that has emerged over the past decade.

*Wessely*: Then, we were talking about factors such as heart rate variability, but you haven't mentioned those.

*Steptoe*: No, but we still measure them.

*Wessely*: George's point is a good one that those earlier things haven't lasted the distance. So why should we find the current story more compelling?

*Steptoe*: We are now looking more directly at the processes which we think are really involved in the disease pathology, instead of just looking at the global markers.

*White*: We have already complained that cardiologists aren't too interested in the BPS model. However, my experience in talking to cardiologists recently is that one story they are interested in is the link between CHD and depression. Does depression cause CHD and does it kill people who already have CHD? You hinted that there is a problem of measurement in this area. I would be interested to hear more on this. My impression is that the Beck Depression Inventory (BDI) seems to be the most commonly used measure. Yet we know that the BDI is full of non-depressive items. Is there as good evidence for categorical depressive disorder being as much of a risk factor for these two outcomes as a high BDI score?

*Steptoe*: These are different issues. The original evidence in this area was more on categorical diagnostic-type criteria.[5] Since then, there have been quite a number of studies trying to look more at depressive symptoms as a continuum in the period immediately following myocardial infarction.[6] Quite a few studies show associations and there is a smaller number of studies that don't. There are also possibly national differences in this. Many people working in this area suspect that there could be important variations to do with how doctors interact with their patients in different countries.

*Lewin:* It is a legitimate question that needs to be sorted out by systematic review. Has the association with depression been mainly found in studies that have used the BDI, or is there equally good evidence using other measures of depression?

*Creed:* I think you are right to say that the evidence is still in the balance. If you talk to American cardiologists, they say that it is all cut and dried, but the studies that have shown this have either used the BDI or have only been done on people who have been selected for a higher tendency to have arrhythmias, so these results are not generalizable. We couldn't find the effect in Manchester. The timing of the measurement is also an issue: how do you measure depression over the last 2 weeks when you only have a week to do this.

*White:* In a big enough study one could look at the individual items in the BDI and concentrate on the more core items of depression. Has this been done?

*Steptoe:* Not that I know of. You are also hinting at a more general issue about why clinicians don't assess these factors in normal practice. One of the issues is very much a measurement one: psychologists and others who assess these factors haven't produced tools that are particularly user friendly.

*Stansfeld:* When we looked at the General Health Questionnaire (GHQ) predicting CHD in the Whitehall study, one of the first things we thought was that it might be that GHQ tended to lead to more smoking and then that would lead to CHD. We didn't find this. The GHQ is a rather non-specific measure. Lots of these longitudinal studies looking at aetiology of CHD have found that measures of depressive symptoms seem to predict CHD over very long periods of time. This raises another kind of methodological issue, which is whether these symptom scales pick up much more severe conditions, but using a rather non-specific scale, and is it the severe conditions that are pathogenically important? Or is it that these much milder depressive symptoms are in fact important. For instance, in Ford's study there is a 30-year period between depressive symptoms and CHD. I was very interested to hear you talk about the endothelial dysfunction. Could endothelial dysfunction then be the underlying mechanism for a much more longitudinal effect rather than the short-term psychophysiological responses that may be subject to adaptation?

*Steptoe:* That is certainly possible. It could be that experiencing moderate psychological distress for a long time is associated with a chronic, low-level disturbance in inflammatory processes which might increase risk, just as other chronic risk factors through life lead to endothelial dysfunction. The other possibility is that depression is not the driver here, but that the person's life exposure to chronic difficulties is leading in parallel both to emotional upset and to a disturbance of physiological function. These responses aren't necessarily tightly linked. Some people can be quite reactive biologically, but do not show very much disturbance in their mood.

*Malmgren*: Do any of these studies include antidepressant medication? This could influence the cytokines in a positive way, so you should be able to say something more about the direction of the causal relationship.

*Steptoe*: The most recent study of endothelial function has actually looked at people with treated depression.[7] They still had impaired endothelial function, even though their depression had been successfully treated. There is a serious discrepancy here that needs to be resolved.

*Main*: To what extent are the acute stress models applicable to the chronic conditions? And a related but separate question, in terms of these sorts of parameters is there any evidence, as there is in psychophysiology, of habituation towards stressors?

*Steptoe*: What we typically find is that if we repeat testing we find smaller responses. But we also find reasonable stability of individual differences. The person who was more responsive at time 1 is also among the more responsive at time 2; although there is a reduction, the gradation remains the same. In terms of chronic conditions, this has always been troubling. This area of research has been very much moulded around the primary aetiology of disease. An interesting approach is to focus on how these psychobiological processes contribute to flares in chronic autoimmune conditions or disturbances in function. In these cases, the model is not of a causal kind, but involves the modulation of pre-existing pathology.

*Main*: Has stimulus specificity been a problem in terms of variation among individuals in response to different experimental strategies?

*Steptoe*: It is if you look at it in the laboratory studies of healthy young people, but we don't know much about stimulus specificity in other groups.

## References

1. Suls J, Wan CK. The relationship between trait hostility and cardiovascular reactivity: a quantitative review and analysis. *Psychophysiology* 1993; **30**: 615–26.
2. Celermajer DS, Sorensen KE, Georgakopoulos D *et al.* Cigarette smoking is associated with dose-related and potentially reversible impairment of endothelium-dependent dilation in healthy young adults. *Circulation* 1993; **88**: 2149–55.
3. Tsuda A, Steptoe A, West R *et al.* Cigarette smoking and psychophysiological stress responsiveness: effects of recent smoking and temporary abstinence. *Psychopharmacology* 1996; **126**: 226–33.
4. Bermudez EA, Rifai N, Buring J *et al.* Interrelationships among circulating interleukin-6, C-reactive protein, and traditional cardiovascular risk factors in women. *Arterioscler Thromb Vasc Biol* 2002; **22**: 1668–73.
5. Frasure-Smith N, Lespérance F, Talajic M. Depression following myocardial infarction: impact on 6 month survival. *JAMA* 1993; **270**: 1819–25.

6. Bush DE, Ziegelstein RC, Tayback M *et al.* Even minimal symptoms of depression increase mortality risk after acute myocardial infarction. *Am J Cardiol* 2001; **88**: 337–41.

7. Broadley AJ, Korszun A, Jones CJ *et al.* Arterial endothelial function is impaired in treated depression. *Heart* 2002; **88**: 521–3.

# 5  The biopsychosocial approach: a note of caution

## George Davey Smith

## Summary

This chapter will provide a cautionary critique of whether the biopsychosocial (BPS) model is useful in understanding aetiological factors in chronic diseases. I will illustrate the arguments by referring to studies of peptic ulcer and ischaemic heart disease. I will show that bias and confounding can generate spurious findings and associations, especially in observational studies. When interventional studies have been used to examine the efficacy of a psychosocial approach the results have been disappointing.

## Introduction

This presentation concerns one area where I feel we need to be cautious about the BPS approach. This is when considering the aetiological importance of some of the factors postulated within the BPS model. Choose whatever term you like: stress, psychosocial factors, social anxiety, and so on. They have similar resonance, and, in my view, problems. I am sure that these factors are related to a general sense of well-being, happiness, or quality of life and that through their effects on health-related behaviours, such as smoking, drinking, drug use, sexual behaviour, risk taking, and adherence to medical care, they will have an effect on mortality and major disease outcomes. However, I think the evidence is less good that psychosocial factors have a direct aetiological effect on diseases like peptic ulcer or coronary heart disease.

One illustration of how such factors are related to particular health outcomes comes from a study of differentials according to characteristics of areas.[1] We used an indicator of material deprivation, the Townsend Index, and an index of social fragmentation, the Congdon Index, and examined how these correlated with different causes of death. When we examined small areas across the UK, material deprivation correlated more strongly with overall mortality than social fragmentation (Table 5.1). Because social fragmentation

**Table 5.1** Correlation between indices of social fragmentation and deprivation with standardized mortality ratios for all-cause and cause-specific mortality

| | Simple correlations | | Partial correlations | |
|---|---|---|---|---|
| | Townsend Index | Congdon Index | Townsend Index | Congdon Index |
| **Women** | | | | |
| All cause | 0.82 | 0.35 | 0.85 | −0.50 |
| Coronary heart disease | 0.66 | 0.12 | 0.81 | −0.62 |
| Stroke | 0.58 | 0.12 | 0.68 | −0.46 |
| Lung cancer | 0.81 | 0.51 | 0.73 | −0.12 |
| Stomach cancer | 0.60 | 0.15 | 0.69 | −0.45 |
| Suicide | 0.38 | 0.58 | −0.04 | 0.48 |
| Cirrhosis | 0.63 | 0.56 | 0.40 | 0.23 |
| **Men** | | | | |
| All cause | 0.87 | 0.46 | 0.86 | −0.40 |
| Coronary heart disease | 0.67 | 0.13 | 0.80 | −0.60 |
| Stroke | 0.67 | 0.24 | 0.71 | −0.40 |
| Lung cancer | 0.84 | 0.44 | 0.82 | −0.34 |
| Stomach cancer | 0.60 | 0.15 | 0.69 | −0.45 |
| Suicide | 0.58 | 0.71 | 0.18 | 0.53 |
| Cirrhosis | 0.70 | 0.67 | 0.45 | 0.36 |

From Reference 1.

is related to deprivation, it was also related to all-cause mortality. But if we took deprivation into account, the association between social fragmentation and all-cause mortality actually reversed (Table 5.1). However for outcomes that are plausibly related to social fragmentation—suicide and cirrhosis—social fragmentation stayed related to mortality.

The psychosocial environment does appear to be associated with those causes of death that common sense would suggest it should be related to, through its influence on dispositions and behaviours. But what is the evidence that psychosocial factors are direct aetiological factors in chronic diseases, acting through psychoneuroendocrinological (or other currently fashionable) mediating mechanisms? Is stress an important determinant of population health?

I would like to quote from an article George Engel wrote a year after his seminal *Science* paper,[2] where he talked about our need to think about psychosocial factors.[3] He said,

> Predicated on a systems approach, the BPS model dispenses with the scientifically archaic principles of dualism and reductionism, and replaces the simple cause and effect explanations of linear causality with reciprocal causal models. Health, disease and disability thus are conceptualized in terms of the relative intactness and functioning of each component system on each hierarchical level. Overall health reflects a high level of intra- and inter-systemic harmony.[3]

I would suggest that, contrary to the view that embracing complexity always gets us closer to the truth, much of what we know about disease actually suggests that the utilization of rather simple models of linear causality is often appropriate, particularly when we are considering ways of improving population health. In this regard Engel's quote has some historical resonance. During the first half of the nineteenth century the complex, highly theoretical language of those who opposed the view that diseases like cholera were contagious was contrasted with the crude, reductionist tone of the contagionists.[4]

The more we understand about many diseases, the simpler the models get. The extraordinary detail given in reports in the 1830s about factors related to cholera no longer appeared so mysterious once it was recognized that a proximal transmissible element—associated with a wide variety of factors—was a necessary cause.[4] Some of the factors considered in the complex models are ones that would have influenced whether or not people were exposed to the transmissible agent and in this sense they are acting as distal causes. However, if the chain of causation is broken, then the disease does not occur. For example, many psychological and social factors influence whether people smoke and thus indirectly lead to an increase in lung cancer risk. In different times and different places, though, different economic and psychological factors may influence smoking. The social class gradient of cigarette smoking has, for example, changed greatly in the UK over the last 50 years.[5] Ultimately social and psychological factors will only influence the risk of lung cancer through influencing smoking patterns. Take away the cigarettes, and these factors will not result in lung cancer.

Similarly, consider peptic ulcer or stomach cancer. If you come from a large family where there are poor facilities for maintaining hygiene, you have a much higher risk of acquiring *Helicobacter pylori* infection in childhood. Therefore in some sense these social factors are causally related to acquisition of *H. pylori* and if you acquire *H. pylori* then your risk of peptic ulcer and stomach cancer increases greatly. However, if you treat the infection, or interrupt the transmission route, the link between the underlying social factors and the risk of these diseases will be broken.

Of course not everyone who smokes cigarettes develops lung cancer and not everyone carrying *H. pylori* develops stomach cancer or peptic ulcer. Therefore it might be thought that investigating why certain people develop disease, given these exposures, is the key issue. However, if no one smoked cigarettes in a population, the vast bulk of lung cancer would disappear. Thus in public health terms, cigarette smoking is the cause of the burden of disease and focusing on why some smokers get lung cancer and some do not may be a diversion from a public health intervention that could produce a dramatic improvement in population health.

## Cautionary tales

Over the past 50 years many psychosocial factors have been proposed and accepted as important aetiological agents for particular diseases and then they have quietly been dropped from consideration and discussion. If this meeting had been held 15 years ago we would have discussed type A behaviour at great length. Type A behaviour will hardly be mentioned at this meeting, because it no longer appears to be an important cause of coronary heart disease. People versed in the history of epidemiology will know that conditions such as cholera, pellagra, beri beri, asthma, Down's syndrome, scurvy, yellow fever, typhoid, and peptic ulcer were all at one time seen as diseases that were importantly influenced by stress or (in earlier times) 'moral' factors. In 1832 William Beaumont, for example, considered that such factors underlaid 'the greater proportional number of deaths in the cholera epidemics'.[6] He would doubtless have considered the BPS model an ideal way of conceptualizing the causes of cholera, while pouring scorn over those studying the geographical distribution of cases and relating this to water supply.

An important critic of the BPS model—although she never explicitly talks about it—is Susan Sontag. She published a remarkable book, *Illness as metaphor*,[7] a year after Engel's 1977 article appeared. Sontag wrote about how in plague-ridden England in the late sixteenth and seventeenth centuries, it was believed that a happy man would not get the plague. She stated that,

> The fantasy that a happy state of mind would fend off disease flourished for all infectious diseases before the nature of infection was understood. Theories that diseases are caused by mental state and can be cured by willpower are always an index of how much is not understood about the physical basis of the disease. The notion that a disease can be explained only by a variety of causes is precisely the characteristic of thinking about diseases where causation is not understood.

Diseases that are thought to be multi-determined have the widest scope for becoming metaphors for what is felt to be socially or morally wrong. Sontag was writing at least partially in response to her own diagnosis with cancer. Her reason for being sceptical of the BPS model was that she saw it as a way of putting blame for disease on the people with disease. This metaphorical treatment of disease can lead to internalized blame and guilt. Sontag therefore wanted to strip these metaphors away and see disease principally as a biological, not psychological, phenomenon.

The peptic ulcer story will be well known to most of you. A large amount of epidemiological work, carried out over some 50 years, repeatedly suggested that stress was a major factor in the causation of peptic ulcer. One case–control study was published in 1937.[8] If the study had got the right answer this would be considered an important early classic of the genre. Davies and Macbeth Wilson studied 205 patients with peptic ulcer. They recruited a group of controls with hernias, because they recognized that having an illness would influence the way people reported life events and they matched for age, sex, and social class. They asked people about life events, with an interviewer blinded to the case or control nature of each patient. This was clearly a study that had been well planned and showed evidence of methodological sophistication absent from most such research of its time. They detailed life events that had preceded the diagnosis of disease and demonstrated very strong associations between life events and the risk of peptic ulcer. Using a statistical approach not available to them in 1937, we can now calculate an odds ratio among men of 20 (95% confidence interval (CI), 9–47; $P < 0.0000001$) and among women of 13 (95% CI, 4–41; $P < 0.0000001$). In retrospect it is almost certainly the case that, despite their attempt to account for a possible bias, the associations arose because people who were reporting symptoms of peptic ulcer also tended to over-report problems in other aspects of their lives.

Richard Doll was introduced to epidemiology by Francis Avery Jones, an epidemiologically minded gastroenterologist. Avery Jones was very attuned to thinking about epidemiological patterns of disease and was also someone who appeared convinced that stress was important in peptic ulcer. In his chapter in the 1948 book *Progress in clinical medicine*[9] Avery Jones said,

> There have not been any major advances in the treatment of gastroduodenal ulcer. A better appreciation of the natural history of the disease has directed the treatment away from the ulcer towards the individual as a whole ... ,

which was a fair summary of the BPS approach. He went on to state that,

> Most clinicians agree there is a particular personality associated with peptic ulcer. These patients are tense, possess unusual drive and are over-conscientious in their work. They tend to worry unduly, but do not give way to their emotions ... The recognition of the psychological aspects of peptic ulcer has the virtue of therapeutic application. If the tensed-up, over-active individual can relax, he can ease the strain on his digestion. If the doctor can listen to the unburdening of a tragic tale, often untold to other ears, he may relieve a nervous tension which has been reflected on the stomach. If the patient can learn to appreciate the inter-relation between mind and stomach, he may be able to minimise his dyspepsia at times of stress.

Regarding the management of ulcers, Avery Jones thought that,

> During convalescence the patient should be given a simple exposition of peptic ulcer. A clear understanding of the need for maintaining a calm outlook on life, and of the necessity for not exceeding his natural 'tempo' by accepting too much work or responsibility, will be much more valuable than routine medication. The patient has got to live with his ulcer-forming tendency and it is essential to give him all the information at our disposal ... There is little doubt that healing is accelerated and more commonly completed if real rest is taken, preferably away from home, where the extra work occasioned by the illness may add to the worry of the patient. A period away from home may add perspective to domestic difficulties.

The patient in these quotes was, of course, always a male patient and it would be interesting to know what the wives of these patients thought about 'perspective' being added to their 'domestic difficulties' through absence from home. Avery Jones went on to discuss dietary aspects of treatment:

> It is sufficient to have initial hourly or two-hourly milk feeds, a first diet with small two-hourly purée feeds, and a basic second diet when pain has subsided, still with two-hourly feeds ... The third diet re-directs the emphasis to ordinary meal-times, but maintains the bland characteristics.

This does not sound like an attractive diet. However such was Avery Jones's concern not to increase stress, he added that,

> The diet should be served in as colourful and attractive a way as possible. A bland insipid colourless diet may cause less psychic flow of gastric juice, but it makes the patient depressed and irritable. The sustained resentment is more harmful than the increased psychic secretion.

It is entertaining to look at these discussions with the benefit of hindsight. Perhaps what is not quite so entertaining is the realization that in 400 consecutive admissions for gastroduodenal bleeding to the hospital at which Avery Jones worked, 27 of them died under this regime. This was a disease that killed people. As the dismal pattern of morbidity and mortality due to peptic ulcer continued, many of the epidemiological studies—which should have identified potentially modifiable causes of the disease—continued to focus on stress as a major causal factor. Interestingly, looking at these studies now, they often found that people with peptic ulcers came from large families and had more siblings than people not developing ulcers.[10–13] We now think that this is because the transmission of infection by *H. pylori* is facilitated within large sibships. Indeed, epidemiologists would tend to interpret such data as a possible indicator of the particular dynamics of infection. However, because the belief that peptic ulcer was stress-related was strong, association with family formation were taken to reflect particular psychological exposures,[14,15] thus associations that could have served as an important clue to a modifiable—and key—cause of the disease were unfortunately taken as yet more 'proof' of the pre-eminent role of stress in peptic ulcer.

Another clue to a modifiable cause of peptic ulcer should have come from the pioneering work of Mervyn Susser and Zena Stein in 1962.[16] These authors identified clear birth cohort patterns in the rise (and then fall) of peptic ulcer disease in the UK, with duodenal ulcer lagging approximately 10 years behind gastric ulcer in terms of the birth cohort with the peak disease rates. An analysis of data from 19 countries showed similar cohort patterns, with some variation between countries in precisely when the rises and falls started, but a consistent pattern being seen with respect to the difference between gastric and duodenal ulceration.[17]

The detection of birth cohort phenomena in disease or mortality rates gives important clues as to the disease aetiology—specifically, suggesting aetiological factors operating early in life. Thus other early cohort analyses demonstrated that tuberculosis mortality fell in a cohort-specific fashion,[18,19] which Springett interpreted as indicating that most tuberculosis causing death at older ages was acquired during earlier life.[19]

Despite the work of Springett and others, the initial interpretation of the birth-cohort trends in peptic ulcer rates was strongly influenced by the prevailing paradigm that peptic ulcer was a disease caused by stress. Thus the birth cohort patterns observed by Susser and Stein were interpreted as reflecting the particular experiences of the UK birth cohort demonstrating highest disease risks—the First World War as young adults, then the depression of the 1930s, and the Second World War in middle age[16,20]—rather than an important aetiological factor acting in early life. Now, of course, we would identify *H. pylori* acquisition in early life as this factor.[21]

There were a few vocal sceptics in the stress and peptic ulcer saga. One was Richard Asher. Commenting on a paper by Szasz and Robertson, regarding psychological factors in the aetiology of baldness,[22] Asher wrote, 'It is now fashionable to put forward mental causes for those illnesses where physical causes have not yet been found, such as peptic ulcer.'[23] Richard Doll relates how Asher gave him an article to read about peptic ulcer and its cause by psychological stress and asked, 'Do you think that's a fair account of what people think?' Doll replied, 'Well, it's a bit stilted language, Richard, but yes, it's a perfectly fair account.' Asher replied, 'Actually, it was written in 1850 about general paralysis of the insane. And I merely substituted peptic ulcer for general paralysis of the insane.'[24]

Jerry Morris, Director of the Medical Research Council Social Medicine Research Unit, was also not an enthusiast for stress as a cause of peptic ulcer. A member of his unit, EM Goldberg, carried out a detailed study into the social and psychological background of duodenal ulcer[14] and in the introduction thanked 'Dr JN Morris, whose healthy scepticism, particularly in matters psychological, helped throughout to keep the team's feet on the ground.' Morris considered that time trends in peptic ulcer incidence made little sense if viewed within the stress framework. He stated that these trends

> would suggest to anyone in sympathy with 'psychosomatic' theories ... that the type of personality disposed to the disease is less common—unfortunately not a testable proposition; [or] that the environment is less of a strain—which is scarcely conceivable.[25]

Finally, an anonymous writer in the *British Medical Journal* in 1959 said

> When future work has solved the riddle of chronic peptic ulcer, we may find that the facile explanation sometimes given today that it is a disease of civilization due to mental stress will seem as remote from the truth as the view that malaria is caused by foul vapours ascending from the swamps.[26]

## Enter *Helicobacter pylori*

In 1983, *H. pylori* was introduced as a candidate cause of peptic ulcer. It could be said that as we did not know about *H. pylori* until 1983, what does it matter that until then we had a stress model, because it did not block the development of understanding of the causes of peptic ulcer? But this may not be the case. Spiral bacteria, which clearly were *H. pylori*, were described in the stomach in 1889[27] and the specific hypothesis that peptic ulcers were caused by bacteria had already been advanced, with evidence, in 1875.[27] These early findings were followed by repeated studies published in good journals isolating bacteria, from peptic ulcers, which would now be identified as *H. pylori*.[27] Doctors in Mount Sinai Hospital advocated antibiotic treatment for peptic ulcers, which they claimed worked, in 1948.[28] A patent for an antibiotic formulation for treating peptic ulcers was issued in 1961.[29] However, the stress model served to block people from building on this and moving towards an answer that would have led to a treatment that could have improved the quality of life, dramatically, for millions of people.

Various psychological treatments for peptic ulcer were advocated and large numbers of people were subjected to them. Of course the usual claims for dramatic success were made, but properly conducted randomized controlled trials demonstrated no benefit of such time-consuming and expensive treatments.[30–32] The conclusion of one well-conducted trial was that 'our study demonstrates a need for humility about the degree to which psychological interventions can effect powerful biological processes and impact on patient's lives.'[32]

Things may appear clear with hindsight, but people really were directed away from a treatment for peptic ulcers that worked—antibiotics—to ones that did not. All the pieces fitted together, including the identification of a bacterium, by the 1950s. But the answer that could have led to an effective treatment of the disease was missed because of a particular model—essentially the BPS model—and the mindset that it generated.

## Observational studies of threats to health and the problem of confounding

Now I am going to address problems in observational data relating psycho-social factors to health outcomes. The two major issues are confounding and bias. Confounding is a general issue in epidemiology. It is not something that is of any greater importance in psychosocial epidemiology than in other fields of epidemiology. It is important in all areas where we are studying factors that are very strongly socially patterned. The antioxidant story is relevant here. The epidemiological evidence gave very strong suggestions that antioxidant vitamin intake reduced the risk of cardiovascular disease. Large cohorts of people were followed up and the risk of cardiovascular disease in relation to

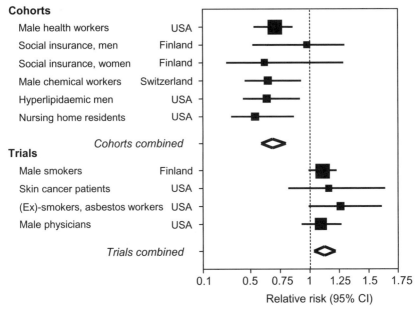

**Fig. 5.1** Meta-analysis of results of observational cohort studies of β-carotene intake and cardiovascular mortality and of randomized controlled trials of the same issue. CI, confidence interval.

β-carotene intake or levels examined. Differences in β-carotene were associated with a large apparent reduction in the risk of cardiovascular disease (Fig. 5.1).[33] Some of these observational study results were adjusted for many potential confounding factors and this apparent protective effect was still shown. Large-scale randomized placebo-controlled trials of β-carotene for up to 13 years showed, if anything, slightly increased risk of cardiovascular disease in those given β-carotene (Fig. 5.1). The most striking finding was that in the first large randomized controlled trial, β-carotene was measured in the blood at baseline in the control group and it predicted cardiovascular disease just as in other observational studies. In the same study that showed that changing β-carotene level had no beneficial effect on cardiovascular disease risk, an observational analysis suggested apparent protection.

'Eating fruit halves the risk of an early death' a UK newspaper recently claimed,[34] in an excited response to a study showing a strong inverse association between blood vitamin C levels and coronary heart disease risk.[35] A subsequent randomized controlled trial of a vitamin supplement that raised

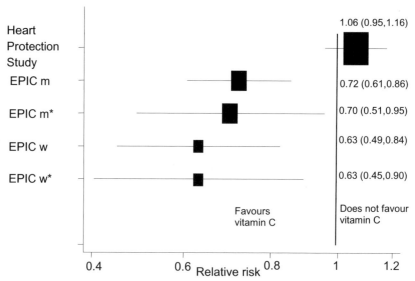

**Fig. 5.2** Estimates of the effects of an increase of 15.7 μmol/l plasma vitamin C on coronary heart disease risk estimated from observational epidemiological EPIC (European Prospective Investigation of Cancer and Nutrition) study and randomized controlled Heart Protection study. EPIC m, men (age adjusted); EPIC m*, men (adjusted for systolic blood pressure, cholesterol, body mass index (BMI), smoking, diabetes, and vitamin supplement use); EPIC w, women (age adjusted); EPIC w*, women (adjusted for systolic blood pressure, cholesterol, BMI, smoking, diabetes, and vitamin supplement use).

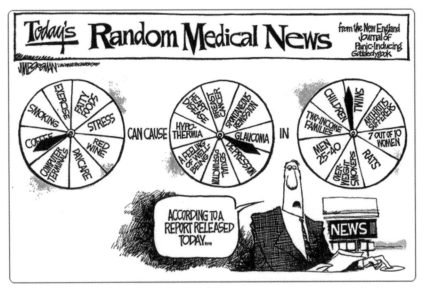

**Fig. 5.3** One view of the value of epidemiology.

blood vitamin C levels by 15.7 μmol/l found 5-year coronary heart disease risk unchanged (relative risk, 1.06; 95% CI, 0.95, 1.16),[36] whereas the equivalent observational findings for this increase in blood vitamin C were coronary heart disease relative risks of 0.63 (95% CI, 0.49, 0.84) in women and 0.72 (95% CI, 0.61, 0.86) in men (Fig 5.2). Again the results from robust experiment and fallible observation are clearly not compatible. Similar stories could be told with respect to vitamin E intake and, famously, hormone replacement therapy (HRT), with observational data suggesting a strong protective influence on cardiovascular disease risk and randomized controlled trials ruling out such protective effects.[37] The repeated publication of claims from epidemiological studies—which get changed as better data accrue—have understandably led to cynicism among the public (Fig. 5.3).

Now I will give an illustration of how confounding can generate associations between socially patterned exposures and outcomes. In the first Whitehall study, Geoffrey Rose, Martin Shipley, and I completed a series of analyses on car ownership.[38] Car ownership was enquired about because Rose thought that if people had cars, they would do less exercise and would be at higher risk of coronary heart disease. Of course, by the time we came to look at the data in the late 1980s, we realized that car ownership would function as an indicator of social circumstances. Car owners had higher incomes and should live longer, and this is what we saw. People without a car had a 40 per cent higher risk of coronary heart disease mortality. If you adjusted for all of the standard risk factors, a statistically robust residual effect remained, with people who did not have cars having a higher risk of mortality. If we randomized people to car ownership, would this reduce their coronary heart disease mortality? Probably not. But if, rather than asking people about car ownership, we had asked them about other socially patterned factors—for example, many of the stress measures we have heard about at this meeting—we would get exactly the same finding. Confounding generates these sorts of associations and conventional approaches for statistically 'controlling' for it do not work.[39,40]

In a study in the west of Scotland set up in the 1970s—known as the Collaborative study—a then popular stress measure called the Reeder Stress Inventory was elicited from nearly 6000 men.[41] It is predominantly a 'psychological' measure of perceptions of negative feelings and, in the few contemporary studies where comparisons can be made, scores on other measures of feelings are highly correlated with those of the Reeder Stress Inventory.[42] In contrast currently popular psychosocial measures—popular, perhaps, because they appear to predict disease—are often more 'social'. That is, they are measures of aspects of the social environment (such as work conditions) that are assumed to provoke negative feelings. Consequently estimates of the effects of these latter measures are inevitably prone to confounding—because poor social environment is likely to be characterized by several potentially health damaging factors in addition to any negative feelings it engenders in the person experiencing it.

An indication that the measure has some meaning was that the people who reported high stress were more likely to be heavy smokers or heavy drinkers, to do less leisure time exercise, and to have worse sleep patterns.[41] The stress measure was related to behavioural risk factors in the way that you would expect. But because of the sort of questionnaire it was, and the context of the time, it was actually associated with a higher socioeconomic position—better-off people reported more stress. If you adjusted the associations of stress with smoking, drinking, and exercise for measures of socioeconomic position, the associations got stronger.[41] This measure was telling us something about how people were feeling, which was reflected in their behavioural patterns.

You would imagine that this stress measure should be associated with higher risk of mortality—it was associated with smoking, heavy drinking, and other risky behaviours. The remarkable thing was that because it was associated with higher socioeconomic position, stress was apparently protective in this study.[43] All-cause mortality was lower in the people with high stress, as was cardiovascular disease mortality. Interestingly, smoking-related cancers were lower in the people with high stress, presumably because of the con-founding by socially patterned risk factors. The point here is that if stress is socially patterned the 'wrong way' then it appears that stress is protective. This is perhaps analogous to the way that type A behaviour ceased to predict coronary heart disease once diagnosed coronary heart disease was no longer a disease apparently of the affluent. In our study, psychiatric hospital admissions were much higher in people with high stress. This stress measure meant something. 'High stress' people also got admitted to hospital more for haem-orrhoids, varicose veins, and other non-mandatory admissions.[44] Stress influenced the way they presented to hospital. It did not influence the onset of cardiovascular disease, however.

How can we get round confounding in observational epidemiology? One way is to reinstate one of Bradford Hill's causal criteria: specificity. If you think that stress processes influence cardiovascular disease, then they should not be related to other outcomes, as most diseases have only a finite number of causes. When exposures are associated in a general way with a wide variety of outcomes it is likely that confounding by socially patterned behavioural and environmental factors are at play. Early on in the HRT debate, Diana Petitti and colleagues pointed out that HRT use apparently protected against accidental and violent deaths in observational studies as much as against coronary heart disease and that given the lack of a plausible biological link between HRT and accidental/violent death both associations may have been confounded,[45] a suggestion later confirmed by the randomized controlled trials.[46]

The great shame in much of the stress literature is that only one endpoint—cardiovascular disease—is usually reported. If in the same study it was shown that stress was related to stomach cancer, or lung cancer, to the same degree as cardiovascular disease, this would suggest that confounding may well be generating the associations. Studies should report multiple outcomes.

## Bias

Finally, I'm going to address the issue of bias, with an illustration of how bias can generate associations in observational studies. In the Collaborative study, the men were followed up after 5 years and Rose's angina questionnaire was given out. There was a 2.5-fold higher risk of incident angina among the men who reported more stress, but no effect on incident ischaemia,[47] or, as we have seen, cardiovascular disease mortality (Table 5.2). Indeed ischaemia and cardiovascular disease mortality showed reversed effects, presumably because the people reporting more stress experienced more favourable social cir-cumstances. The large apparent influence of stress on incident angina was

**Table 5.2** Odds ratios (95% confidence intervals) for incident angina and ischaemia at second screening by reported stress category at first screening (low stress as baseline, mean follow-up period of 5 years 2 months)[47]

| | Incident angina | | Incident ischaemia | | Coronary heart disease mortality | |
|---|---|---|---|---|---|---|
| | Adjusted for age only | Adjusted for age, socioeconomic position, screening interval, and risk factors* | Adjusted for age only | Adjusted for age, socioeconomic position, screening interval, and risk factors* | Adjusted for age, only | Adjusted for age, socioeconomic position, and risk factors* |
| High stress | 2.32 (1.43–3.78) | 2.66 (1.61–4.41) | 0.63 (0.34–1.15) | 0.67 (0.36–1.26) | 0.86 (0.67–1.12) | 0.96 (0.74–1.25) |
| Medium stress | 1.22 (0.82–1.82) | 1.37 (0.91–2.08) | 1.04 (0.73–1.48) | 1.03 (0.71–1.49) | 0.86 (0.72–1.03) | 0.97 (0.81–1.16) |
| Low stress | 1.00 | 1.00 | 1.00 | 1.00 | 1.00 | 1.00 |
| P for trend | 0.002 | <0.001 | 0.27 | 0.37 | 0.14 | 0.72 |

* Risk factors: smoking, alcohol consumption, weekly hours of exercise, cholesterol concentration, diastolic blood pressure, body mass index, forced expiratory volume in 1 second.

**Table 5.3** Incident angina, according to level of perceived psychological stress at baseline, with and without adjustment for reporting tendency[48]

| Perceived stress | Mean reporting tendency score | Incident angina* (odds ratio (95% confidence interval)) | |
| --- | --- | --- | --- |
| | | Adjustment A—age, socioeconomic position, smoking, alcohol consumption, weekly as exercise, blood pressure, cholesterol, body mass index, lung function | Adjustment B as in A, plus reporting tendency score |
| High (n = 739) | 0.77 | 2.63 (1.59–4.33) | 2.28 (1.37–3.80) |
| Medium (n = 3017) | 0.52 | 1.36 (0.90–2.05) | 1.27 (0.84–1.92) |
| Low (n = 1821) | 0.41 | 1.00 | 1.00 |
| P for trend | <0.001 | <0.001 | 0.003 |

probably seen because the people who reported high stress also reported other forms of discomfort in their lives, including chest pain. This was obviously not due to there being any actual stress-related coronary disease, otherwise it would have been revealed in incident ischaemia and cardiovascular disease mortality. We had a good indicator of reporting tendency in this study. A series of symptoms were queried, which were thought to be symptoms of diabetes, but most of these symptoms did not predict mortality.[48] If you want a marker of reporting tendency you want something that does not predict mortality. This measure was quite strongly related to stress reporting. It was also related to reporting other factors, such as low job satisfaction, that we had in the study and seemed to be a marker of a tendency to report high rates of symptoms. It was related to Rose angina, but if you adjusted for reporting tendency, this made very little difference to the results (Table 5.3).[48] The point is that adjustment for measures of negative affectivity in studies does not actually control for reporting tendency. We could have published the 2.5-fold increased risk of angina independent of confounders and reporting tendency, because studies of stress have got into major journals reporting on just this outcome and with similar effect sizes (Table 5.4). Rather than this, we reported these results as demonstrating how it is possible to get misleading findings on stress and disease from observational epidemiology. It is interesting to compare our results using the Reeder questionnaire with the Whitehall study findings for job control (Table 5.5).[49] The two studies got very similar results with a subjective measure—Rose angina. In both studies there was no asso-

**Table 5.4** Recent studies reporting relationships between subjective exposures and subjective health outcomes

| Study | Subjective exposure | Health outcome | Effects described | Comments |
|---|---|---|---|---|
| Collaborative study | Global perceived stress | Odds ratio for incident Rose angina | High stress, 2.28 (1.37–3.80); medium stress, 1.27 (0.84–1.92); low stress, 1.00 | Results adjusted for age, cardiac risk factors, occupational class and reporting tendency |
| Bosma et al. (1997)[49] | Job control | Odds ratio for incident Rose angina | Low control, 2.02 (1.22–3.34); intermediate control, 1.44 (0.86–2.39); high control, 1.00 | Results adjusted for age, cardiac risk factors, employment grade and reporting tendency |
| Bosma et al. (1999)[58] | Psychological attributes | Odds ratio for self-reported adult 'poor general health' by childhood social class | Odds ratio of 1.67 (1.02–2.75) associated with lowest childhood social class reduced to 1.45 (0.87–2.43) on adjustment for locus of control | Results adjusted for age, marital status, urbanisation, religious affiliation and adult social class |
| Evans et al. (2000)[59] | Worry about pressure at work | Self-reported quality of life (SF-36) scores | Trend of decreasing health status with increasing worry about pressure at work for all eight dimensions of SF-36 | Results adjusted for age, sex, ethnicity, marital status, education, occupational class, employment status, disease risk factors, environmental hazards |
| Cheng et al. (2000)[60] | 'Job strain' (job control, job demands, and work-related social support) | Change in self-reported quality of life (SF-36) scores | Physical functioning deteriorated more and mental health improved less in subjects with low compared to high job strain (change in physical functioning with high control, –3.12 (–4.37 to –1.87), low control, –3.76 (–4.95 to –2.57)) | Results adjusted for age, disease risk factors, marital status, educational level, presence of confidant and job insecurity |

**Table 5.5** Associations odds ratios (95% confidence intervals) between perceived stress and job control and subjective and objective outcomes in the West of Scotland Collaborative study and the Whitehall II study[47,49,61]

| Outcome type | Effects in Collaborative study | Effects in Whitehall II study |
|---|---|---|
| *Fully subjective** | | |
| High exposure | 2.66 (1.61–4.41) | 2.02 (1.22–2.34) |
| Medium exposure | 1.37 (0.91–2.08) | 1.44 (0.86–2.39) |
| Low exposure | 1.00 | 1.00 |
| *Fully objective†* | | |
| High exposure | 0.67 (0.36–1.26) | 1.17 (0.8–1.8) |
| Medium exposure | 1.03 (0.71–1.49) | 1.16 (0.8–1.7) |
| Low exposure | 1.00 | 1.00‡ |

* Rose angina in both studies. †Electrocardiogram abnormalities (Minnesota coding system) in both studies. All estimates adjusted for age, social position, and cardiovascular risk factors except for ‡, where only unadjusted estimates were reported in the paper.[61]

ciation between job control and the non-subjective measure of electro-cardiogram (ECG) ischaemia. There is a remarkable parallelism between the findings.

In observational epidemiology, we need to take both confounding and bias into account. If a stress measure is not confounded with social position and other behavioural factors, then one needs to consider bias. If it is both related to reporting tendency and confounded, then both need to be considered. Every time we see an epidemiological result, the β-carotene, vitamin C, and HRT examples should come to mind.

## Evidence from experimental studies and non-human primates

The preceding discussion of approaches to interpretational difficulty in observational data aside, the most powerful strategy to minimize the possibility of confounding is random allocation of exposure level within an experimental study. In this way any confounding factors (measured or unmeasured) should be evenly distributed across the different levels of exposure such that any effect seen is truly that of the exposure. To allow this approach, exposure level must be modifiable through an intervention amenable to random allocation. Arguably, this provides the strongest and most practically relevant evidence on causality, because a positive treatment effect demonstrates both the existence of a causal relation and the effectiveness of an intervention based on this relation.

The number of experimental studies of the effects of psychosocial intervention on objective measures of heart disease is relatively small. Most have assessed effects on prognosis amongst individuals with established heart disease. The factors determining prognosis in people with heart disease may not be the same, or may not have the same relative importance, as those determining disease development. Nevertheless this evidence is still useful as an indicator of the potential of psychosocial interventions to improve population cardiovascular health. In most published examples 'stress reduction' interventions were delivered as part of an intervention package targeting multiple risk factors such as smoking, diet, and exercise and aiming to improve case management. Reviews of these studies have suggested small but significant effects on prognosis, but have not been able to disaggregate the effects of the psychosocial component of the intervention from that of other components.[50,51]

A 'pure' psychosocial intervention was assessed in the recently completed Enhancing Recovery in Coronary Heart Disease Patients (ENRICHD) trial, a study considerably larger than any of those included in the preceding reviews.[52] Depression is perhaps the psychosocial factor with the strongest candidature for a causal relation with heart disease.[53] Because of this, ENRICHD assessed the effect of depression reduction (through cognitive behavioural therapy—with adjunctive use of sertraline at physicians' discretion) on the prognosis of established heart disease. The intervention was effective in reducing depression, but heart disease prognosis was the same amongst controls as in the intervention group. Indeed, lead investigators on ENRICHD acknowledged that the association between depression and heart disease may not be causal and have emphasized that the principal justification for treating depression is improved quality of life, more than reduction in mortality[54]

Patel and colleagues described perhaps the most convincing demonstration of an effect of a psychosocial intervention on coronary mortality amongst subjects without clinical heart disease at study recruitment.[55] Following a stress reduction intervention (relaxation therapy) amongst a group of subjects at high coronary risk, one control subject out of 81 died from heart disease and five out of 81 had ECG changes compatible with myocardial infarction, whereas no intervention subjects died from heart disease and only one out of 88 had ECG changes compatible with myocardial infarction, during a 4-year follow-up. The authors at the time suggested that, 'If the results of this study could be obtained in a larger study the financial and health care implications would be enormous.' Based on their preliminary results this seems a reasonable assertion—however it is noteworthy that almost 20 years later nobody has reported replication of these findings in a larger study.

Finally, primate models of psychosocial stress and coronary heart disease have been used to support the plausibility of various claims about stress and this condition. However, the totality of evidence demonstrates considerable heterogeneity—because as many studies exist that appear to demonstrate effects in one direction as show the opposite. Authors choose to cite the studies that support their hypothesis, ignoring those that run in the exactly opposite direction.[56] As in other areas of epidemiology, biological plausibility, when used in this way, is a very weak criteria for causality and animal evidence should be treated with as much respect as evidence from humans—through systematic reviewing, rather than the current and highly unsatisfactory pick-and-mix approach.[57]

## Coda: which type of doctor?

In this presentation I have suggested that the epidemiological evidence supporting important contributions of psychosocial factors as direct causes of disease is limited. However, it might be suggested that despite this, a doctor who is influenced by the BPS is the sort of doctor one would like to consult when sick. I am not so certain about this. When writing about a myocardial infarction patient whom he had seen, Engel stated, 'In the end, whether the patient lives or dies, the biopsychosocial model further provides the physician with the conceptual tools to clearly think and plan the implications of the cardiac arrest.'[3] If I have a heart attack, I want to be treated by a doctor who cares about whether the patient lives or dies. I'm not really concerned about whether the doctor has the above-mentioned conceptual tools, I would rather have a doctor who keeps up to date with the best evidence on somatic treatments and gives me morphine, a thrombolytic, and aspirin, then puts me on appropriate long-term treatments.

## Acknowledgements

Many thanks to John Macleod for comments on an earlier draft of this chapter.

## References

1. Davey Smith G, Whitley E, Dorling D, Gunnell D. Area based measures of social and economic circumstances: cause specific mortality patterns depend on the choice of index. *J Epidemiol Commun Health* 2001; **55:** 149–50.

2. Engel GL. The need for a new medical model: a challenge for biomedicine. *Science* 1977; **196:** 129–36.

3. Engel GL. The biopsychosocial model and the education of health professionals. *Ann NY Acad Sci* 1978; **310:** 169–87.

4. Davey Smith G. Behind the Broad Street pump: aetiology, epidemiology and prevention of cholera in mid-19th century Britain. *Int J Epidemiol* 2002; **31**: 920–32.

5. Lawlor DA, Frankel S, Shaw M, Ebrahim S, Davey Smith G. Smoking and ill health: does lay epidemiology explain the failure of smoking cessation programs among deprived populations? *Am J Pub Health* 2003; **93**: 266–70.

6. Rosenberg CE. *The cholera years: the United States in 1832, 1849 and 1866*. Chicago: University of Chicago Press; 1962.

7. Sontag S. *Illness as metaphor*. New York: Random House; 1978.

8. Davies DT, Macbeth Wilson AT. Observations on the life-history of chronic peptic ulcer. *Lancet* 1937; **11th December:** 1353–60.

9. Avery Jones F. Gastro-intestinal disorders including liver diseases. In: Daley R, Miller HG, ed. *Progress in clinical medicine*. London: Churchill; 1948. pp. 53–93.

10. Monson RR. Familial factors in peptic ulcer. II Family structure in duodenal ulcer. *Am J Epidemiol* 1970; **91**: 460–66.

11. Adami H-O, Bergström R, Nyrén O, Forhaug K, Gustavsson S, Lööf L, Nyberg A. Is duodenal ulcer really a psychosomatic disease? A population-based case–control study. *Scand J Gastroenterol* 1987; **22**: 889–96.

12. Nasiry R, Piper DW. Social aspects of chronic duodenal ulcer. A case control study. *Digestion* 1983; **27**: 196–202.

13. Paffenbarger RS Jr, Wing AL, Hyde RT. Chronic disease in former college students. XIII Early precursors of peptic ulcer. *Am J Epidemiol* 1974; **160**: 307–15.

14. Goldberg EM. *Family influences and psychosomatic illness. An inquiry into the social and psychological background*. London: Tavistock; 1958.

15. Mirsky IA. Physiologic, psychologic, and social determinants in the etiology of duodenal ulcer. *Am J Digest Dis* 1958; **3**: 285–314.

16. Susser M, Stein Z. Civilization and peptic ulcer. *Lancet* 1962; **20 January:** 115–19 (reprinted in *Int J Epidemiol* 2002; **31**: 13–17).

17. Sonnenberg A, Muller H, Pace F. Birth cohort analysis of peptic ulcer mortality in Europe. *J Chron Dis* 1985; **38**: 309–17.

18. Frost WH. The age selection of mortality from tuberculosis in successive decades. *Am J Hyg* 1939; **30**: 91–96.

19. Springett VH. An interpretation of statistical trends in tuberculosis. *Lancet* 1952; **March 15:** 521–25.

20. Susser M. Causes of peptic ulcer. A selective epidemiologic review. *J Chron Dis* 1967; **20**: 435–56.

21. Harvey RF, Spence RW, Lane JA, Nair P, Murray LJ, Harvey IM *et al.* Relationship between the birth cohort pattern of *Helicobacter pylori* infection and the epidemiology of duodenal ulcer. *Q J Med* 2002; **95**: 519–25.

22. Szasz TS, Robertson AM. A theory of the pathogenesis of ordinary human baldness. *Arch Dermatol Syphilol* 1950; **61**: 34–48.

23. Asher R. Is baldness psychological? In: *A sense of Asher: A new miscellany*. London: Keynes Press; 1983 (originally published in 1951).

24. Christie DA, Tansey EM. *Wellcome witnesses to twentieth century medicine. Peptic ulcer: rise and fall*. London: Wellcome Trust Centre for the History of Medicine; 2002. Vol. 14.

25. Morris JN. *Uses of epidemiology*. 3rd edn. Edinburgh: Churchill Livingstone; 1975.

26. Anonymous. Georgraphy of peptic ulcer. *BMJ* 1959; **October 10:** 668.

27. Kidd M, Modlin IM. A century of *Helicobacter pylori*. *Digestion* 1998; **59:** 1–15.

28. Ewald PW. *Plague time: the new germ theory of disease*. New York: Anchor Books; 2002.

29. Rigas B, Feretis C, Papavassiliou ED. John Lykoudis: an unappreciated discoverer of the cause and treatment of peptic ulcer disease. *Lancet* 1999; **354:** 1634–35.

30. Lööf L, Adami HO, Bates S, Fagerström KO, Gustavsson S, Nyberg A *et al*. Psychological group counseling for the prevention of ulcer relapses: a controlled randomized trial in duodenal and prepyloric ulcer disease. *J Clin Gastroenterol* 1987; **9:** 400–7.

31. Wilhelmsen I, Haug TT, Ursin H, Berstad A. Effect of short-term cognitive psychotherapy on recurrence of duodenal ulcer: a prospective randomized trial. *Psychosom Med* 1994; **56:** 440–48.

32. Wilhelmsen I, Haug TT, Berstad A, Ursin H. Increased relapse of duodenal ulcers in patients treated with cognitive psychotherapy. *Lancet* 1990; **336:** 307.

33. Egger M, Schneider M, Davey Smith G. Spurious precision? Meta-analysis of observational studies. *BMJ* 1998; **316:** 140–4.

34. Laurence J. Eating fruit halves the risk of an early death. *Independent* 2001; **March 4:** 13.

35. Khaw K-T, Bingham S, Welch A, Luben R, Wareham N, Oakes S, Day N. Relation between plasma ascorbic acid and mortality in men and women in EPIC-Norfolk prospective study: a prospective population study. *Lancet* 2001; **357:** 657–63.

36. Heart Protection Study Collaborative Group. MRC/BHF Heart Protection Study of antioxidant vitamin supplementation in 20 536 high-risk individuals: a randomised placebo-controlled trial. *Lancet* 2002; **360:** 23–33.

37. Davey Smith G, Ebrahim S. Data dredging, bias, or confounding. *BMJ* 2002; **325:** 1437–38.

38. Davey Smith G, Shipley MJ, Rose G. Magnitude and causes of socio-economic differentials in mortality: further evidence from the Whitehall Study. *J Epidemiol Commun Health* 1990; **44:** 265–70.

39. Phillips A, Davey Smith G. How independent are 'independent' effects? Relative risk estimation when correlated exposures are measured imprecisely. *J Clin Epidemiol* 1991; **44:** 1223–31.

40. Phillips AN, Davey Smith G. Confounding in epidemiological studies. *BMJ* 1993; **306:** 142.

41. Heslop P, Davey Smith G, Carroll D, Macleod J, Hyland F, Hart C. Perceived stress and coronary heart disease risk factors: the contribution of socio-economic position. *Br J Health Psychol* 2001; **6:** 167–78.

42. Metcalfe C, Davey Smith G, Wadsworth E, Sterne JAC, Heslop P, MacLeod J *et al*. A contemporary validation of the Reeder stress inventory. *Br J Health Psychol* 2003; **8:** 83–94.

43. Macleod J, Davey Smith G, Heslop P, Metcalfe C, Carroll D, Hart C. Are the effects of psychosocial exposures attributable to confounding? Evidence from a prospective observational study on psychological stress and mortality. *J Epidemiol Commun Health* 2001; **55:** 878–84.

44. Metcalfe C, Davey Smith G, Macleod J, Heslop P, Hart C. Self-reported stress and subsequent hospital admissions as a result of hypertension, varicose veins and haemorrhoids. *J Pub Health Med* 2003; **25:** 62–68.

45. Petitti DB, Perlman JA, Sidney S. Postmenopausal estrogen use and heart disease. *N Engl J Med* 1986; **315:**131–32.

46. Beral V, Banks E, Reeves G. Evidence from randomised trials on the long-term effects of hormone replacement therapy. *Lancet* 2002; **360:** 942–4

47. Macleod J, Davey Smith G, Heslop P, Metcalfe C, Carroll D, Hart C. Psychological stress and cardiovascular disease: empirical demonstration of bias in a prospective observational study on Scottish men. *BMJ* 2002; **324:** 1247–51.

48. MacLeod J, Davey Smith G, Heslop P, Metcalfe C, Carroll D, Hart C. Limitations of adjustment for reporting tendency in observational studies of stress and self reported coronary heart disease. *J Epidemiol Commun Health* 2002; **56:** 76–77.

49. Bosma H, Marmot MG, Hemingway H, Nicholson AC, Brunner E, Stansfeld SA. Low job control and risk of coronary heart disease in Whitehall II (prospective cohort) study *BMJ* 1997; **314:** 558–65.

50. Linden W, Stossel C, Maurice J. Psychosocial interventions for patients with coronary artery disease: a meta-analysis. *Arch Intern Med* 1996; **156:** 745–52.

51. Dusseldorp E, van Elderen T, Maes S, Meulman J, Kraaij V. A meta-analysis of psychoeducational programs for coronary heart disease patients. *Health Psychol* 1999; **18:** 506–19.

52. Writing Committee for the ENRICHD Investigators. Effects of treating depression and low perceived social support on clinical events after myocardial infarction: the Enhancing Recovery in Coronary Heart Disease Patients (ENRICHD) randomized trial. *JAMA* 2003; **289:** 3106–16

53. Wulsin LR, Vaillant GE, Wells VE. A systematic review of the mortality of depression. *Psychosom Med* 1999; **61:** 6–17.

54. Lesperance F, Frasure-Smith N. The seduction of death. *Psychosom Med* 1999; **61:** 18–20.

55. Patel C, Marmot MG, Terry DJ, Carruthers M, Hunt B, Patel M. Trial of relaxation in reducing coronary risk: four year follow-up. *BMJ* 1985; **290:** 1103–6.

56. Petticrew M, Davey Smith G. Monkey Business: what do primate studies of social hierarchies, stress, and the development of CHD tell us about humans? Society for Social Medicine Abstract. *J Epidemiol Commun Health* 2003; **57**(Suppl 1): A1–21.

57. Pound P, Ebrahim S, Sandercock P, Bracken MB, Roberts I. Where is the evidence that animal research benefits humans? *BMJ* 2004; **328:** 514–17.

58. Bosma H, van de Mheen HD, Mackenbach JP. Social class in childhood and general health in adulthood: questionnaire study of contribution of psychological attributes. *BMJ* 1999; **318:** 18–22.

59. Evans J, Hyndman S, Stewart-Brown S, Smith D, Petersen P. An epidemiological study of the relative importance of damp housing in relation to adult health. *J Epidemiol Commun Health* 2000; **54:** 677–86.

60. Cheng Y, Kawachi I, Coakley EH, Schwarz J, Colditz G. Association between psychosocial work characteristics and health functioning in American women: prospective study. *BMJ* 2000; **320:** 1432–6.

61. Stansfeld SA, Fuhrer R, Shipley MJ, Marmot MG. Psychological distress as a risk factor for coronary heart disease in the Whitehall II study. *Int J. Epidemiol* 2002; **31:** 248–55.

## Discussion

*Wessely*: That was a powerful and uncomfortable paper. We should remember a couple of things, though. You presented a strong argument against hubris and accepting fashionable trends, merely because they are fashionable. There will undoubtedly be many people, including, for example, those who one might call 'CFS activists', who would have loved every word you were saying. There is a popular and seductive Whiggish view of medical history in which we move implicitly from unknown diseases which are thought to be psychiatric and as we become brighter, better scientists they are finally accepted in the pantheon of real diseases. You should remember that there is an opposite trend as well, which you didn't mention. You ignored the history of visceral proptosis, floating kidney, autointoxication, or focal sepsis, for example. There are also lots of other things that are seen as very clearly organic and which switch the other way.

*Stansfeld*: I realize that we have to take into account both negative affectivity and confounding. This is really important but do they really explain away all the effects of psychosocial factors. Are you saying, then, that psychosocial factors are going to have no impact on the aetiology of physical illness? For example, George Brown and others have worked on symbolic loss, in terms of events like not being promoted to a job, or if your partner is unfaithful, in relation to mental illness. The evidence for psychosocial factors as causal factors in mental illness, particularly depression, is quite strong. If I didn't feel that, I would get another job. But in relation to physical illness I wonder about work like Jane Ferrie's on job insecurity, where she has shown effects of perceived job insecurity on indices of coronary heart disease risk. What do you think about the possibility of these sorts of effects? If psychosocial influences don't lead directly to physical illness, what about effects on ageing, for example?

*Davey Smith*: First, I certainly think psychosocial factors are plausible contributors to mental illness. I have no doubt this is the case. Psychosocial factors are also importantly related to how people rate their quality of life, which is probably more important in countries with high longevity than is merely living longer. My main point was about disease aetiology. As a disease epidemiologist I want to get the right answers about this. As an aside, I think we know massively more about disease aetiology now than we did in 1977. The constant quoting of nihilistic statements about us having 'lost the war on cancer' and so on is wrong. We know the causes of some 70% of world-wide cancers. This is remarkable.

As I said, with mental illness I think psychosocial factors are aetiologically important. They are also clearly aetiologically important in many other illnesses, but as factors which influence the distribution of known exposures, not as direct causes, in my view. Most illness is related to specific exposures. The example I started off with was cholera. People in epidemiology are generally taught about John Snow and cholera. The Whiggish view is that Snow came along, found that cholera was transmissible by water and dealt with it. What is remarkable about Snow's writings was that he had an extraordinarily nuanced view of how exposures came about.[1] First, he didn't just think that cholera was waterborne, but that it could also be faecally–orally transmitted. Where he worked, as a general practitioner during the 1832 outbreak, was near a mining community, and he noticed that miners had a high rate of cholera. He went down the pit and observed the conditions in which they had to eat and excrete. He noticed how these conditions ensured that transmission would occur. Snow's recommendation for dealing with cholera in miners was to give them work breaks so they could use proper toilet facilities. This is a beautiful and overlooked exposition of a simple model. Social factors were of key importance, but in the end they worked through influencing the distribution of exposures. In my view susceptibility has been overplayed and exposure has been under-appreciated in social epidemiology.

*Marmot:* I would emphasize Simon Wessely's point. It is easy to look back and say, 'Gosh how silly they were in the past to think all these silly thoughts; aren't we clever now!' There are many examples of people being silly all over the place, not just in the past. Your logic seems to be to seize on the notion of stress and say that people were silly about it before, therefore we should never think about stress ever again. I have a problem with your logic. The fact that not all diseases that were thought to be due to autoimmunity are so, does not mean that none is. The question is not could diseases be influenced by stress, of course they could, but instead what is the evidence for it? Research has advanced beyond the examples you cite because there have been many advances in conceptualization and measurement of psychosocial factors. Given those advances, I find it curious that you chose to illustrate the fallibility of self-reported stress measures with the Reeder scale. We conducted a systematic review of psychosocial factors and coronary heart disease using only studies that passed through a quality filter.[2] Not a single article linked the Reeder scale with incidence of coronary heart disease. To show then that in your data the Reeder scale is not related to hard evidence of coronary disease is hardly surprising. If your point is that it illustrates that if the reported stress is self reported and the disease outcome is self reported, there could be bias, my answer is, of course. The fact that there could be a spurious association does not mean there is. Yes, of course there can be reporting bias. The fact that you can illustrate it does not mean that either it is the whole story in the studies you cite (my own, for example), or in the wealth of other literature on this subject. That's why in my chapter I spent some time discussing the systematic review of the evidence that actually looked at validated endpoints. Self-reported measures of psychosocial factors predict validated diagnoses of heart disease and mortality.

Your other criticism is confounding—a problem recognized by the founders of epidemiology, by Durkheim, by philosophers, by most scientists. We know confounding can occur. What one could take away from what you said is the message that controlled trials get it right, while observational studies get it wrong. You used the well-known example of the failure of the trials of β-carotene to prevent disease. Observational studies suggest a protective effect. Trials do not. One suggestion is that that β-carotene might be a marker for dietary intake, but it is not the β-carotene that has the protective effect. Your conclusion, though, was that if the trials didn't give the same results as the observational studies then the latter must have had incomplete control for confounding. In a technical sense that is true if the exposure is carotene. It is confounded by other dietary elements. If, however, the exposure is diet—fruit and vegetables perhaps—then the mistake the trials made was to intervene on an indicator, rather than the real exposure. The trouble is to do a dietary trial of prevention of heart disease does not solve the confounding problem. Enrol people in a dietary trial and they mess you up by taking up jogging. Trials are *an* answer to some questions. They are not *the* answer to all questions. You have delighted and stimulated your many admirers with a raft of observational studies about the life course, including parents' social class, education, childhood growth, voting patterns, social disruption, and disease. Are you now saying that all these studies of yours are wrong because they were observational studies, not controlled trials and therefore had incomplete control for confounding? Surely not? One of course needs to be careful in controlling for confounding. As an example, take the Finnish study that I cited that showed a link between low control and coronary mortality.[3] Reporting bias is unlikely with death as an endpoint. Would your other criticism of confounding by social class apply? It showed exactly what you would expect: that the association between job control and heart disease weakens when you control for social class and social position. This is what you would expect if low control were on the pathway between low social position and coronary disease. The association weakens but it doesn't go away.

*Davey Smith*: For medical treatments such as hormone replacement therapy (HRT) the randomized trials with long-term follow-up do get the right answer. Doctors told women that HRT reduced the risk of cardiovascular disease on the basis of observational data producing about the same relative risk as seen in the Finnish study of job control you refer to. The relative risks in the observational HRT studies changed in about the same way on adjustment for confounding factors as do the relative risks in the job control studies. However there were massively more observational data on HRT, consistently suggesting that it was protective against coronary heart disease. If any doctors are now giving advice on the basis of this observational data, I think they are doing their patients a disservice. The randomized trials of HRT give the right answer to the question 'will my patients experience reduced coronary heart disease risk if they take HRT?' The answer is 'no'.

In the β-carotene example, of course β-carotene is a marker of something else—this is the definition of confounding! Millions of people in the USA were taking β-carotene supplements on the basis of the observational studies. The best test of the effect of β-carotene supplements comes from randomized trials, which do give evidence on cause and effect. I think epidemiology as a whole needs to revisit the issue of the importance of confounding. There are approaches to data analysis such as sensitivity analysis that could really help observational epidemiology. This is now a tractable approach. The specificity issue is also key: I'd really like to see reports of other outcomes than coronary heart disease in many of these observational studies of psychosocial factors. There are also novel ways of using genetic markers as ways of testing causal effects of environmental exposures.[4] So we can get more robust evidence from observational studies, but these approaches have not really been utilized in the psychosocial field.

*Elwyn:* You raised very interesting issues about aetiology. We have heard other presentations about interventions. We may have to differentiate in the biopsychosocial model between aetiology, where it is a weaker kind of model and intervention for complex diseases such as back pain, cardiac syndromes, and depression. We have yet to grapple with the design of interventions.

## References

1. Davey Smith G. Behind the Broad Street pump: aetiology, epidemiology and prevention of cholera in mid-19th century Britain. *Int J. Epidemiol* 2002; **31**: 920–32.
2. Kuper H, Marmot M, Hemingway H. Psychosocial factors in the aetiology and prognosis of coronary disease: a systematic review. *Semin Vasc Med* 2002; **2**: 267–314.
3. Kivimaki M, Leino-Arjas P, Luukkonen R, Riihimaki H, Vahtera J, Kirjonen J. Work stress and risk of cardiovascular mortality: prospective cohort study of industrial employees. *BMJ* 2002; **325**: 857–60.
4. Davey Smith G, Ebrahim S. 'Mendelian randomization': can genetic epidemiology contribute to understanding environmental determinants of disease? *Int J Epidemiol* 2003; **32**: 1–22.

# 6 Can neurobiology explain the relationship between stress and disease?

## Stafford Lightman

## Summary

Events that have occurred early in life, perhaps during a period of prolonged stress, may affect biological processes, sometimes permanently. The central nervous system (CNS) is the prime candidate for both being the sensor for these and also the major controller of the response to both physiological and pathological stimuli. There is good evidence that these responses include changes to midbrain neurotransmitter concentrations, the hypothalamic–pituitary–adrenal (HPA) axis, and the autonomic nervous system. These are both determined and differentiated by acute and chronic stressors, particularly those experienced at an early age. I will use animal models of stress to demonstrate these changes.

## The stress response

Extreme stress can bring about intense emotion, which causes a variety of physiological reactions. There is central activation of the hypothalamus, which will have two major outputs. One is direct neural activation through both the sympathetic nervous system, affecting blood vessels and the adrenal medulla and the parasympathetic nervous system. The second is a humoral route through which the hypothalamus releases corticotrophin-releasing hormone (CRH) and arginine vasopression (AVP). These act on the anterior pituitary, which then releases adrenocorticotrophin (ACTH), which acts on the adrenal glands to secrete cortisol, which then circulates around the body. This is the output of stress.

I will focus firstly on what is controlling this output, rather than the output itself. I should add here that I do not like the word 'stress' and what I am really referring to are 'stressors' that impact on the CNS. All sorts of stressors in the internal or exterior environment can affect us by activating the brainstem,

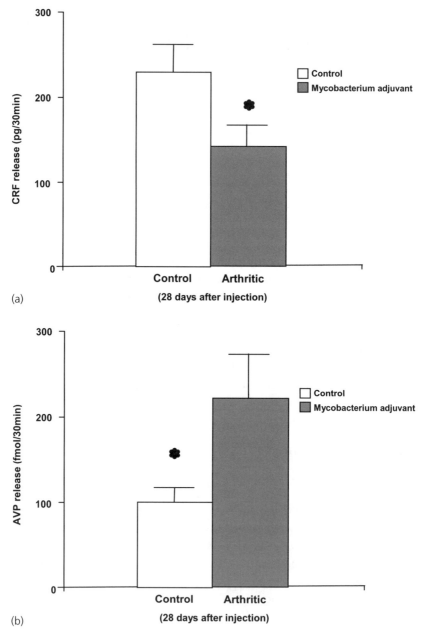

**Fig. 6.1** Hypophysial portal blood concentrations of corticotrophin releasing factor (CRF) (a) and arginine vasopressin (AVP) (b) in control animals and animals with chronic inflammatory stress secondary to injection with mycobacterial adjuvant (Freund's adjuvant) in the tail base 28 days previously. Note the reduction in CRH and the increase in AVP during chronic stress.

hippocampus, or amygdala. These activate the hypothalamus, which secretes CRH and AVP, which in turn act on the pituitary gland. If we suffer an acute stressor, this is what we expect to happen. For example, if you give rats an injection of endotoxin, this will result in an increase in CRH messenger ribonucleic acid (mRNA) in the hypothalamus and the concentration of ACTH precursor pro-opiomelancortin mRNA increases in the anterior pituitary, followed by ACTH and then corticosterone increasing in the plasma. This response is adaptive and it is good for us.

We are more interested in maladaptation to chronic stress. It is difficult to do good experiments with chronic stress in animals, but we have been able to do this using a model of autoimmune arthritis. Rats were treated with an injection of Freund's adjuvant in the tail base. About 11 days later, they developed arthritis. Their blood levels of ACTH rose very rapidly and corticosterone levels were also elevated. This chronic stress was maintained for a prolonged period, resulting in chronic activation of the HPA axis that was maintained as long as they had the arthritis. The odd thing here is that there was a huge increase of CRH mRNA in the hypothalamus with an acute stress, but with chronic stress the CRH levels plummeted and AVP rose (see Figs 6.1(a) and 6.1(b)).[1] From the brain's perspective, what happens in an animal with chronic stress is completely different from acute stress. The chemistry of that part of the brain completely changes. The details do not matter: the significant factor is that what turns on the stress response has changed. The normal stress response, mediated by CRH, has been replaced by a totally different mediator, AVP, which has taken over the activation of the HPA axis. The hypothalamus has detected that the stress is chronic, rather than acute and has changed the way it is responding to this stress.

This does not only happen in induced disease. We see a similar effect in mice with spontaneous systemic lupus erythematosus, a chronic autoimmune disease. As they get older the disease gets more severe. Despite increased levels of plasma corticosterone, CRH mRNA actually goes down and AVP mRNA goes up.[2]

## The effect of time on the stress response

The hypothalamic response is not only determined by what happens acutely, but also by past experience, even things that happened a very long time ago. Shanks and colleagues gave newborn rats a small injection of endotoxin on days 2 and 5 of their lives and gave littermate controls corresponding saline injections.[3] This endotoxin injection had no immediate effect other than a slight temperature rise and the rats were still looked after normally by their mothers. They were brought up together with their littermates and showed no distinguishing features. When they were adult, she examined the CRH mRNA levels in these rats and showed that those given endotoxin had an increased level of CRH mRNA. This mild infection early on in their lives had affected their brains for the whole of the rest of their lives, so they had been 'hard-wired' differently from an early age.

## Brain–body communication of the stress response

How does all this information get into the brain? How does the brain know what is going on in the body? There has been a lot of interest in the fact that if you activate the immune system, this causes the release of many cytokines, which flood the body and affect the brain. This makes sense as a default pathway when you are very ill, but it does not seem to explain the sickness behaviour and raised body temperature seen in mild and even very localized disease processes. Somehow your brain knows what is going on.

Work done by Dantzer and others suggests that the peripheral nervous system and in particular the vagus nerve is important in mediating some of these responses.[4] We have been very interested in finding out how the messages from the periphery get to the brain, how the brain might know what is going on in the body, and how this might affect the way the brain responds and ultimately alters behaviour. We have studied the role of the peripheral nervous system in mediating some of these responses, using the lungs as our model system. Lungs have a large vagal innervation and we can actually give mice a mild and short-term infection similar to tuberculosis, by using a closely related bacterium *Mycobacterium vaccae*. This results in a large but temporary increase in corticosterone. We wanted to know the pathway through which this infection activates the brain. The first thing we did was to look at the site in the brain that receives the input from the vagus nerve. This is called the nucleus of the solitary tract. We found that simply causing a mild inflammation in the lungs rapidly activates (within 12 hours) a lot of cells in the nucleus of the tractus solitarius in the brainstem.

Where else was the brain activated? The dorsal raphe nucleus, part of the serotonergic system in the midbrain, which projects to a major degree to the limbic system and the locus coeruleus, a huge noradrenergic group of cells projecting to the forebrain, were also activated. We therefore have very good evidence that inflammation in the lungs affects some very important cell groups within the CNS. These project to areas of importance not only for neuroendocrinology but also for mood and behaviour. We therefore have a mechanism through which the peripheral nervous system can mediate both the behavioural and neuroendocrine effects of illness.

Is this all that goes on? We know that CRH in the hypothalamus controls the HPA axis, but it also projects back down to the brainstem. Indeed, there is a reciprocal system in which cells in the brainstem project to and activate the hypothalamus, which in turn can activate cells in the brainstem. We can look at these cells in the brainstem electrophysiologically. If we infuse CRH onto serotonergic neurones in the midbrain (remember there is a projection from the hypothalamus to the brainstem) we find an activation of these cells, with a dose–response relationship. We can see therefore that there are responses in the brainstem that can be modulated by activity of the stress-responsive cells in the hypothalamus. These can be blocked by an antagonist of CRH.[5]

## Brain–endocrine plasticity

What is the effect of recent experience on these brainstem neurones? We looked at rats that had a daily episode of restraint for 5 days. A normal rat, given a low dose of CRH, showed no activation of brainstem cells at all. In contrast, a rat restrained for 5 days, which was therefore under chronic stress, showed a major response when given the same very low dose of CRH. The experience of the animal changed its responsivity within the CNS. Not only did stress change the mixture of chemicals that were present within the hypo-thalamus, but it also affected the brainstem—the area that perceives all the external influences—by becoming hypersensitive to the signals coming into it. This changes completely the way this part of the CNS perceives the outside world.

These data reflect the plasticity of the brain in its responses to what is going on in the outside world. Different patterns of stress can change the way that different neurones, in very important parts of the brainstem and hypo-thalamus, respond to being activated. Does this have effects on the output? The most convenient outputs for us to look at are corticosterone in the rat and cortisol in man. We studied rats that had long-term cannulas and were in a room with no disturbances from human visitors. Blood samples were taken under computer control and this could be programmed as often as we wanted, without stressing the animals. The pattern of the secretion of corticosterone was not what would be expected (see Fig. 6.2). Most previous studies involved occasional blood samples from humans or rats and these suggest a smooth transition of plasma levels from morning to the evening. In reality, however, there are huge peaks and troughs.[6] In the dark phase, when rats were awake, there was a much higher concentration of corticosterone. When they were asleep, the level was lower. In humans we found just the same picture of peaks and troughs of cortisol throughout the day.

The pattern by which receptors perceive corticosterone determines the response of the tissue. This is important for our understanding of the nor-mality and abnormality of HPA function. Male and female rats, interestingly,

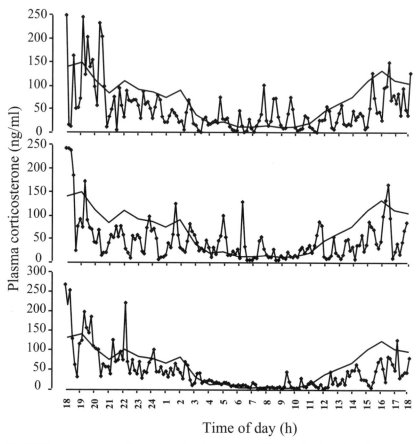

**Fig. 6.2** Plasma concentrations of corticosterone over 24 hours in three female Sprague–Dawley rats. Note the marked pulsatility of plasma corticosterone levels throughout the day. The smooth lines denote the mean levels averaged out for each of the three animals.

show quite different patterns, with females having much greater peaks of corticosterone than males. This may be an important determinant of the susceptibility to disease. There are also different patterns of hormone secretion with ageing. There is a marked diurnal rhythm of corticosterone in young rats, which is completely gone by middle age. What happens in disease? A normal rat will show typically 13 pulses of corticosterone in 24 hours, but an animal with chronic activation of the HPA axis (rats with arthritis) show 21 pulses per day and the patterning has completely changed.[7]

Lactation is an important and fascinating time of physiological change. Lactating humans and rats have a major difference in the regulation of the HPA axis. Most importantly, they do not respond to stress. When we looked in detail at 24-hour rhythms in lactating individuals, there was huge plasticity. They lost their circadian rhythm and had as much corticosterone secreted in the day as in the night. Seventy-two hours after the pups had gone their rhythm returned; even stronger than they had had it before. The HPA axis is a highly plastic system.[8]

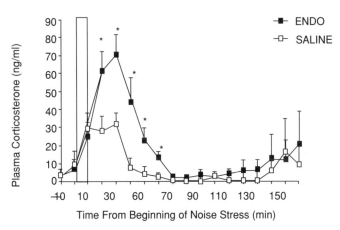

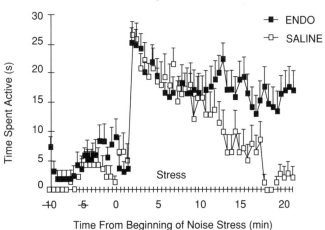

**Fig. 6.3** Plasma corticosterone levels in response to noise stress and measures of behavioural activity in animals that as neonates were injected with either saline or endotoxin. Reprinted from Reference 3. Copyright (2000) National Academy of Sciences, U.S.A.

Earlier, I described the data of Shanks and colleagues, when they gave newborn rats endotoxin on day 2 and day 5 of life.[3] When they became adults, they had elevated CRH levels in the hypothalamus. Shanks joined us and repeated this experiment and we then did 24-hour sampling in her animals to see what was actually happening to their hormonal activity. Was it causing an effect? The littermate controls have a totally normal 24-hour rhythm of corticosterone secretion, whereas the endotoxin-exposed animals had a little more in the daylight period and much greater corticosterone secretion at night.[3] This early intervention had not only changed the hard-wiring of the hypothalamus for the rest of their lives, but it had also changed the endogenous activity of the HPA axis throughout the whole of their lives. The implications of this are that the stress response change could affect susceptibility to affective disorders, autoimmune diseases, cardiovascular disease, and so on.

We have stressed these animals, giving them a noise stress of 105 decibels of white noise.[8] There was a normal stress response in the controls, but a much larger corticosterone response in the neonatally treated endotoxin animals (see Figure 6.3). It was not just hormones that changed—their behaviour was completely different. The endotoxin-exposed animals continued to be hyperactive after the noise stress was turned off, unlike the controls, which rapidly returned to their normal basal behaviour activity. Thus they exhibited a hardwired difference in their behaviour. Is this relevant to disease? I described earlier how we can cause arthritis in these animals with an adjuvant injection into the tail base. When we did this with the endotoxin-exposed animals they were completely resistant to arthritis! Early life events can therefore hard wire changes in hormone regulation, behaviour. and even disease susceptibility.

## Conclusion

In conclusion, I have shown that the brain is always receptive and is permanently listening to the body. It knows about things like infection and changes its own biochemical signature in response. If things happen in the neonatal period, the brain knows about it and this changes the brain for the rest of life. If over the last few weeks you have been undergoing some form of stressful stimulus, your brain knows about it and not only does it change its chemical signature, it changes its responsiveness to any new signal that is received by the brain. The way the brain responds, particularly in terms of corticosterone signalling by way of the HPA axis, has major effects on the pattern of hormone release. These are initially important for the responses of target tissues and changes in these patterns can alter susceptibility to and progression of disease.

# References

1. Chowdrey HS, Larsen PJ, Harbuz MS *et al*. Evidence for arginine vasopressin as the primary activator of the HPA axis during adjuvant-induced arthritis. *Br J Pharmacol* 1995; **116**: 2417–24.

2. Shanks N, Moore PM, Perks P *et al*. Alterations in hypothalamic–pituitary–adrenal function correlated with the onset of murine LSE in MRL +/+ and lpr/lpr mice. *Br Behav Immunol* 1999; **13**: 348–360.

3. Shanks N, Windle RJ, Perks PA *et al*. Early-life exposure to endotoxin alters hypothalamic–pituitary–adrenal function and predisposition to inflammation *Proc Nat Acad Sci* 2000; **97**: 5645–50.

4. Bluthé RM, Walter V, Parnet P, Laye S, Lestage J, Verrier D, *et al*. Lipopolysaccharide induces sickness behaviour in rats by a vagal mediated mechanism. *CR Acad Sc Paris, Sci de la Vie* 1994; **317**: 499–503.

5. Lowry CA, Rodda JE, Lightman SL *et al*. Corticotropin-releasing factor increases *in vitro* firing rates of serotonergic neurons in the rat dorsal raphe nucleus: evidence for activation of a topographically organized mesolimbocortical serotonergic system. *J Neurosci* 2000; **20**: 7728–36.

6. Windle RJ, Wood SA, Shanks N *et al*. Ultradian rhythm of basal corticosterone release in the female rat: dynamic interaction with the response to acute stress. *Endocrinology* 1998; **139**: 443–50.

7. Windle RJ, Wood SA, Kershaw YM *et al*. Increased corticosterone pulse frequency during adjuvant-induced arthritis and its relationship to alterations in stress responsiveness. *J Neuroendocrinol* 2001; **13**: 905–11.

8. Windle RJ, Wood S, Shanks N *et al*. Endocrine and behavioural responses to noise stress: comparison of virgin and lactating rats during non-disrupted maternal activity. *J Neuroendocrinol* 1997; **9**: 407–14.

## Discussion

*Drossman*: The key question for me is the issue of plasticity. You implied that if something happens in early life you are that way from that point on. But aren't we learning that there are ways of changing this back?

*Lightman*: Yes and also recent events can change the response. But these early life experiences can make you more susceptible to being this way whatever happens. The key manifestation is that it will change susceptibility. Unless other things supervene you will be more likely to be more responsive to stimuli for the rest of your life.

*Elwyn*: Has similar detailed work been done on humans in terms of looking at changes in corticosteroid levels under stress and in individuals from different social backgrounds?

*Lightman*: There has been some as yet unpublished work by Elizabeth Young at the University of Michigan on patients with depression, but otherwise no. The problem is that it is incredibly expensive and time intensive to do this work. In order to see these pulses we have to take blood samples every 15 minutes or so throughout 24 hours.

*Elwyn*: The patients I see, in a very deprived urban council estate, say that they smoke because this is the only way that they can cope with their life. There might be some way in which this is a signal of the stress they are under.

*Lightman*: This is an important question that needs to be answered.

*Wessely*: You said that you had some rats and that you gave them a tiny bit of endotoxin, which gave them a mild fever for a short time and which didn't affect their behaviour. Then later their corticotrophin-releasing hormone (CRH) messenger ribonucleic acid (mRNA) shoots up and this looks very significant. But if the trigger for that change is something as seemingly insignificant as an infection, it is difficult to extrapolate this to humans: babies and young children have infections the whole time. Is this at all relevant?

*Lightman*: The parallel would be in the Third World where many children get major endotoxin-related diseases early on in life. This would be an important area to look at.

*Wessely*: Is it just a way of switching on that system? It could be that the non-stressed rats are actually the abnormal ones.

*Lightman*: Deciding what is normal is a very difficult question. It depends what you are adapted for or maladapted for. Of course, I would agree that a laboratory rat is only well adapted for being in a laboratory. I was just saying that the two rats were different.

*Marmot*: The answer to Simon Wessely's question about young rats might come from Michael Meaney's work. He shows that if you can stimulate the mother into excessive grooming by temporarily removing the pup and giving it back, this seems to damp down the hypothalamic–pituitary–adrenal (HPA) axis.[1] So with children exposed to infection, protective maternal responses might alleviate a subsequently over-reactive HPA axis.

*Lightman*: Maternal behaviour is extremely important. We looked at this but we didn't do the detailed studies that Michael Meaney did. There was no obvious change in maternal behaviour with these animals. We were worried that the mothers might treat them differently from their littermates, but we saw no evidence for this.

*Lewin*: I've read that there is growing evidence that children not exposed to microbes and dirt are more likely to develop asthma.

*Lightman*: There are good data showing that as 'cleanliness' improves the rate of asthma rises.[2]

*Steptoe*: As I understand it there are some conditions associated with stress in humans, such as post-traumatic stress disorder (PTSD), where cortisol levels tend to be much lower than expected. What is the mechanism there?

*Lightman*: There are data from Rachel Yehuda.[3] What we don't know about patients with PTSD is what happens at the moment that they experienced the acute stress. There could have been some very powerful response at the time that had effects which subsequently resulted in sustained low levels of cortisol. No one understands what is going on. I should add we still need further studies to confirm Rachel Yehuda's fascinating data.

*Wessely*: We should also be careful about assuming that the neuro-endocrinology of PTSD is clear. It is not. The evidence base is intriguing, but not compelling. It is also not specific: several groups have found the same as Rachel Yehuda, but in chronic fatigue syndrome.

*Marien*: How much do you think this is part of conditioning? The autonomic nervous system, amygdala, and hippocampus might be being conditioned to a particular specific trigger, which stimulates exactly the same response if it recurs. We know that the immune and autonomic nervous systems are both inter-related and very prone to conditioning. Theoretically, you only need one exposure to get the conditioned response. One of the benefits is that this conditioning, with its associated alterations in midbrain activity and autonomic changes, is responsive to treatment. One of the treatments is graded exposure. You can give humans cognitive behavioural therapy, which will use repeated exposure to extinguish the conditioned response. Have you any views on this?

*Lightman*: That is an interesting thought. In rats, if you give a homotypic stressor—the same stressor repeatedly—they adapt and lose their response to that particular stressor. If you then give them a heterotypic (a different stimulus to which they have not adapted) stressor they have an exaggerated response.

They will down-regulate the same activation from the same stressor, but underlying this they are sensitized to novel stressors.

*Chalder*: I find it refreshing to talk about physiological and behavioural aspects of development in individuals, given that I work in cognitive behavioural psychotherapy, where the emphasis today seems to be more on cognition. I was brought up more in the behaviour/physiological paradigm. What is your perspective on how one should intervene and what would be the most powerful intervention?

*Lightman*: We have done some studies in humans, including studies on carers of patients with Alzheimer's disease. We have found them to have a very poor immunological response to influenza vaccine.[4] We have found that by giving behavioural therapy to these subjects we can improve their response to vaccination.[5]

*Chalder*: Is your intervention more behavioural or cognitive? I know it is difficult to differentiate between them, but it is quite important, given that current therapists seem to be leaving behaviour and physiology behind.

*Lightman*: Predominantly cognitive.

*Marien*: What is the effect of having chronically raised arginine vasopression (AVP) as opposed to CRH?

*Lightman*: I can give you a theoretical answer but it is a bit teleological. Central CRH has all sorts of effects. If you give CRH centrally it causes all the responses associated with the stress response: the animal is active, anxious, and shows all the symptoms of being 'stressed'. This, of course, would serve as an adaptive response to short-term stresses. If you are chronically stressed, however, you don't want to be like that all the time. So in order to maintain the activation of your HPA axis, without the unwanted maladaptive effects of chronically raised CRH, you control your pituitary via AVP and let the CRH levels go down. One can rationalize that this is a useful and adaptive way for the animal to respond to a chronic stressful situation.

*Aylward*: In your experiments you describe using a physical stressor and making observations afterwards. You only described one experiment in which you used a psychosocial stress with isolated rats. Have you or anyone else done an experiment in which you simulate a psychosocial stress instead of a physical one and then make observations aftterwards?

*Lightman*: These sorts of studies have been done with resident–intruder paradigms.[6]

*Aylward*: But have people done experiments similar to yours where the original stress was not physical but psychosocial?

*Lightman*: I don't know about that.

*Lorig*: There was a classic study by Riley published back in 1975 in *Science*.[7] He took some rats that had been bred to develop cancer. He randomized and treated half of them to simulate the experience of wild rats, with night-time feeding and very limited human contact. The other half were treated the way lab rats are normally treated. The lab rats developed their cancers and died on schedule and the other rats lived their normal life-span before dying.

*Lewin*: Animal studies are often misleading and interpreted to fit the myths of the particular age. In the 1960s there appeared to be evidence from studies on monkeys that executive stress produced gastric ulcers.[8] When pairs of monkeys received electric shocks for failing a task, only the executives, the ones who had to make the decision for both animals, went on to develop peptic ulcers. In my opinion there is just too little ecological validity in biopsychosocial research done in labs with animal models for us to consider it in our thinking about disease in humans.

*Lightman*: I certainly wasn't trying to do that. My goal is to try to understand the neural substrate that stressors or life events are acting on. I wouldn't want to make this a model for human disease.

*Wessely*: Michael Marmot earlier gave us the epidemiological underpinnings of a relationship between job hierarchy and disease, from which Andrew Steptoe was talking about some of the possible mediators. You are talking about some of the mechanisms, but what I haven't quite got is what is the epidemiological underpinning of it? It is as if we have a mechanism searching for a disease? Where would you put your evidence to implicate HPA activity in human disease?

*Lightman*: I only had a limited time for my talk and I tried to describe the neurological substrate that responds to afferent activation from the sensory system of the body. In terms of development of disease, the picture would be a different one altogether. Studying rats is useful for understanding tissue mechanisms; you'd have to go back into humans to answer the type of question you are asking.

*Marmot*: One potential answer to Simon Wessely's question is in the metabolic syndrome and insulin resistance. There is ample reason to believe that these cortisol effects have effects on insulin resistance and the pattern of other changes that occur with the metabolic syndrome. This is one tangible way this can be translated into what I was talking about.

*Marien*: It seems to me that we spend all this time at medical school learning about the autonomic nervous system and its associated physiology and the rest of our clinical career ignoring it, except in regard to certain side-effects of drugs. This is actually a potential explanatory model for a lot of medically unexplained physical symptoms, through the HPA axis and autonomic dysfunction. Perhaps this is the area that will make the biopsychosocial model more acceptable to people because there is a clear mechanism through which it is actually functioning.

*Chalder:* I could see the link instantly. If you think about how easily conditioned we are as babies, this will influence our physiology and behaviour for the rest of our lives. Rather than starting with middle-class businessmen, we should be starting with babies and children and following them up in order to understand more clearly the link between physiology and behaviour. Cognition comes much later in one's development. Given that cognition develops so much later, how should we then intervene most powerfully?

*Lightman:* I would agree that these are important things to study.

*White:* I want to make a link between rats and humans, related to the study you described of the response to white noise stress of endotoxin-treated rats compared to control rats. The levels of behavioural activity were the same during the white noise, but it was the endotoxin rats that showed both persistently elevated activity and cortisol levels after the stressor was removed. There are human data showing a similar thing. In a study of work-related stress, the concentrations of noradrenalin remained elevated after work in stressed individuals.[9] Perhaps the pathology of stress does not occur during a stressor itself, but occurs because stressed individuals can't switch off their arousal mechanisms.

*Lightman:* I agree. One of the major problems is not the acute response to stress, but that some individuals are not very good at turning it off and it is this that causes the pathology.

## References

1. Campagne F, Meaney MJ. Like mother, like daughter: evidence for non-genomic transmission of prenatal behavior and stress responsivity. *Prog Brain Res* 2001; **133**: 287–302.
2. Bach JF. The effect of infections on susceptibility to autoimmune and allergic diseases. *N Engl J Med* 2002; **347**: 911–20.
3. Yehuda R. Biology of post-traumatic stress disorder. *J Clin Psychiat* 2000; **61**: 14–21.
4. Vedhara K, Cox KNK, Wilcock GK *et al*. Chronic stress in elderly carers of dementia patients is associated with increased vulnerability to infectious disease. *Lancet* 1998; **353**: 627–31.
5. Vedhara K, Bennett PD, Clark S *et al*. Enhancement of antibody responses to influenza vaccination in elderly carers of dementia patients following a cognitive–behavioural stress management intervention. *Psychother Psychosom* 2003; **72**: 245–52.
6. Raab AR, Dantzer B, Michaud P *et al*. Behavioural, physiological and immunological consequences of social status and aggression in chronically co-existing resident-intruder dyads of male rats. *Physiol Behav* 1986; **2**: 223–8.
7. Riley V. Mouse mammary-tumors—alteration of incidence as apparent function of stress. *Science* 1975; **189**: 465–67.
8. Brady JV. Ulcers in executive monkeys. *Sci Am* 1958; **199**: 95–8.
9. Lundberg U, Frankenhaeuser M. Stress and workload of men and women in high-ranking positions, *J Occup Health Psychol* 1999; **4**: 142–51.

## 7 Fear and depression as remediable causes of disability in common medical conditions in primary care

### Michael Von Korff

## Summary

This chapter argues that psychological states, in particular fear and depression, are potentially remediable causes of social role disability among primary care patients. I use a common and chronic condition, chronic low back pain, as an example. Recognizing and treating depression can improve disability and quality of life for primary care patients with this and many other chronic conditions. Doctors are less skilled in recognizing and addressing dysfunctional illness beliefs, such as the fear-avoidance beliefs of low back pain patients. Adequately addressing such fears is central to the doctor's role as adviser and healer. Sustained reductions in fear-avoidance beliefs can be achieved through relatively brief, educational interventions. As primary care doctors increase their skills in managing these common causes of social role disability, their traditional role as doctors who assume responsibility for the whole person and all aspects of health that affect quality of life will be strengthened.

Finally, it is important to remember that doctors usually have no more basis for inferring that psychological illness is the cause of pain than that there is an underlying physical cause. Focusing on what can help the patient feel and do better is more appropriate than convincing patients that pain is a 'psychosomatic' disorder.

## The definition of disability

Disability has been defined by the World Health Organization as an inability or limitation in performing daily activities and social roles due to physical and/or psychological impairment.[1] In its most severe forms, disabled people may be completely unable to perform basic activities of daily living such as bathing, dressing, and feeding. Such individuals may be institutionalized or may require substantial personal care from family members. Somewhat less severe forms of disability may include substantial limitations in mobility and in instrumental activities of daily living such as inability to shop for groceries or to prepare meals. These forms of disability are most common in elderly populations afflicted by major chronic medical conditions. A much broader spectrum of disability is surprisingly common among younger adult populations. These more common forms of disability include interference with functioning in key social roles, including carrying out family, household, and work responsibilities. The range of such social role disability extends from people unable to carry out these social roles, to others who sustain social role performance, while frequently missing days of work or housework, to yet more people whose social role performance is significantly impaired even though they are rarely absent due to illness. On a population basis, the disability costs of common chronic conditions such as back pain, headache, diabetes, arthritis, asthma, and depressive and anxiety disorders are greatest for these less severe forms of social role disability because they are so common.

## How do psychological states cause disability?

The word disability tends to conjure up images of people who are wheelchair bound due to spinal cord injury or bed-ridden due to a terminal disease. Psychological states such as fear, depression, and anxiety can also cause significant social role disability because psychological illness impairs the highest order human capacities including concentration, motivation, energy, and self-confidence.[2] Common mental disorders are associated with substantial increases in disability in the population at large and in primary care populations.[3,4] Longitudinal studies have shown that as psychological status improves, disability is reduced, while chronic psychological illness is associated with chronic disability.[2,5] More recently, prospective studies have shown that depressive illness predicts subsequent onset of functional disability among people with initially low disability levels.[6–10] Numerous randomized controlled trials have now found that enhanced treatment of depressive illness reduces not only depressive symptoms, but also associated social role disability.[11–15]

### Mental and physical co-morbidity and disability

Chronic physical disorders, such as heart disease, arthritis, and diabetes, are often co-morbid with depressive and anxiety disorders.[16] Chronic pain disorders, such as back pain and headache, are also often co-morbid with psychological disorders.[17] There is increasing understanding of the important role that psychological illness plays in producing disability among people with co-morbid chronic medical conditions. A growing body of research shows that depressive illness is often a stronger predictor of social role disability than the severity of disease-related impairments among people with common chronic medical conditions.[18–20] Randomized controlled trials of depression treatments among patient populations with a high prevalence of chronic medical conditions have also found that effective treatment of depression is associated with improved disability outcomes when co-morbid physical disease is present.[12,15]

This research is leading to a more integrated understanding of the effects of physical disease and psychological illness on disability. On the one hand, chronic physical diseases and chronic pain conditions can be viewed as major stressors that can induce or exacerbate psychological illness, particularly among people with a prior history of psychological illness. On the other hand, depression and anxiety may amplify pain and chronic physical symptoms that contribute to increased disability. Depressive illness is also associated with adverse health risk behaviours such as smoking, obesity, and infrequent exercise. This perspective suggests that the debate about whether psychological illness causes physical disease or physical disease causes psychological illness may be missing the mark. Psychological disorders are a contributing factor for some chronic physical diseases, perhaps through increased exposure to behavioural risk factors such as tobacco use or obesity, through stress-mediated mechanisms, or through shared neurophysiological pathways (see Chapters 3–6). It is virtually certain that chronic physical illness can induce or exacerbate depression and anxiety disorders, particularly when chronic physical symptoms are present. In the remainder of this chapter, we consider this interplay of physical and psychological illness in their effect on social role disability.

## The host, agent, and environment

Physical disease can impair physical capacities such as muscle strength, fine and gross motor coordination, respiratory capacity, vision, and hearing. However, disability levels often show only low to moderate correlation with objective measures of physical impairment.[18–20] In contrast, mental illness tends to impair high-order capacities central to carrying out diverse social roles. Impairments caused by mental illness include loss of motivation and energy, reduced ability to engage in planned action, loss of self-confidence, fears that lead to activity avoidance, reduced ability to interact effectively, and reduced ability to sustain effort toward achieving goals.[21] The often weak association of observed physical impairments with role disability may be due to individual differences in both resilience and social circumstances. Jette proposed that determinants of disability be conceptualized using the epidemiological triad of *host* (resilience or vulnerability factors), *agent* (impairments initiating disability), and *environment* (social mediators of adaptive or maladaptive response to impairments).[22] From this ecological perspective, psychological impairments, particularly among persons with co-morbid physical impairments, may be critically important because they reduce both host resilience and ability to effectively utilize resources in the social environment. Using the example of chronic back pain, the remainder of this chapter will consider how psychological states can affect social role disability and will suggest useful approaches to managing these adverse psychological states in the primary care setting.

### Why is fear disabling? The example of chronic low back pain

Fear-avoidance beliefs are cognitions leading to avoidant behaviours.[23–25] Fear-avoidance beliefs have been shown to contribute to activity limitations among low back pain patients.[26] Some hypothesize that fear-avoidance beliefs are a more potent cause of disability than pain *per se*.[27] Vlaeyen and colleagues propose a cognitive–behavioural model of fear avoidance in which pain appraisal consists of 'catastrophizing' cognitions in some patients and more adaptive cognitions in others.[23,28,29] Those patients with more adaptive cognitions are less likely to avoid exercise and normal activities. Those who fear increased pain during movement are more likely to avoid activities, potentially leading to deconditioning, disability, and depression. This model is supported by studies showing that fear-avoidance beliefs predict functional outcomes.[23,24,30–32] Fear-avoidance beliefs are likely to be important in other chronic medical conditions including arthritis, chronic obstructive pulmonary disease, heart failure, and headache (for example, avoidance of activities that may trigger severe headache), among others.

### Putting theory into practice: biopsychosocial treatment of low back pain

Many primary care patients with low back pain continue to have significant fears and worries long after seeking care. As shown in the Table 7.1, these fears and worries are common and are accompanied by activity limitations that can significantly impair quality of life and ability to carry out important social roles in work and family life. Randomized trials have shown benefits of interventions that address these fear-avoidance beliefs. Providing written

**Table 7.1** Percentage of primary care back pain patients reporting specific worries about back pain and activity limitations 2 months after a primary care back pain visit

| | |
|---|---|
| *Worries about back pain (n = 226)* | |
| The wrong movement might cause a serious problem with my back | 64% |
| Avoiding unnecessary movements is the safest way to prevent back pain from worsening | 51% |
| My body is indicating that something is dangerously wrong | 50% |
| I might become disabled for a long time due to back pain | 47% |
| I am unable to do all the things normal people do because it is too easy to be injured | 44% |
| I am afraid of injuring myself if I exercise | 31% |
| My back pain may be due to a serious disease | 19% |
| | |
| *Activity limitations (n = 481)* | |
| Doing less housework | 45% |
| Difficulty standing for short periods of time | 38% |
| Difficulty walking short distances | 26% |
| Decreased sexual activity | 24% |
| Doing no housework | 23% |

Data source: studies in References 36 and 38.

information alone to reduce fears has been found to have some, albeit limited, benefit.[33] More intensive, multi-faceted interventions have proven more effective in reducing fears related to back pain and in improving functional outcomes.[34–40] Deyo and colleagues found that simple advice to return to normal activities, when compared to prescribed bed rest, reduced work loss short term.[41] This finding contributed to revised thinking regarding the role of bed rest and activation in back pain care.[42,43] Numerous studies have tested educational–behavioural interventions to return patients to normal activity. Information alone does not appear to be as effective as 'graded activity'.[34–48] Graded activity programmes gradually increase activity levels, setting initial exercise levels according to the patient's baseline capacity. The effect size in these intervention studies has typically ranged from small to moderate, suggesting the difficulties in increasing activity levels in an often sedentary patient population impaired by back pain.

*In-vivo* exposure to feared activities may offer an approach to increase the effect size of activating interventions. Crombez and colleagues found that repetition of exercises at maximal force lowered future predictions of back pain.[49] Single-case studies have found that *in-vivo* exposure to feared activities is more effective than graded activity.[50] In this study, fear reduction only happened during exposure and not during graded activity. In addition, reductions in pain-related fear were accompanied by reductions in pain vigilance and disability and by increases in physical activity. In a single-case cross-over design, treatment gains produced during exposure generalized to the home setting.[51]

Many back pain patients seek care with unrealistic expectations. They believe that back pain is often due to a slipped disc or trapped nerve. Most expect a doctor to order an X-ray and to be able to tell them exactly what is wrong.[52] However, patients often bring realistic expectations to the visit as well, typically viewing the most important things physicians do in the back pain visit as offering reassurance and advice.[52] An observational study that audiotaped primary care back pain visits found that the fear-avoidance beliefs of patients were rarely elicited nor were they adequately addressed, even through the physicians frequently recommended physical exercise.[53]

## Depression and low back pain: chicken or egg?

There has been considerable confusion about whether depression is a cause of chronic back pain or a consequence. There can be little doubt that discussing pain with patients as if it were simply 'masked' depression can alienate patients who might otherwise accept treatment of depression co-morbid with chronic back pain. Many patients with chronic back pain will accept depression treatment if the depression is discussed as an understandable consequence of persistent pain, rather than as an underlying cause of pain of unknown origin. The inference that pain of unknown origin is necessarily caused by co-morbid depression is not a sound assumption, nor does it necessarily lead to good patient care. The physician usually has no more basis for inferring that psychological illness is the cause of pain than that there is an underlying physical cause of the pain. Focusing on what can help the patient feel better and do better is more appropriate than convincing patients that back pain is a 'psychosomatic' disorder, in the traditional sense of that term.

## Remediable causes of disability

This chapter has presented ideas and evidence supporting the idea that psychological states, in particular fear and depression, are potentially remediable causes of social role disability among primary care patients. We have focused on a common chronic or recurrent condition in primary care: chronic low back pain. For primary care patients with a broad range of chronic conditions, recognizing and treating major depression can improve disability outcomes. Recognizing and treating major depression is also important, of course, for depressed primary care patients who do not have a co-morbid physical illness.

Many, if not most, primary care physicians in the USA and the UK are now proficient in recognizing depressive illness and they are increasingly skilled in first-line treatment of this disorder. Recognizing and treating depression, if the treatment is evidence based and sustained over at least a 6-month period, can make an important contribution to reducing social role disability and improving patients' quality of life.

Primary care physicians are less skilled in recognizing and addressing dysfunctional illness beliefs, such as the fear-avoidance beliefs of back pain patients. Adequately addressing such fears of patients is central to the physician's role as adviser and healer. Recent research suggests that sustained reductions in fear-avoidance beliefs can be achieved through relatively brief, educational interventions. Many primary care physicians are now routinely recommending exercise to their back pain patients. This is a step in the right direction. However, without adequately addressing underlying fear-avoidance beliefs that inhibit resumption of normal activities, many patients will worry that they may experience a severe recurrence of back pain if they are active. Research is needed to determine how physicians can efficiently elicit the fear-avoidance beliefs of their patients and address these fears in ways that help patients restore normal functioning in their daily lives.

While neither depression nor chronic back pain can be cured with existing medical treatments, depressive illness can usually be controlled. Primary care physicians may also help patients with social role disability by addressing common fears that inhibit activities that are important for maintaining a high quality of life. As primary care physicians increase their proficiency in managing these common causes of social role disability, their traditional role as physicians who assume responsibility for the whole person and all aspects of health that affect quality of life will be solidified and strengthened.

## Acknowledgement

This research was supported by NIH grant P01 DE08773.

## References

1. World Health Organization. *International classification of impairments, disabilities and handicaps.* Geneva: World Health Organization; 1980.
2. Von Korff M, Ormel J, Katon W, Lin EHB. Disability and depression in medical patients: a longitudinal analysis. *Arch Gen Psychiat* 1992; **49:** 91–100.
3. Wells KB, Golding JM, Burnham MA. Psychiatric disorder and limitations in physical functioning in a sample of the Los Angeles general population. *Am J Psychiat* 1988; **145:** 712–17.

4. Ormel J, Von Korff M, Ustun TB, Pini S, Korten A, Oldehinkel T. Common mental disorders and disability: a strong and cross-culturally consistent relationship. Results from the WHO Collaborative Study. *JAMA* 1994; **272**: 1741–8.

5. Ormel J, Von Korff M, Van Den Brink W, Katon W, Brilman E, Oldehinkel T. Depression, anxiety and disability show synchrony of change: a 3 1/2 year longitudinal study in primary care. *Am J Pub Health* 1993; **83**: 385–90.

6. Bruce ML, Seeman TE, Merrill SS, Blazer DG. The impact of depressive symptomatology on physical disability: MacArthur Studies of Successful Aging. *Am J Pub Health* 1994; **84**: 1796–9.

7. Manninen P, Heliovaara M, Riihimaki H, Makela P. Does psychological distress predict disability? *Int J Epidemiol* 1997; **26**: 1063–70.

8. Ormel J, Von Korff M, Oldehinkel AJ, Simon G, Tiemens TG, Ustun TB. Onset of disability in depressed and non-depressed primary care patients. *Psychol Med* 1999; **29**: 847–53.

9. Armenian HK, Pratt LA, Gallo J, Eaton WW. Psychopathology as a predictor of disability: a population-based follow-up study in Baltimore, Maryland. *Am J Epidemiol* 1998; **148**: 269–75.

10. Penninx BW, Guralnik JM, Ferrucci L, Simonsick EM, Deeg DJ, Wallace RB. Depressive symptoms and physical decline in community-dwelling older persons. *JAMA* 1998; **279**: 1720–6.

11. Coulehan JL, Schulberg HC, Block MR, Madonia MJ, Rodriguez E. Treating depressed primary care patients improves their physical, mental, and social functioning. *Arch Intern Med* 1997; **157**: 1113–20.

12. Katzelnick DJ, Simon GE, Pearson SD, Manning WG, Helstad CP, Henk HJ *et al.* Randomized trial of a depression management program in high utilizers of medical care. *Arch Fam Med* 2000; **9**: 345–51.

13. Lin EHB, Von Korff M, Russo J, Katon W, Simon GE, Unutzer J *et al.* Can depression treatment in primary care reduce disability? A stepped care approach. *Arch Fam Med* 2000; **9**: 1052–8.

14. Wells KB, Sherbourne C, Schoenbaum M, Duan N, Meredith L,Unützer J *et al.* Impact of disseminating quality improvement programs for depression in managed primary care: a randomized controlled trial. *JAMA* 2000; **283**: 212–20.

15. Unützer J, Katon W, Callahan CM, Williams JW, Hunkeler E, Harpole L *et al.* for the IMPACT Investigators. Collaborative care management of late-life depression in the primary care setting: a randomized controlled trial. *JAMA* 2002; **288**: 2836–45.

16. Westert GP, Satariano WA, Schellevis FG, van de Bos GA. Patterns of comorbidity and the use of health services in the Dutch population. *Eur J Publ Health* 2001; **11**: 365–72.

17. Von Korff M, Simon G. The relationship between pain and depression. *Br J Psychiat* 1996; **168 (suppl 30)**: 101–8.

18. Sullivan MD, LaCroix AZ, Baum C, Grothaus LC, Katon WJ. Functional status in coronary artery disease: a one-year prospective study of the role of anxiety and depression. *Am J Med* 1997; **103**: 348–56.

19. Molenaar ET, Voskuyl AE, Dijkmans BA. Functional disability in relation to radiological damage and disease activity in patients with rheumatoid arthritis in remission. *J Rheumatol* 2002; **29**: 267–70.

20. Sokka T, Kankainen A, Hannonen P. Scores for functional disability in patients with rheumatoid arthritis are correlated at higher levels with pain scores than with radiographic scores. *Arthr Rheum* 2000; **43**: 386–9.

21. Von Korff M. Disability and psychological illness in primary care. In: Tansella M, Thornicroft G, ed. *Common mental disorders in primary care: essays in honour of Professor Sir David Goldberg.* London: Routledge Press; 1999.

22. Jette AM. Disablement outcomes in geriatric rehabilitation. *Med Care* 1997; **35**: JS28–37.

23. Vlaeyen JW, Linton SJ. Fear-avoidance and its consequences in chronic musculoskeletal pain: a state of the art. *Pain* 2000; **85**: 317–32.

24. Crombez G, Eccelston C, Baeyens F, van Houdenhove B, van den Broeck A. Attention to chronic pain is dependent upon pain-related fear. *J Psychosom Res* 1999; **47**: 403–10.

25. Waddell G, Newton M, Henderson I, Somerville D, Main CJ. A Fear-Avoidance Questionnaire (FABQ) and the role of fear-avoidance beliefs in chronic low back pain and disability. *Pain* 1993; **52**: 157–68.

26. Vlaeyen JW, Crombez G. Fear of movement/(re)injury, avoidance and pain disability in chronic low back pain patients. *Man Ther* 1999; **4**: 187–95.

27. Crombez G, Vlaeyen JW, Heuts PH, Lysens R. Pain-related fear is more disabling than pain itself: evidence of the role of pain-related fear in chronic back pain disability. *Pain* 1999; **80**: 329–39.

28. Vlaeyen JWS, Kole-Snigders AMJ, Boeren RGB, van Eek H. Fear of movement/(re)injury in chronic low back pain and its relation to behavioural performance. *Pain* 1995; **62**: 363–72.

29. Vlaeyen JWS, Linton SJ. Fear-avoidance and its consequences in chronic musculoskeletal pain: a state of the art. *Pain* 2000; **85**: 317–32.

30. Klenerman L, Slade PD, Stanley IM, Pennie B, Reilly JP, Atchison LE *et al.* The prediction of chronicity in patients with an acute attack of low back pain in general practice setting. *Spine* 1995; **20**: 478–84.

31. Linton SJ, Hallden K. Can we screen for problematic back pain? A screening questionnaire for predicting outcome in acute and subacute back pain. *Clin J Pain* 1998; **14**: 209–15.

32. Fristz JM, George SZ, Delitto A. The role of fear-avoidance beliefs in acute low back pain: relationships with current and future disability and work status. *Pain* 2001; **94**: 7–15.

33. Roland M, Dixon M. Randomized controlled trial of an educational booklet for patients presenting with back pain in general practice. *J R Coll Gen Pract* 1989; **29**: 244–6.

34. Indahl A, Velund L, Reikeraas O. Good prognosis for low back pain when left untampered. A randomized clinical trial. *Spine* 1995; **20**: 474–7.

35. Indahl A, Haldorsen EH, Holm S, Reikeras O, Ursin H. Five-year follow-up study of a controlled clinical trial using light mobilization and an informative approach to low back pain. *Spine* 1998; **23**: 2625–30.

36. Von Korff M, Moore JE, Lorig K, Cherkin DC, Saunders K, Gonzalez VM *et al.* A randomized trial of a lay person-led self-management group intervention for back pain patients in primary care. *Spine* 1998; **23**: 2608–15.

37. Burton AK, Waddell G, Tillotson KM, Summerton N. Information and advice to patients with back pain can have a positive effect. A randomized controlled trial of a novel educational booklet in primary care. *Spine* 1999; **24**: 2484–91.

38. Linton SJ, Andersson T. Can chronic disability be prevented? A randomized trial of a cognitive–behaviour intervention and two forms of information for patients with spinal pain. *Spine* 2000; **25**: 2825–31.

39. Moore JE, Von Korff M, Cherkin D, Saunders K, Lorig, K. A randomized trial of a cognitive–behavioural program for enhancing back pain self care in a primary care setting. *Pain* 2000; **88**: 145–53.

40. Von Korff M, Moore JC. Stepped care for back pain: activating approaches for primary care. *Ann Intern Med* 2001; **134**: 911–17.

41. Deyo RA, Diehl AK, Rosenthal M. How many days of bed rest for acute low back pain? A randomized clinical trial. *New Engl J Med* 1986; **315**: 1064–70.

42. Quebec Task Force on Spinal Disorders. Scientific approach to the assessment and management of activity-related spinal disorders. A monograph for clinicians. Report of the Quebec Task Force for Spinal Disorders. *Spine* 1987; **12 (suppl 7)**: S1–59.

43. Abenhaim L, Rossignol M, Valat JP, Nordin M, Avouac B, Blotman F *et al.* The role of activity in the therapeutic management of back pain. Report of the international Paris task force on back pain. *Spine* 2000; **25**: S1-S33.

44. Frost H, Klaber Moffett JA, Moser JS, Fairbank JC. Randomised controlled trial for evaluation of fitness programme for patients with chronic low back pain. *BMJ* 1995; **310**: 151–4.

45. Malmivaara A, Hakkinen U, Aro T, Heinrichs ML, Koskenniemi L, Kuosma E *et al.* The treatment of acute low back pain——bed rest, exercises, or ordinary activity? *New Engl J Med* 1995; **332**: 351–5.

46. Cherkin DC, Deyo RA, Battie M, Street J, Barlow W. A comparison of physical therapy, chiropractic manipulation, and provision of an educational booklet for the treatment of patients with low back pain. *New Engl J Med* 1998; **339**: 1021–9.

47. Moffett JK, Torgerson D, Bell-Syer S, Jackson D, Llewlyn-Phillips H, Farrin A *et al.* Randomised controlled trial of exercise for low back pain: clinical outcomes, costs, and preferences. *BMJ* 1999; **319**: 279–83.

48. Rossignol M, Abenhaim L, Seguin P, Neveu A, Collet JP, Ducruet T *et al.* Coordination of primary health care for back pain. A randomized controlled trial. *Spine* 2000; **25**: 251–9.

49. Crombez G, Vervaet L, Baeyens F, Lysens R, Eelen P. Do pain expectancies cause pain in chronic low back patients? A clinical investigation. *Behav Res Ther* 1996; **34**: 919–25.

50. Vlaeyen JW, de Jong J, Geilen M, Heuts PH, van Breukelen G. The treatment of fear of movement/(re)injury in chronic low back pain: further evidence on the effectiveness of exposure in vivo. *Clin J Pain* 2002; **18**: 251–61.

51. Vlaeyen JW, de Jong J, Geilen M, Heuts PH, van Breukelen G. Graded exposure *in vivo* in the treatment of pain-related fear: a replicated single-case experimental design in four patients with chronic low back pain. *Behav Res Ther* 2001; **39**: 151–66.

52. Klaber Moffett JA, Newbronner E, Waddell G, Croucher K, Spear S. Public perceptions about low back pain and its management: a gap between expectations and reality? *Health Expect* 2000; **3**: 161–8.

53. Turner J, Le Resche L, Von Korff M, Saunders K, Ehrlich K. Back pain in primary care: patient characteristics, content of initial visit, and short-term outcomes. *Spine* 1998; **23**: 463–9.

## Discussion

*Marien*:  It seems to me that a lot of this boils down to a sort of dualism. We haven't really talked about Descartes. One of the interesting things is the unitary linear causality. The medical model is actually a very cosy place for doctors to be. The work by Chris Main, Kendall, and Linton shows that objective medical data are not a good predictor of disability in back pain.[1] But our default is to look at objective medical data. The best predictors of disability are so called 'psychological' yellow flags, such as fear avoidance. I think there is another aspect to this—another fear avoidance, but this time on the part of the doctors and physiotherapists. We, as professionals, are comfortable in our arena, because this is where we have been educated. I think we (doctors) have a fear avoidance about emotion and actually 'opening the can of worms'. This is because we are not educated as to how to do this. When I was working in primary care myself, I remember that if I tripped over something that was emotionally distressing for the patient I changed the subject very quickly and talked about something else. What we should be doing, however, is homing in on this as emotional data and then teasing out the patient's fears and worries. It is no good just telling people to 'open the can of worms'; we actually need to help people overcome their own fear avoidance. An interesting piece of work would be looking at the doctors' fear avoidance about addressing these issues.

*Aylward*:  Yesterday we discussed some important issues, but today we have hit on what I think are the crucial issues. These aspects of the biopsychosocial (BPS) model have had the greatest impact in developing social and welfare policy in the UK. These techniques are simply described and one can communicate them to our colleagues, and even our politicians, who sometimes find it difficult to grasp these issues. This sort of work will strongly influence how social policy and rehabilitation will develop over the next year or so. Importantly, we should consider the work by Buchbinder and colleagues in Victoria, Australia.[2] This showed the utility of a multi-media public educational programme for low back pain rehabilitation and prevention. We hope that we will be able to repeat some of this here. It is expensive, but the results that were obtained in Victoria were remarkable. I welcome this part of this meeting.

*Von Korff*:  If you take interventions that individually are modest in their effects and you have the healthcare system and the social welfare system using these approaches consistently, you end up with a larger effect. This is a very important aspect.

*White*:  Exercise or activity programmes are the archetypal BPS interventions. This was shown to us in our trial when we used graded exercise therapy in chronic fatigue syndrome.[3] We showed that if we improved exercise capacity or performance, there was a closely associated reduction in sub-maximal cardiovascular response to exercise. In other words, there was a physical change—they became fitter. On the psychological side we found that getting fitter was not associated with feeling better. The psychological improvement came purely from being exposed to the programme: a behaviour therapy of graded exposure. Being exposed to the programme was the best predictor of feeling better and it wasn't associated with actually getting fitter. There are two ways to change beliefs. You can look at and change beliefs first using cognitive behavioural therapy (CBT), which leads to behaviour changes, which is perhaps is what happened in your programme. The other way is rather than using 'C-BT', using instead 'B-CT': changing the behaviour first, which then changes the cognition. We also found on the programme that social function improved as well. The social side is that people on these programmes are getting out of the home and meeting people.

*Lewin:* Thirty years of research in cardiac rehabilitation shows that exercise programmes alone, although they restored function to the heart, had practically no effect on return to work, anxiety, and depression. It is a very seductive idea, but in reality it doesn't work. There is no long-term effect in terms of hard outcomes.

*Aylward:* This is largely because many of the studies have not actually included return to work as an outcome measure.

*Lewin:* They abandoned it deliberately because they weren't able to influence it.

*White:* There are two possible explanations. Perhaps there is a differential effect in different diseases. So, exposure is needed to the particularly avoided behaviour, which is exercise or physical activity in chronic fatigue syndrome and perceived stressful activities in heart disease. Or perhaps we need to look carefully at how an intervention programme is delivered for each disease.

*Lewin:* You may have delivered the exercise programme in a far more psychological way, with more understanding on the patients' part. But purely physical exercise programmes do not have very much effect.

*Wessely:* The highly successful *BMJ* trial of exercise was a CBT trial.[4]

*White:* It was educational, telling people why exercise gets people better and then giving the exercise.

*Wessely:* We are talking about barriers. Michael Von Korff, you showed a very convincing relationship between fear avoidance and disability. If I was one of my patients who saw that data, I would immediately say that is right and the reason would be because this is true. That's the way it is. I would say I avoid activity because if I don't, this is what happens. This is the reality: I am more disabled because I am more sick. This is the huge barrier that we haven't considered. The people we see just don't believe us.

*Von Korff:* Many patients seen in primary care settings are highly receptive to information that addresses their fear-avoidance beliefs and to encouragement to resume normal activities. We shouldn't generalize too quickly from the most difficult patients seen in tertiary care settings to the more typical patients with recurrent or chronic pain problems seen in primary healthcare settings. If we start with the assumption that all chronic pain patients are motivated largely by secondary gain and are difficult and demanding individuals, then we will miss the broader opportunity to fundamentally change the way chronic pain and other chronic symptoms are managed in the healthcare and social welfare systems.

*Lorig:* This is where we have to develop very key messages, which the healthcare system gives consistently. The key message I would give any patient that says this to me is that I understand their position, but I would ask what more can they do without having more pain at the end? Every patient can tell us this, even if it is only that they can walk for a minute. In this case I'd suggest that they try walking one minute an hour while they are awake. We are giving them the control to modify the program and the assurance that this is safe. If you do this it is incredible what you can do.

*Wessely:* We accept that. This is what we do in treatment programmes. But we also know that even getting patients to see us is a challenge because of their fear-avoidance beliefs.

*Sharpe:* In relation to this, I'd like to get the word iatrogenesis on the table; doctors do cause harm by their psychological interventions as well as by their medical ones. People often do not get consistent messages from their various medical attendants. In fact, in the UK at least, there are substantial numbers of doctors and others who give people exactly the opposite advice, in terms of this evidence, that is, to rest. When Simon Wessely is trying to tell his patients one thing, they can read something entirely different on the Internet or see someone else who will tell him or her exactly the opposite. That inconsistency of apparently authoritative information is an important part of the problem.

## References

1. Accident Compensation Corporation and the National Health Committee. *New Zealand acute low back pain guide.* Wellington: Accident Rehabilitation and Compensation Insurance Corporation of New Zealand and the National Health Committee, Ministry of Health; 1997.

2. Buchbinder R, Jolley D, Wyatt M. Population based intervention to change back pain beliefs and disability: three part evaluation. *BMJ* 2001; **322**: 1516–20.

3. Fulcher KY, White PD. Randomised controlled trial of graded exercise in patients with the chronic fatigue syndrome. *BMJ* 1997; **314:** 1647–52.
4. Powell P, Bentall R, Nye FJ, Edwards RHT. Randomised controlled trial of patient education to encourage graded exercise in chronic fatigue syndrome. *BMJ* 2001; **322:** 387–92.

# 8 How important is the biopsychosocial approach? Some examples from research

Jos Kleijnen

## Summary

The biopsychosocial (BPS) approach can appear to be a complex idea at first glance, although it can be deconstructed into relatively simple single factors. One of the important single factors is the context in which healthcare is delivered. This chapter will explain some of the research I have been involved in when investigating the effects of contextual factors on health outcomes. I will particularly review the contextual effects on the 'placebo response' in trials, which can vary remarkably across trials and countries. These healthcare contexts include communication by doctors, the expectations of both doctors and patients, and the means of administration of interventions.

## Background

Giving a definition of the BPS approach that encompasses everything is difficult, but I see a lot of parallels between the holistic approach of some alternative practitioners and the BPS approach. In the early days of my career as a researcher, we were preparing what we now call systematic reviews, in the area of alternative medicine. When talking with homeopaths and acupuncturists in those days (around 1988), we said that their treatments should be evaluated using randomized double-blind trials, if at all possible. In one discussion a homeopath said, 'if you do such a trial you have to get informed consent and explain to patients what is going to happen, and this changes the context and setting in which I apply my practice to such an extent that I will not be as effective as I am in normal life.' Although this sounded implausible to me, I thought they might have a case (there are even more implausible aspects of homeopathy than just the context). At that time, these discussions triggered my interest in what I now prefer to call contextual effects: the role of the circumstances in which studies take place and how this may influence any difference between a placebo and a drug response. In clinical practice, contextual effects address the roles that the doctor–patient relationship and the circumstances in which it takes place play as part of the total healing response of the patient.

Earlier on we discussed *Helicobacter pylori*. This reminded me of an interesting study done by Professor Dan Moerman, a medical anthropologist from Michigan.[1] He looked at studies of ulcer healing by cimetidine, with quite a different viewpoint to that of a clinical epidemiologist. He noticed that if you examine the 60 or 70 cimetidine studies from different countries, some of them reported significant effects on ulcer healing rates, relative to placebo and some of them did not. The effect of cimetidine was fairly constant across all studies, with about 80 per cent of ulcers healing. The difference between the significant and non-significant studies came from the placebo group. The placebo groups in German-speaking countries had much higher ulcer healing rates, up to 70 per cent, solely from being on placebo. In contrast, in Dutch, US, or English studies the placebo healing rates are around 40–50 per cent. This is quite a difference. Moerman hypothesized that in Germany people might be much more susceptible to placebo effects and their self-healing properties were stimulated better than in other countries. This was quite interesting and it sounded plausible enough to me until I discussed it with a professor of gastroenterology in Amsterdam. He had a completely different explanation, which was that the people in the German studies behaved differently in the trials. These trial protocols forbade people from taking other medication at the same time. So the Germans stopped taking the aspirin, which was causing the ulcers in the first place, whereas the Dutch simply carried on taking them. Depending on your perspective, you can have very plausible but quite different explanations for the same phenomenon. Perhaps both explanations have some truth in them.

## The healing process and context in randomized controlled trials

What happens in the healing process? One simple model is an additive model containing three main elements. One of these—and probably the most important one—is the natural course of disease, with the self-healing properties of the body. The second one would be everything else that happens in the context of interactions between healthcare professionals and patients. I would include placebo effects in this as a subgroup. Third, there are specific treatments that may have a little extra effect. I think for most diseases, this still holds. For most people they see, general practitioners (GPs) do not have to do anything specific because things get better by themselves.

If we translate these components into the setting of evaluating interventions by means of a randomized controlled trial (RCT), then the total effect that is measured at the end of a study is built up of the following factors: the natural course of disease, the placebo and contextual effects, the specific effects, and then other things such as bias and random errors.[2] If you randomize subjects and give one group a placebo, everything is supposed to be identical except for the specific effects of the intervention to be tested. This is the aim of a RCT.

There are a number of assumptions here. We assume that there is an additive model, that is, if we leave out the specific treatment for one group (receiving a placebo instead) the difference from the group with the active treatment is a fixed, specific effect. We also assume that everything is equal between the two groups except this specific effect. Most scientists will know that the longer a trial goes on, different things happen in the different groups and therefore this basic assumption may be optimistic. We also assume that we will be able to make a perfect placebo. In reality, many so-called double-blind trials are not at all 'blind', because for many interventions no convincing placebo is available. Another assumption is that the placebo given is inert. We could have a long discussion about what 'inert' means in this context.

In real life, I do not think these assumptions are valid, that is, that the components of the overall effect are really additive, that you can add up specific and contextual effects and the natural course of disease to arrive at the total effect. It is more likely that these components interact. If we wish to allow for this when evaluating new treatments, then we need to take account of the context in which the evaluation takes place, because this interaction does occur. Context X will differ from context Z, so interactions will be different and thus you will be measuring different effects. In theory, I could do a trial and randomize a group of people in pain to receive either an analgesic (group A) or a placebo (group B). If we take a visual analogue scale of 10, which represents lots of pain and 0, which signifies no pain, we might find an effect. Group A might have an average outcome of 5 and group B 7 on this scale. You might say that the specific effect in this study is 2 (7 − 5) on this scale. But what would happen if I were to manipulate the context at the same time? I might say to the people who will receive the analgesic and placebo in groups C and D that this new medication is a new drug available from the USA and it is very expensive and they are very lucky to be the first people to benefit from this new treatment. We have then manipulated the context in which the treatment takes place. If there is any effect of a statement like this, we might measure pain at outcome at a level of 3 in the treated group and 6 in the placebo group and the difference is now 3. So the specific effect we are measuring, if we assume that there is no scale effect, is more in one situation compared with the other. If this is a phenomenon that takes place in normal life, it is something that trials do not take account of at all. Let us look into this further.

A number of years ago we searched for studies in which there was a two-by-two design and both drug and placebo were randomized along with the context in which the study was done. We found about 10 trials, dating back as far as 1953. The quality was variable and on average quite low, but the trials seemed to confirm that these interactions between contextual interventions and specific drug interventions do take place. There are a lot of contextual effects that could be considered here, including how treatment is administered, the setting and patient characteristics, and the patient–practitioner interactions. These are all part of the context in which treatments take place.[3]

## Interactions between context and specific treatments

We then prepared another systematic review where we tried to see whether manipulations of doctor–patient interactions had any effect on patient outcomes.[4] The difference between this and the previous review was that we did not demand two-by-two balanced placebo designs. So if people were randomized to have message A versus message B, as long as they were patients and health outcomes were measured, these studies were included. Quite a few studies that we included were in fact balanced placebo designs. We set this in the theoretical framework of Leventhal's self-regulatory theory, in which there are various mental components such as cognitive and emotional responses whenever people experience illness.[5] Cognitive responses are questions about what is causing it, am I going to die, and how long is this going to last? The emotional responses are things like fear, anxiety, and depression. There could be interventions with both of them. This is a dynamic model where the relationships go in all directions and in the end you have a health outcome. But it is a useful model that may give some ideas about what is actually going on in a theoretical framework. We looked at communication and information given regarding treatment by health professions to patients. For example, giving a clear and definite diagnosis versus giving an unclear or no diagnosis. Another example regards prognosis: whether this is communicated or not and if it is, whether it is positive or negative. Then there are interventions in which expectations of patients are changed. Emotional care is the other element here: providing support, compassion, and reassurance may have positive effects on the emotional aspects of the patients' responses.

On the basis of this model we studied RCTs, examining contextual effects in healthcare interactions, to assess whether they had any influence on patients' health through the two pathways of cognitive and emotional care.[4] We did an extensive search strategy. Studies had to be RCTs to be included and they had to be related to patient–practitioner interactions conducted in a clinical population with a physical condition. We developed a data abstraction tool and found 23 000 references. Two of our research fellows selected 624 articles that appeared to be potentially relevant and these were assessed for inclusion. Twenty-five of them fulfilled our inclusion criteria and they were abstracted independently by the two reviewers. There was a lot of heterogeneity in the studies, so we did not do a meta-analysis but took a more descriptive approach. A lot of the trials used only cognitive interventions. Some of them used a combination of cognitive and emotional interventions. About half of the studies reported significant effects. We did not find any harmful effects from emotional interventions. Without being able to statistically pool these studies, all in all there is a strong indication that something happens to health outcomes. We assessed study quality according to a number of items and this was variable. In terms of cognitive interventions, the typical study would be drug versus placebo with raised or non-raised expectations of a positive outcome.

One good example is a study about informed consent, by Bergmann and colleagues in France, who told half of the people they were in a study; the other half were not told.[6] This work was done in 1988 when French regulations 'did not require systematic informed consent', that is, the authors say it was still possible not to inform patients that they were going to be included in a placebo-controlled study. From a scientific perspective, I think we need more of these studies because they teach us a lot. So, what were the results? In terms of pain, the group that were told they were part of a study had much less pain. The placebo group who were informed actually had less pain than the group treated with the active drug in the uninformed study arm. Also, the specific effect (difference between active and placebo) looked much larger in the non-informed group. So the very act of giving informed consent may greatly influence the result of a study.

We used this study to convince the medical ethics committee in Amsterdam that we should be allowed to do a similar study, which we did.[7] This was also in pain patients, with two randomizations, the first between tramadol or placebo and the second between two statements. The first statement said, 'This is a medication that recently became available in the Netherlands. This drug, according to my experience, is very effective and will decrease the pain quickly after taking it.' The second statement said, 'My own experience with this medication is limited and my impression is that it will not be beneficial in all patients. The pill becomes effective almost immediately, if it is going to have an effect.' The study included 112 patients. The medical ethics committee allowed us not to inform patients about the cognitive intervention, on the understanding that we would mention in the informed consent that there was another randomization, apart from tramadol or placebo, that it was guaranteed that this would have no harmful effect, and that the medical ethics committee had approved it. If the patients insisted, they could be told the other randomization and still participate in the study. Only two out of 112 patients wanted to know what the other intervention was.

At this point I would like to mention another aspect of using both blinding and placebos. We asked the company who provided tramadol to give us placebos for this. This drug comes in capsules and if you open the capsule you see something that looks like a white salt. If you opened the placebo capsule, something appeared that looked like a powder. The salt tasted sour, bitter, and nasty, but the powder did not taste of anything. We asked the company to confirm that all their tramadol studies were done with these placebos. They confirmed that this was the case. Many of these studies were cross-over trials and we were not impressed, so we asked them to make new placebos for us, which were more convincing. The company refused to do this. As an alternative, our hospital pharmacy made our placebos for us. These placebos contained quinine and citric acid. This looked like a salt and tasted bitter and sour. We thought this was a much more convincing placebo.

The results of this study showed that there was no significant difference between the tramadol and placebo group. We also found no difference between the positive and negative messages. The intention was to measure interactions, but because there were no actions we could not measure interactions! This was a totally negative study and we had to try five journals before one accepted it for publication.[7] We need more of these sorts of studies because we can learn a lot about doctor–patient interactions and how they influence what we think is the specific effect of a treatment. They also teach us to question what we really mean by a placebo.

## Cognitive care and emotional care

Our review showed that when giving a diagnosis, most of the studies did not find an effect unless the diagnosis was accompanied by a prognosis.[4] On this question, a beautiful trial by a GP in the South of England called Thomas was published in the *British Medical Journal*.[8] Thomas found that patients who had been given a firm diagnosis as well as a positive prognosis reported feeling significantly better at 2 weeks compared to patients who were told 'I cannot be certain what is the matter with you'. Regarding emotional care interventions, we did not find a single study in a clinical patient population that actually investigated emotional care in an RCT, but four studies involved a combination of cognitive and emotional care. Three of these four studies showed that enhancing the patient's expectations, while providing either support or reassurance, significantly enhanced the health outcomes measured. What we found in the review was that there was a lot of inconsistency regarding the kinds of emotional and cognitive care that have been tested. But a relatively consistent finding is that physicians who adopted a warm, friendly, reassuring manner were more effective than those who kept their consultations formal and did not offer reassurance. We need a lot more research to investigate these contextual effects in doctor–patient interactions where expectations themselves are also being assessed. Interestingly, we found that when people did try to manipulate expectations of patients, they did not measure what the expectations were and whether they actually changed. There is still a lot to do in doctor–patient interaction studies.

## Administration of drugs

Does the route of administration alter efficacy? We studied this in patients with migraine, looking at whether it makes a difference giving a pain killer as a tablet or a subcutaneous injection.[9] We found that subcutaneous delivery reduced pain more than the oral pill. In the same paper, we also looked at hospital versus home care for migraine. We expected that hospital care would produce greater pain reduction, being a more intensive context, but we found no evidence for this. In a different study, studying stomach ulcers, we compared the ulcer healing rates of the placebo groups of ulcer trials where they had either two placebos a day, or three and four placebos a day.[10] All these studies had used similar protocols. We found that there was a significant 8 per cent difference (95 per cent confidence interval, 4.6–11.3 per cent) with four (44.2 per cent with healed ulcers) as opposed to two (36.2 per cent with healed ulcers) placebos per day. This suggests that both the mode and frequency of administration of drugs can affect efficacy.

## The colour of medicines

Does colour affect efficacy? We asked pharmaceutical companies who make sedative and antidepressant drugs to send us samples of their most frequently prescribed medicines. We looked at what colour they were. We wrote to all the companies and asked them whether they had any research available on whether the colour of medication had any effects at all. Nobody knew of any. Antidepressants seemed to have bright colours, such as red, orange, or yellow, more often than sedatives or anxiolytics, which were green, purple, or blue.[11] These differences were statistically significant. We also tried to answer the question as to whether different coloured formulations of the same drug produce a different effect in randomized clinical trials. However, the six trials that we identified showed inconsistent differences between colours. A few years later Viagra came on the market: it could not have been any other colour but blue ...

## Conclusions

I hope that our studies have been useful in helping to understand the BPS model. It is a different approach than that used by some other groups. Apart from the usual hypotheses on how to explain differences between the effects reported in different randomized trials addressing the same question (variations in patient characteristics, outcome measures, random variation) one should also consider the effects of variations in context. Knowledge resulting from further studies that take the BPS model into account will improve clinical trials methodology and might increase the applicability of trial results in clinical practice. In addition, an optimal mixture of context and active treatment might improve outcomes for patients.

## References

1. Moerman DE. General medical effectiveness and human biology: placebo effects in the treatment of ulcer disease. *Med Anthropol Q* 1983; **14:** 13–16.

2. Ter Riet G, Kleijnen J, Knipschild P. Over klinisch effectiviteitsonderzoek en placebo effecten. *Integraal* 1988; **1:** 94–101.

3. Kleijnen J, de Craen AJM, van Everdingen J *et al.* Placebo effect in double-blind clinical trials: a review of interactions with medications. *Lancet* 1994; **344:** 1347–49.

4. Di Blasi Z, Harkness E, Ernst E *et al.* Influence of context effects on health outcomes: a systematic review. *Lancet* 2001; **357:** 757–62.

5. Leventhal H, Nerenz D, Straus A. Self regulation and the mechanisms for symptom appraisal. In: Mechanic D, ed. *Monograph series in psychological epidemiology 3: symptoms, illness, behaviour, and help-seeking.* New York: Neale Watson; 1982. pp. 55–86.

6. Bergmann JF, Chassany O, Gandiol J *et al.* A randomised clinical trial of the effect of informed consent on the analgesic activity of placebo and naproxen in cancer pain. *Clin Trials Meta-analysis* 1994; **29:** 41–7.

7. De Craen AJM, Lampe-Schoenmaeckers AJEM, Kraal JW *et al.* Impact of experimentally-induced expectancy on the analgesic efficacy of tramadol in chronic pain patients: a 2 * 2 factorial, randomized, placebo-controlled, double-blind trial. *J Pain Symptom Man* 2001; **21:** 210–17.

8. Thomas KB. General practice consultations: Is there any point in being positive? *BMJ* 1987; **294:** 1200–2.

9. De Craen AJM, Tijssen JGP, De Gans J *et al.* Placebo effect in the acute treatment of migraine: subcutaneous placebos are better than oral placebos. *J Neurol* 2000; **247:** 183–8.

10. De Craen AJM, Moerman DE, Heisterkamp SH *et al.* Placebo effect in the treatment of duodenal ulcer. *Br J Clin Pharmacol* 1999; **48:** 853–60.

11. De Craen AJM, Roos PJ, De Vries AL *et al.* Effects of coloured medication. *BMJ* 1996; **313:** 1624–6.

## Discussion

*Aylward*: I was delighted to hear your talk because many of the things that you spoke about have been common in my experience too. During the 1970s when there was a plethora of new analgesic non-steroidal anti-inflammatory drugs (NSAIDs) on the market in the UK, we were all asked to do many double-blind cross-over controlled studies against a placebo with the new drugs. I rapidly began to lose all faith in many of the new NSAIDs because we found in patients with rheumatoid disease, who were well selected with severe finger joint reversible swelling, that the response to a placebo was almost the same as the response to the new NSAIDs. We also discovered that the location where we assessed the patient altered the response markedly and the hospital setting produced the better response for both placebo and drug treatment. We measured changes in the circumference of the proximal inter-phalangeal joints in the hands. Not only did we have a good response in regard to pain in the hospital setting, but also reductions in measures of the level of inflammation. In addition, we found the characteristics (that is, attitudes and beliefs etc.) of the doctor who was the blinded observer also had a significant effect. Doctors with empathy and a caring attitude enhanced the placebo effect to a greater extent than the drug effect. We tried to get these studies published, but no journal would publish our results in the 1970s because it was assumed that the failure to demonstrate a significant difference from the placebo effect meant that the study was done badly.

*Kleijnen*: The hospital versus home study we did was a systematic review looking at sumatriptan for migraine, which is quite different. Our hypothesis in advance was that the hospital-treated patients would do better than those treated at home, but we didn't find that. We had quite a bit of difficulty in publishing our randomized trial; it was only the fourth or fifth journal that took it. We have had trouble in getting our articles published a number of times, but we have always persevered. The record is being rejected by seven journals for our paper on hyperbaric oxygen treatment for multiple sclerosis. Eventually one of the top neurology journals accepted it.

*Furnham*: In the French study, the hypothesis was that the process of gaining informed consent changed expectations in some way and the expectation had the effect. How did they know this was the case?

*Kleijnen*: You can only know this if you measure it and they didn't in that study.

*Furnham*: What is it about the informed consent process that changes expectations?

*Aylward*: In the sorts of studies that we did we engaged the patient, telling them about what was going on. We warned them about adverse effects and so on.

*Furnham*: You can do this in writing. So is this the effect of the information or the effect of the dialogue?

*Aylward*: I don't know, but I would think it is the dialogue.

*Furnham*: So it may not have anything to do with the informed consent. It could be the dialogue, which is what the compliance literature suggests. The single most predictive factor in patient compliance is the nature of the doctor–patient communication. As a sort of aside, in relation to your comments about colour, there is a product sold by chemist's shops in the UK called 'Night Nurse'. This is green and liquid in the UK and the name suggests a busty matron tucking you up. The manufacturers will tell you that they have had to radically change the name and colour across cultures and they don't have any explanation for this. The Swiss wanted a blue suppository and the Germans wanted something else.

*Kleijnen*: Cultural differences like this are well documented. What is also known is that although some colour meanings may differ by culture, many do have consistent meanings across almost all cultures. In the same issue of the *British Medical Journal* in which our colour article was published,[1] another group published an article about the names of drugs.[2]

*Wessely*: You have actually taken us further in the biopsychosocial (BPS) model than from where we began. I was expecting you to end up with a review of how brilliant cognitive behaviour therapy (CBT) is and how fantastic models based on the BPS model are. In fact, you have gone even beyond this to genuinely 'touchy–feely' qualities in clinical interactions. On the way, did you go through interventions that explicitly use the BPS model as opposed to what you have done, which is to look at the non-tangible factors of clinical interactions?

*Kleijnen*: Not really. We often do systematic reviews of different therapies, as you well know. But this is not part of the path that colleagues and I have been following in exploring contextual elements. The starting point here was a discussion about holistic cultures and so on, in discussions of complementary medicine. This gave us the stimulus to go along the lines that we have been going.

*Wessely*: There is a view that the explicit models of BPS interventions are not touchy–feely; that in themselves they are rigorous and have a theoretical basis. They are based on a certain model of how the body and mind interact, which they then seek to alter, as opposed to yours which are almost dealing with metaphysical qualities. You are attempting to measure the unmeasurable.

*Kleijnen*: It always helps to have a theory and to try to fit things you have to the theory. Theories are only valid, though, for as long as they last. They come and go. As an epidemiologist, I just try to do the perfect study, measuring in the least biased way whatever happens. The mechanism is not the primary focus.

*Davey Smith*: There is a review being carried out for the Cochrane heart group that I am involved in concerning behavioural and psychological interventions in cardiovascular disease. The bottom line is that randomized controlled trials (RCTs) across a range of psychological interventions show little convincing evidence of benefit.[3] We heard from Andrew Steptoe about observational studies that are constantly showing that depression is positively associated with coronary heart disease risk. The largest trial that has been carried out on this issue is the ENRICHD study.[4] This included around 2500 people after a myocardial infarction (MI) and with evidence of depression, randomized to CBT (plus selective serotonin reuptake inhibitors if deemed necessary) or usual care. The follow-up looked at their ratings of depression over the subsequent months or years and showed that CBT did indeed reduce depression. However, it had no effect on reinfarction or mortality.

This field is one that is beset with publication bias, or 'small study' bias.[5] Small studies produce results unlike those from big studies for several reasons. One of these is that they are often carried out by enthusiasts and they may not be subject to the same sorts of external quality control. In somatic therapies there have been dramatic effects in small studies that aren't replicated in bigger and better studies. For example, in randomized trials of intravenous magnesium after MI, small studies reported a halving of mortality. Then when a much larger study was done it showed no benefit.[6] One reason is that small negative studies are not published; another is that biases are introduced into small studies carried out by enthusiasts. In studies of behavioural therapy and stress management in cardiovascular disease, evidence of publication bias is seen, with the large, well-done randomized studies such as ENRICHD showing no benefit at all.

*Lewin*: I'm sure that is true, but there are two important points to make. Firstly there is a problem in describing what qualifies as a psychological intervention. Too often anything that isn't medical or surgical is described as psychological, anything from education to relaxation therapy however appropriate or inappropriate and these are often applied to an unselected group of people, regardless of their actual psychological needs or profile. Research quality issues related to size should be controlled by the review process but these more technical issues are rarely dealt with by reviewers. These studies bias the results of the systematic reviews of the efficacy of psychological treatments in medical patients. For example, in heart disease there have been several very large studies that either did not use recognized CBTs targeted at those patients demonstrated to be in need of that treatment, or were not delivered by specially trained and suitably experienced clinicians, or did not show any significant effect on the psychological variables hypothesized as being the intervening variable.[7,8] Secondly, the failure to improve survival is sometimes used to dismiss the value of CBT for medical patients. Studies like ENRICHD have clearly shown that high-quality CBT can reduce depression and improve quality of life in patients screened for those target problems. OK, it didn't keep people alive longer; some of us didn't expect it to (and have yet to be convinced that stress or depression play a primary role in the aetiology of heart disease), but it did show that an appropriate psychological treatment delivered to well-defined groups of patients by well-trained and supervised psychologists can restore people to a better quality of life and psychological health. Reducing suffering and, when it is necessary, improving a patient's health-related quality of life should be justification enough for providing these treatments.

*Chalder*: I agree that it's not just the size of the studies that counts. Just because you have a large RCT that shows a different result to some of the smaller RCTs that have been done, it doesn't mean that the result in the larger RCT is necessarily more accurate. It may not just be the intervention that is delivered that is important but also the quality of the intervention and the way it is delivered. The larger the study the more latitude there is for variation in the quality of the intervention.

*Davey Smith*: The Frasure-Smith example is a fascinating one. As you know, her group carried out a small intervention study that showed a big benefit with respect to mortality reductions.[9] This study was cited as demonstrating that such interventions could prevent subsequent cardiac events and mortality; the authors themselves stated that the evidence that psychosocial interventions could reduce mortality 'is at least as strong as the evidence for exercise'.[10] The same team then carried out a larger study, which was published in *The Lancet*[8] and if anything showed a detrimental effect of the intervention on mortality. The conclusion of this paper was that 'future trials will need to address outcomes other than survival'. The methods of the intervention were also criticized, even though they were similar to the ones in the earlier trial that remained uncriticized because it obtained the 'right' result.

*Lewin*: This is one of the studies I alluded to, the intervention was to give MI patients a General Health Questionnaire (GHQ) over the phone and if they scored more than 5 a nurse was sent round to try to help the patient.[8] As this intervention didn't have any effect on any of the psychological variables that they measured and the nurses had no psychological training, the study has nothing to say about the hypothesis. Yet, because of its size and prominence, it is regarded as evidence that psychological interventions have no value. Incidentally, the pilot study contained a basic flaw, a social class imbalance and it was this, not the size of the study, that probably accounted for the misleading finding.

*Davey Smith*: I agree that one thing that can contribute to 'small study bias' is that smaller studies actually deliver the intervention better than larger studies.[11] The point is correct about the Frasure-Smith study, although that didn't stop people citing the earlier one, which used basically the same methods. The thing to do in a meta-analysis is to score the trials in terms of methodological rigour, not just in terms of size. Size isn't itself a quality factor; it does, however, influence the probability of publication—very large studies are likely to get published even if they get negative results. The ENRICHD study is a high-quality study that collected appropriate process measures and showed that the intervention actually influenced depression. I agree that people might feel better with the intervention, which is all fine and good. But one of the claims made is that these psychological factors are aetiological factors for disease. If they are, then the strongest test of causality is that if you modify or remove them, you change disease outcomes. There are many examples in medical care where the evidence from observational studies was much greater than anything we have heard about today, but randomized trials failed to confirm the causal nature of the associations under investigation. In observational studies hormone replacement therapy (HRT) was consistently associated with a 50 per cent lower risk of coronary heart disease (CHD). Taking HRT is confounded by socioeconomic and behavioural factors to probably about the same degree as are some stress measures (such as job control). In large randomized studies with long follow-up, HRT is associated with, if anything, a small increase in CHD risk. The observational studies were done to the best standards possible and were multiply adjusted for a range of potential confounding factors. The body of observational evidence was much greater and more convincing than we have for many of these psychological factors. This should be salutary to us and we should recognize that the best evidence comes from experimental manipulations.

*Wessely*: If I read George Davey Smith correctly, he is taking the 'bio' bit out of BPS.

*Lorig*: The whole emphasis on using meta-analysis to push forward or put down a field has real problems when we are talking about psychosocial elements. This is for four reasons. First, with most psychosocial interventions the population is highly heterogeneous, unlike most clinical trials. Second, we are also throwing together interventions that are heterogeneous. When we do a meta-analysis of statins, we know what we are talking about, but when we are doing a meta-analysis of psychosocial interventions for heart conditions we have no idea what we are talking about. Third, we are often using insensitive measures. Until very recently most measures in this field have come from epidemiology and were not developed for sensitivity. If we don't see change, it may be an instrument problem. The fourth problem here is that when we are looking at something like statins, we are always looking at their effect after a washout period: we are not looking at them on top of usual care. None of us doing psychosocial interventions are ever allowed to do our interventions after a washout period. We do it only on top of usual care. Thus we should be careful about using meta-analysis to disprove a field.

*Kleijnen*: I understand what you are saying. We thought that meta-analysis was not appropriate here. You shouldn't do meta-analysis in circumstances where there are big differences in patients and interventions. This is being done way too often. I think the general approach of systematic reviews always makes sense, though. Where meta-analysis happens it is actually quite interesting that it actually comes from the social and psychological sciences.

*Von Korff*: I almost never disagree with Kate Lorig, but I will here. I think a negative meta-analysis would be a tremendous boon to this field. It would push us to think of things such as end-points and interventions. What are the interventions? Can we describe our interventions? With regard to end-points, this field shot itself in the foot by jumping on David Spiegel's trial.[12] This was a small trial that showed an effect on mortality. When people tried to replicate it, they failed. Spiegel did find that it improved quality of life, but this was a subtext. We really have to get clear about what our end-points are. Meta-analysis forces us to think about what our end-points should be. Psychosocial interventions are a mess, especially when we get into the real world of delivering them. We don't have a clue what is being delivered. Some trials are done with integrity and may be described in a way that people can replicate them. Once they move out into the real world, all bets are off. Unless these interventions are developed in a way that they can be disseminated into the real world, who cares? These are some issues that hard-hitting meta-analyses will raise for us and will help us improve our methods. As long as this field is so defensive about the fact that that we have negative findings, people are going to throw it out. No one will listen to us and we won't make progress. We have to face the problems with our methods and start moving towards larger trials that can be definitive.

*Salmon*: Your analysis of RCTs has led to a stimulating discussion about the power of expectations. But a lot of those RCTs weren't intended to manipulate expectations in the way they did. Clinically, a lot of the people here are in the business of just trying to change expectations. What are the implications of your analysis for what designs we should use if we want to change expectations? To pin this down to a particular comparison, in one hospital after hip replacement people are in hospital for about 10 days. In another it is about 3 days. The hypothesis is that a very charismatic surgeon in the second hospital changed expectations not only of the patients he works with, but also the whole clinical team. Therefore, expectations could be a much more powerful influence on recovery from surgery than any of the processes that have been studied in the psychological literature beforehand.

*Kleijnen*: Ideally, we would like to do this in an RCT as well. But this is difficult if there is an elaborate manipulation of expectation. It is not possible to blind. This is probably why the studies that have been done have tried to keep the intervention quite subtle and simple.

*Salmon*: The danger is that if we stick with the RCT model, we study only things that can be done in that way. I have been involved in studies where we randomized tape recordings that people listened to before surgery—just because this was possible to do in a randomized way. But interventions like this seem trivial by comparison with what this surgeon may be achieving by changing the whole system.

*Kleijnen*: I'm quite a pragmatic person. I think we try to do the best possible study in the most unbiased way. With these more complex interventions you could probably still randomize, but you should probably forget blinding of practitioners and patients. Perhaps you could try blinding people who assess the outcomes in order to approach the ideal as closely as possible. But you have to remain pragmatic. I think it makes sense to test whether simple interventions have any effect first.

*Sharpe*: I take that viewpoint entirely, that is, we do need randomized studies. But given that the main business of clinical medicine is doing consultations with patients and given that many of us believe that there are psychological aspects of the consultation that are very important, am I right in assuming that there is only a tiny amount of randomized research on how those psychological aspects of the consultation should be used? And if so, why is that?

*Elwyn*: There are some systematic reviews of the patient-centred approach that Vicky Entwistle at Aberdeen has carried out.[13] She found 12 randomized trials that could be included in this review, but she didn't think much of their quality and came out with very little in terms of effect size. Simon Griffin and colleagues in Cambridge have done another systematic review of a wider based patient-centred approach to consultation mostly done in general practice.[14] He also found that the interventions were very poor quality in terms of process measures and also have variable effect size. They can't draw any conclusions from this research because the quality of the work doesn't hold out.

*Waddell*: As this discussion continues, I am getting increasingly confused. I naively thought the BPS model tried to address the inadequacies of the biomedical model because that focused solely on disease and treated human beings as machines. I thought the BPS model was trying to reintroduce both mind and body and operationalize that into social, psychological, and biological issues. But after we got the history and philosophy out of the way this morning, almost the whole of the rest of the day seems to me to have been trying to force social and psychological factors back into a proper biomedical model. It has been about physiological and neurohormonal mechanisms and trying to link psychological and social factors to disease. I was beginning to be encouraged by Jos Kleijnen's paper, which was talking about expectations and people. Of all people, I never expected that Simon Wessely would promptly try to block that discussion and suggest that we should forget about all this ethereal nonsense and get back to medicine. Since about 11 this morning, no one has mentioned the mind!

*Marien*: It is interesting that at this meeting we have so few papers on emotion or emotional care. If you look at CBT, what it is trying to do is to influence emotion through cognition. What behavioural experiments are trying to do is manipulate emotion. What this demonstrates is that we are actually very uncomfortable with addressing emotion. When you scan brains of people and they are emotional, there is a huge chemical change in their midbrain. Simon Wessely accused Jos Kleijnen of being ethereal and moving into a woolly domain. I don't think it is woolly. Placebos and nocebos are about beliefs, meanings, and attributions. These are cognitive. What complementary and alternative medicine does is to create context in which people feel comfortable. They talk a language they want to hear, they feel understood, and they experience connectedness that they don't feel with doctors, who are being very clinical and detached. We need to start bringing emotion into this discussion, because everyone is skirting around it. I would agree with Gordon Waddell. This is about recognizing emotional health and well-being. Contexts, beliefs, and meanings have a powerful effect on this. Complementary medicine is an environment where a lot of people feel very safe, whereas they don't feel comfortable in a medical environment.

*Wessely*: Let me try to sum up where we are, then. We all agree that warm, caring doctors get better results than Sir Lancelot Spratt. Jos Kleijnen's studies and those by many others in this room suggest that something rather more definable can also dramatically improve outcomes such as quality of life, in symptom-based conditions in particular. George Davey Smith's challenge is to say we have not shown similar certainty in improving harder outcomes of the type that tend to convince the Sir Lancelot Spratts of this world, but we have also heard that this doesn't necessarily matter: perhaps this isn't what we are about. Is that fair?

*Lewin*: There is another issue that came out, that there may be long-term developmental processes that are not necessarily going to have an impact on primary prevention of disease.

*Steptoe*: I have been very interested in the way that the discussion has gone back and forth. It would be premature to consider the sort of thing I was describing about mechanisms in the context of trials. The understanding still has quite a way to go. I only know about certain areas. Doug Drossman mentioned the gastrointestinal area and we are learning much more about the biology. That type of knowledge has yet to be implemented in these interventions. I am not even sure that a stress management type of intervention would be appropriate.

*White*: I would like to make one point about the biology of placebos, which should help us to think about whether we go with either the psychosocial or biomedical model. Either would be a mistake, particularly when we are dealing with chronic disabling conditions. The model is biopsychosocial and we mustn't lose the biology. One example from the biology of placebos is a recent study showing that functional brain scans of placebo responders have changes in cerebral blood flow not seen in the non-responders.[15] In other words, here is a good example of how the psychological mind can affect the physical brain; we are back to the brain as the organ of the mind. We have come full circle back to the BPS model.

*Main*: We seem to be caught up in trying to unentangle the relationship between the bio- and the psychosocial and how they actually link. But what are these models for? Models have a number of different purposes, ranging from explanatory to predictive. The sorts of models we have talked about function in quite different ways. Perhaps later we can discuss what we are actually trying to do with these BPS models.

## References

1. de Craen AJ, Roos PJ, Leonard de Vries A *et al.* Effect of colour of drugs: systematic review of perceived effect of drugs and of their effectiveness. *BMJ* 1996; **313**: 1624–26.

2. Holm S, Evans M. Product names, proper claims? More ethical issues in the marketing of drugs. *BMJ* 1996; **313**: 1627–9.

3. Rees K, Bennett P, West R *et al.* Psychological interventions for coronary heart disease. (Cochrane Review). In: *The Cochrane Library, Issue 2.* Chichester: Wiley; 2004.

4. Writing Committee for the ENRICHD Investigators. Effects of treating depression and low perceived social support on clinical events after myocardial infarction. The Enhancing Recovery in Coronary Heart Disease patients (ENRICHD) randomized trial. *JAMA* 2003; **289**: 3106–16

5. Egger M, Davey Smith G, Schneider M *et al.* Bias in meta-analysis detected by a simple, graphical test. *BMJ* 1997; **315**: 629–34.

6. Egger M, Davey Smith G. Misleading meta-analysis. *BMJ* 1995; **310**: 752–54.

7. Jones DA, West RR. Psychological rehabilitation after myocardial infarction: multicentre randomised controlled trial. *BMJ* 1996; **313**: 1517–21.

8. Frasure-Smith N, Lespérance F, Prince RH *et al.* Randomised trial of home-based psychosocial nursing intervention for patients recovering from myocardial infarction *Lancet* 1997; **350**: 473–9.

9. Frasure-Smith N, Prince R. The ischemic heart disease life stress monitoring program: impact on mortality. *Psychosom Med* 1985; **47**: 431–45.

10. Frasure-Smith N, Lesperance F. Prognosis and management after a first myocardial infarction. *New Engl J Med* 1990; **323**: 548–9.

11. Egger M, Davey Smith G, Schneider M *et al.* Bias in meta-analysis detected by a simple, graphical test. *BMJ* 1997; **315**: 629–34.

12. Spiegel D, Bloom JR, Kraemer HC *et al.* Effect of psychosocial treatment on survival of patients with metastatic breast cancer. *Lancet* 1989; **2**: 888–91.

13. Lewin SA, Skea ZC, Entwistle V *et al.* Interventions for providers to promote a patient-centred approach in clinical consultations. *Cochrane Database Syst Rev* 2001; **4**: CD003267.

14. Griffin S, Gillard S, Veltman M *et al.* A systematic review of trials of interventions to improve the interactions between patients and practitioners. In: *The 29th Annual Scientific Meeting of the Association of University Departments of General Practice.* Bournemouth: CBC Oxford Ltd, on behalf of the AUDGP; 2000.

15. Mayberg HS, Silva JA, Brannan SK *et al.* The functional neuroanatomy of the placebo effect. *Am J Psychiat* 2002; **159**: 728–37.

# 9 Complementary and alternative medicine: shopping for health in post-modern times

Adrian Furnham

## Summary

There has been a steady documented and international increase in the popularity of complementary and alternative medicine (CAM). This rise seems to be related to dissatisfaction with orthodox medicine (OM), particularly the consultation. An attempt is made to compare and contrast the stereotypical CAM and general practitioner (GP) consultation in an attempt to understand the appeal of CAM. This chapter looks at the philosophy and beliefs behind CAM and contrasts them with the approach of OM. It also seeks to answer four questions. What is it? How does it work? How is it different from OM? Who seeks it? Finally, the psychology of CAM is discussed.

## The dramatic rise of complementary and alternative medicine

Complementary and alternative medicine has gained wide recognition and is now big business;[1] it seems to be favourably perceived by many GPs.[2] The rise of CAM led to a UK House of Lords enquiry into six aspects of CAM: evidence, information, research, training, regulation and risk, and National Health Service (NHS) provision.[3]

There has been a considerable rise in public and research interest in complementary medicine.[4-6] One index of this is the 'theme issue' of the *Journal of the American Medical Association* in 1998.[7]

In 1993, 34 per cent of all Americans visited a CAM therapist; this accounts for more visits than to all US primary care physicians put together. Expenditure was estimated at US$13.7 billion per annum.[8] By 1997, an estimated 47 per cent of all Americans visited a CAM practitioner.[9] Annual visits rose from 427 million in 1990 to 629 million in 1997.[9]

In France the use of homeopathy (the most popular CAM) rose from 16 per cent of the population in 1982 to 29 per cent in 1987 and 36 per cent in 1992.[10] In the Netherlands 6 per cent of the population attended a CAM therapist in 1981, rising to 9 per cent in 1985 and 16 per cent in 1990. In the UK around 25 per cent of the UK population have used some form of CAM, while around 80 per cent of the public are satisfied with CAM therapies compared to 60 per cent being satisfied with OM.[1,11]. Two-thirds of UK hospital doctors believe that CAM has a place in mainstream medicine. About 93 per cent of GPs have suggested a referral to CAM and nearly 67 per cent of local health authorities in the UK are purchasing at least one form of CAM.[11] Individuals spend £1.6 billion per annum on CAM therapies, the NHS spends about £400, and £500 million is spent on products and services.[1,11]

## What is complementary and alternative medicine?

The great range of CAM inevitably means there is a considerable diversity of therapies and their attendant theories and philosophies. Yet there are common themes in the philosophies of CAM. Aakster believes that they differ from OM in five ways.[12]

1. *Health.* Whereas conventional medicine sees health as an absence of disease, alternative medicine frequently mentions a balance of opposing forces (both external and internal).

2. *Disease.* Conventional medical professionals see disease as a specific, locally defined deviation in organ or tissue structure. Complementary and alternative medicine practitioners stress body-wide signs, such as body language indicating disruptive forces and/or restorative processes.

3. *Diagnosis.* Regular medicine stresses morphological classification based on location and aetiology, while alternative interpretations often consider problems of functionality to be diagnostically useful.

4. *Therapy.* Conventional medicine often claims to destroy, demolish, or suppress the sickening forces, while alternative therapies often aim to strengthen the vitalizing, health-promoting forces. Complementary and alternative medicine therapists seem particularly hostile to chemical therapies and surgery.

5. *The Patient.* In much conventional medicine the patient is the passive recipient of external solutions, while in CAM the patient is an active participant in regaining health.

Aakster described three main models of medical thinking.[12] The *pharmaceutical* model is a demonstrable deviation of function or structure than can

**Table 9.1** Results from the four ratings of complementary and alternative medicine therapies

| Therapy | Have you heard of it? (% 'yes') | Does it work? (% 'yes') | Have you tried it? (% 'yes') | Mean effectiveness (1 = not effective, 10 = very effective) |
|---|---|---|---|---|
| 1. Acupuncture | 98 | 90 | 9 | 6.3 |
| 2. Acupressure | 56 | 57 | 9 | 5.0 |
| 3. Alexander technique | 43 | 42 | 9 | 4.9 |
| 4. Aromatherapy | 97 | 80 | 52 | 5.7 |
| 5. Art therapy | 38 | 29 | 8 | 4.3 |
| 6. Autogenic training | 5 | 6 | 1 | 2.9 |
| 7. Ayurveda | 11 | 12 | 4 | 3.2 |
| 8. Bach flower remedies | 33 | 28 | 17 | 3.9 |
| 9. Biochemic tissue salts | 4 | 14 | 4 | 3.5 |
| 10. Biorhythms | 49 | 31 | 6 | 3.5 |
| 11. Chiropractic | 74 | 63 | 16 | 5.8 |
| 12. Chelation and cell therapy | 11 | 11 | 0 | 3.2 |
| 13. Colonic irrigation | 73 | 56 | 4 | 4.4 |
| 14. Colour therapy | 44 | 35 | 7 | 3.6 |
| 15. Crystal and gem therapy | 46 | 26 | 7 | 3.0 |
| 16. Dance movement therapy | 45 | 44 | 9 | 4.4 |
| 17. Healing | 80 | 56 | 17 | 4.9 |
| 18. Herbal medicine | 97 | 80 | 38 | 5.8 |
| 19. Homeopathy | 87 | 30 | 30 | 5.6 |
| 20. Hypnosis | 96 | 77 | 18 | 5.7 |

**Table 9.1** *Continued*

| Therapy | Have you heard of it? (% 'yes') | Does it work? (% 'yes') | Have you tried it? (% 'yes') | Mean effectiveness (1 = not effective, 10 = very effective) |
|---|---|---|---|---|
| 21. Magnetic therapy | 28 | 19 | 4 | 3.6 |
| 22. Massage | 95 | 91 | 65 | 7.0 |
| 23. Meditation | 93 | 81 | 35 | 6.1 |
| 24. Music therapy | 55 | 52 | 15 | 5.1 |
| 25. Naturopathy | 17 | 20 | 4 | 3.5 |
| 26. Nutritional therapy | 43 | 46 | 11 | 5.1 |
| 27. Osteopathy | 72 | 63 | 17 | 5.8 |
| 28. Ozone therapy | 7 | 6 | 2 | 2.8 |
| 29. Reiki | 17 | 15 | 6 | 3.3 |
| 30. Reflexology | 88 | 68 | 25 | 5.6 |
| 31. Relaxation | 93 | 86 | 54 | 6.4 |
| 32. Shiatsu | 56 | 38 | 10 | 4.6 |
| 33. Spiritual healing | 81 | 46 | 13 | 4.5 |
| 34. Talk therapies/counselling | 85 | 78 | 30 | 6.3 |
| 35. Traditional Chinese medicine | 84 | 57 | 12 | 5.2 |
| 36. Therapeutic touch | 34 | 26 | 3 | 3.7 |
| 37. Visualization | 32 | 29 | 12 | 4.0 |
| 38. Voice and sound therapy | 26 | 20 | 4 | 3.6 |
| 39. Yoga | 96 | 79 | 32 | 6.2 |

be diagnosed by careful observation. The causes of disease are mainly germ like and the application of therapeutic technology is all-important. The *integrational* model resulted from theorists attempting to reintegrate the body. This approach is not afraid of allowing for psychological and social causes to be specified in the aetiology of illness. The third model has been labelled *holistic* and does not distinguish between soma, psyche, and social. It stresses total therapy and holds up the idea of a natural way of living.

Furnham used factor analysis to see how the public classified 39 different types of CAM based on whether they had heard of it, whether they knew how it worked, whether they had tried it, and whether they believed it worked (see Table 9.1).[13] A pattern emerged with art therapies (for example, music and dance), talk therapies (for example, counselling), and 'foreign techniques' (for example, Reiki and Shiatsu). The 'big six' most established therapies (acupuncture, chiropractic, homeopathy, medical herbalism, naturopathy, and osteopathy) were often grouped together, presumably because they were seen as most established and regulated, despite the fact that they are based on very different methods and philosophies.

Perhaps the most interesting of the four columns is the fourth referring to perceived efficacy. Three things are worthy of note. First, only five of the 39 therapies received scores of 6 out of 10 or above, suggesting only modest efficacy. They were massage, relaxation, talk therapies/counselling, acupuncture, and yoga. Second, 22 therapies had scores of 5 out of 10 or less, suggesting that the general public were not overly impressed by the curative efficacy of CAM. Third, there did seem to be a consistent correlation between the various columns, which is as would be expected. However, it remains unclear whether people try a CAM therapy after they explore its efficacy and methodology or beforehand.

Turner believed all CAM therapies could be classified first by 'emphasis' (structural, biochemical, energetic, and mind–spirit) but also by their care systems.[14] Gray argued there are currently four quite different perspectives on CAM.[15]

1. *The biomedical perspective.* This is concerned with curing of disease and control of symptoms where the physician–scientist is a technician applying high-level skills to their patient. This perspective asserts (1) that the natural order is autonomous from human consciousness, culture, morality, psychology, and the supernatural; (2) that truth or reality resides in the accurate explanation of material (as opposed to spiritual, psychological, or political) reality; (3) that the individual is the social unit of primary importance (as opposed to society); and (4) that a dualistic framework (for example, mind/body) is most appropriate for describing reality. This approach is antagonistic toward and sceptical of CAM, believing many claims to be fraudulent and many practitioners unscrupulous.

2. *The complementary perspective.* Though extremely varied, those with this perspective do share certain fundamental assumptions:

   (a) believing in the importance of domains other than 'the physical' for understanding health;

   (b) viewing diseases as symptomatic of underlying systematic problems;

   (c) a reliance on clinical experience to guide practice; and

   (d) a cogent critique of the limits of the biomedical approach. Interventions at the psychological, social, and spiritual level are all thought to be relevant and important, supporting the idea of a biopsychosocial (BPS) model. Many advocates are critical of biomedicine's harsh and often unsuccessful treatments and point out the paradox of biomedicine often not being based on 'solid scientific evidence'.

3. *The progressive perspective.* Proponents of this perspective are prepared to support either of the above, depending entirely on the scientific evidence. They are hardened empiricists who believe it is possible to integrate the best of biomedicine and unconventional approaches. Like all other health care professionals, their approach is not value free—the advocates of this approach welcome the scientific testing of all sorts of unconventional therapies.

4. *The post-modern perspective.* This approach enjoys challenging those with absolute faith in science, reason, and technology and deconstructing traditional ideas of progress. Followers are distrustful of, and cynical toward, science, medicine, the legal system and institutionalized religion, and even parliamentary democracy. Post-modernists see truth as a socially and politically constructed idea and believe orthodox practitioners to be totalitarian persecutors of unconventional medicine. Proponents of this position argue

   (a) to have a complementary perspective in any debate is healthy;

   (b) that CAM practitioners are also connected to particular economic and theoretical interests;

   (c) that a variety of values and criteria for assessing success is beneficial; and

   (d) that ill people themselves should be the final arbiters of the success of the therapy.

There is more diversity than unity within CAM. Whilst there have been calls to find regulatory bodies to oversee all CAM practices, this has proved very difficult because of the theoretical, historical, and political differences between the various CAM specialties.

# Research in complementary and alternative medicine

The popular interest in CAM has been matched by a relatively sudden and dramatic increase in research into the two central questions in this area.

## Does it work?

Is there good evidence from double-blind, placebo-controlled, randomized studies that the therapy 'cures illness' as it says it does? That is, is there any indisputable scientific evidence that documented findings of success are due to anything more than a placebo effect? Properly designed and executed studies are complex, very expensive, and similar to the research effort to determine the efficacy of psychotherapy. Indeed it is the extensive research into the placebo effect that makes psychological input particularly valuable.[5,6] The answer to the question is that either very little or no good evidence is available for the efficacy of most CAM, with the possible exception of herbalism. However, as more and more sophisticated meta-analyses are published, there does seem to be clear evidence for small but robust positive effects of specific CAM treatments.[16]

## Why choose it?

If the evidence is limited, equivocal, and indeed often points to lack of efficacy, the central question must be why do patients choose at their own expense to visit a CAM practitioner? What do they get from the treatment? Why do they persist? This is where there have been many psychological studies.[6,17] These concern the often mixed motives that patients have in shopping for health treatments.

The principal reason for individuals beginning any CAM treatment appears to be that they regard it as more natural and effective and it allows a more active role for them.[6,17] The second reason is the failure of OM to provide relief for specific (usually chronic) complaints. The adverse effects of OM and a more positive patient–practitioner relationship are also important for many patients. There is little to support the widely held view that CAM-seeking patients are especially gullible or naïve, or have unusual (neurotic) personalities or (bizarre) value or belief systems. However, comparisons of users and non-users of CAM have shown evidence of different beliefs about health and disease in general[6] (see section 'Who seeks complementary and alternative medicine?').

# Complementary and alternative medicine and the medical profession

There have been a limited number of studies of practising doctors' (usually GPs') attitudes to CAM.[18–20] Wharton and Lewith found a high level of interest in CAM among GPs.[21] In total, 38 per cent of the 145 respondents had received some training in CAM and 15 per cent wished to arrange training. In the previous year, 76 per cent had referred patients for alternative treatment to a doctor, 72 per cent had referred patients to non-medically qualified practitioners, and 70 per cent thought that the more acceptable techniques (for example, hypnosis, acupuncture, spinal manipulation, and homeopathy) should be available through the UK NHS. It should be noted that homeopathic treatment has been available through the NHS from its inception. Anderson and Anderson also found a high level of interest in, knowledge of, and referral of patients for CAM by GPs.[22] Of the 222 respondents, 41 per cent had attended lectures or classes in CAM, 12 per cent had received training, 42 per cent wanted training in an alternative form of medicine, 16 per cent were practising a form of CAM, and 59 per cent had referred one or more patients to complementary practitioners within the previous year.

Although these studies were relatively small scale, they yielded comparable results, showing a generally high level of interest in CAM among GPs. Critics have noted many quite orthodox techniques (for example, manipulation and counselling) were wrongly classified as complementary, so exaggerating the interest in truly complementary techniques. General practitioners may also not be representative of the orthodox medical profession.[23] Visser and Peters suggested that GPs have a more pragmatic attitude to medicine than their hospital colleagues, which makes them more willing to accept CAM, although they may remain sceptical of its efficacy.[24]

More recent studies have been reported from the USA, Australia, Canada, Israel, New Zealand, and the UK.[25–27] The consistent message from these studies is that most GPs seemed favourably disposed towards CAM therapies, particularly the better established therapies like acupuncture, chiropractic, and osteopathy, with homeopathy being the most popular.

There is also growing literature on the attitudes, beliefs, and expectations of medical students, as opposed to qualified practitioners, towards CAM.[28,29] Complementary medicine has even been introduced to the curriculum of some medical schools. Medical students most commonly identified acupuncture and acupressure, yoga, biofeedback, and meditation as CAM therapies.[30] Most believed that CAM was effective because of a combination of scientific, therapeutic, and placebo effects. Halliday and colleagues studied 592 Scottish medical students.[31] In all, 77 per cent thought CAM was useful— increasingly so as they progressed through their training. Of these students, 69 per cent said they would like it in their curriculum and 63 per cent were in favour of it being available within the NHS. The greatest doubt among the students was whether they would refer patients to an alternative practitioner outside the NHS; 41 per cent said they would, while 39 per cent were unsure.

Furnham and colleagues found a positive attitude among pre-clinical medical students to established CAM therapies in general.[29] In another study, Furnham and colleagues examined pre-clinical medical students' attitudes specifically to the following five complementary therapies: herbalism, homeopathy, hypnosis (hypnotherapy), osteopathy, and acupuncture.[23] They found very few statistically significant differences in the students' attitudes to the five therapies. In another study, Furnham and colleagues compared the attitudes to CAM of both medical and social science students.[29] There were few differences between them and both groups strongly believed that psychological factors were often the cause of illness. Both were supportive of, but also sceptical of, some aspects of OM. However they had more positive attitudes to CAM. Compared to GPs, they believed that CAM practitioners were more sympathetic, had more time to listen, were more sensitive on emotional issues, and were better at explaining treatments. Both student groups seemed particularly positive toward dietary and exercise treatments.

## Differences in the consultation between complementary and alternative medicine and orthodox medicine

Are the popularity of CAM and its powerful placebo effects due to the often fundamental and dramatic differences between the stereotypic CAM and OM consultation? There is only a limited amount of research in this area.[5] Is it possible to generalize? Is there indeed such a thing as a typical consultation? Is the variation within each group (that is, CAM versus OM) different from or greater than the variation between each group? The differences between the consultations of an aromatherapist compared to an osteopath, or a psychiatrist compared to an orthopaedic surgeon, are considerable. Indeed there may be different 'schools of thought', which results in different types and styles of consultations within each CAM or OM specialty. Then there may be differences depending on the biography, demographics, and training of the individual practitioner. A typical consultation may be hard to define. Consultations are so varied that any generalizations about the difference are only stereotypical, possibly misleading, or meaningless.

And yet patients and practitioners acknowledge, even celebrate, the particular and peculiar approaches to the consultation. Table 9.2 shows 16 different criteria by which CAM and OM may differ and may in part explain the popularity of CAM. General practitioners all too often have too little time, may be perceived as patronising, and may not examine (touch) the patient. Further, patients are often not asked the full set of questions they

**Table 9.2** The prototypic complementary and alternative medicine and orthodox medicine consultation

|  | Complementary and alternative medicine | Orthodox medicine |
|---|---|---|
| Time | More | Less |
| Touch | More | Less |
| Money | More | Less |
| History taking | Holistic, affective | Specific, behavioural |
| Language | Healing, holistic, subjective, personal story, wellness | Cure, dualistic, objective, case history, illness |
| Patient role | Consumer | Sick role |
| Decision-making | Shared/consumer | Doctor/paternalistic |
| Bedside manner | Charismatic, empathic | Cool, professional |
| Sex ratio/role | F = M/feminine | M > F/masculine |
| Time spent talking | Patient ≥ practitioner | Practitioner > patient |
| Style | Authoritative, supportive, counselling | Authoritarian, information/advice giving |
| Confidence in method/outcome | Very high | High |
| Client relationship | Long term | Short term |
| Consulting rooms | Counselling | Clinical |
| Practitioner history | Second profession | First profession |
| Ideology | Strong, left wing | Moderate, middle way |

expect to be asked for a 'full' diagnosis. In short they are not treated like a modern adult consumer. Complementary and alternative medicine practitioners have longer consultations and appreciate the patient's need to talk, to be examined and touched, and so on. The question is how the traditional or average CAM consultation is different from (better than) the traditional orthodox consultation. It is possible to compare and contrast the typical GP and CAM consultation across a number of variables (history-taking approach, language used, patient role, decision-making process, bedside manner, and so on) to show how different they are, which may account for the popularity of the latter. Research is needed to confirm the view that it is very much the nature of the consultation that both differentiates CAM from OM *and* makes it attractive. Current evidence supports this view.

# Why do people use complementary and alternative medicine?

There is some evidence that frequent CAM users are more health conscious and believe more strongly that they can influence their own state of health, both by lifestyle and through maintaining a psychological equilibrium. Complementary and alternative medicine patients appear to have less faith in 'provider control', that is, in the ability of medicine (specifically orthodox doctors) to resolve problems of ill health.[5] Patients with cancer using CAM were more likely to believe cancer was preventable through diet, stress reduction, and environmental changes and to believe that patients should take an active role in their own health.[5] Results from various studies reported by Furnham and colleagues show the following.[5,6,17,18]

## People shop for health

People want to use all possible (and affordable) options in health care. People are not loyal to a brand, to OM, or to any particular therapy. They shop, try out, and experiment. To many people, CAM is just another product or service. The question is how the particular brand offers something quite different, which no other product or service offers. This raises the question as to what makes an individual 'brand loyal'; that is loyal to a therapy, a therapist, or indeed a place of treatment.

## People want a cure without side-effects or pain

This may offer a very strong, unique selling point for homeopathy over herbalism and acupuncture (and so on) because of the scare stories about poisoning with herbs or minerals and pain or infection with acupuncture. It is for instance the 'gentleness' of homeopathy and its dilutions that may be particularly attractive to people. The possible contradiction between being harmless *and* effective is not often confronted.

## People have chronic illnesses or conditions they have difficulty living with

Many patients with chronic painful conditions or addictions have tried many other cures. They turn to CAM sometimes as a last hope. Some therapies have a powerful psychological component, particularly those associated with touch (that is, massage and reflexology).

## People are disappointed by the traditional orthodox consultation

As shown in Table 9.2, there are many reasons for patients' disappointment with OM, but it seems that the nature and style of the consultation is the primary explanation for this.

## Patients want to learn more about self-care (fitness, wellness, and prevention)

Orthodox medicine is seen as narrow and disease (complaint) orientated, which aims to destroy, demolish or suppress 'sickening forces', through such things as chemical therapies and surgery. But many people prefer an emphasis on natural restorative processes to strengthen the vitalizing health-promoting forces. The emphasis is quite different—illness versus wellness. Psychologists have long recognized this. Complementary and alternative medicine is often seen as restorative, balancing, natural, and preventative, which fits in with the particular zeitgeist.

## Patients believe in the 'holistic' message

It seems obvious to most patients that lifestyle, personal relationships, and work operate together and simultaneously to have an impact on health. Equally they believe that there are many and manifold signs of wellness and illness from digestion, sleep patterns, and body appearance, to more subtle non-verbal signs associated with gait, balance, body odour, and so on. The implication is that the diagnostic interview needs to have questions about all aspects of a person's life, not only the physical symptoms.

# Who seeks complementary and alternative medicine?

It is foolhardy to talk about 'typical' patients as CAM rejoices in differences, individuality, and the uniqueness of people's lives. However, there are patterns and a higher probability that particular types of people are likely to seek out, use, and benefit from CAM.

## Demography

Complementary and alternative medicine patients are more likely to be women rather than men, aged 30–40 rather than older or younger, middle and upper rather than working class, well educated, and urban rather than rural.[17]

## Medical history

First, patients seeking CAM have chronic rather than acute problems. Second, their health problems are often non-specific or have a psychological component. Third, many patients have a 'thick file' in the sense that their interest in health issues has led them to seek out various remedies from many different sources.[17]

## Beliefs, attitudes, and values

To a large extent it seems the CAM practitioners have tapped into the zeitgeist of people's beliefs about health. Many patients seem to be sympathetic with green issues, ideas, and understanding.[5] These include environmentalism, one-world-ism, and anti-materialism. Pro-CAM beliefs may also include issues of inequality, alienation, and social exclusion. Complementary and alternative medicine patients also seem to be interested in general consumer affairs and may even belong to bodies that lobby in favour of a certain position. They appear to be sensitive to consumer rights, bad practice, and poor treatment. Complementary and alternative medicine patients appear to be particularly interested in the 'life of the mind'. They certainly believe the maxim of 'a healthy mind in a healthy body'. Complementary and alternative medicine patients are, because of their own medical condition, likely to be very empathic to the plight of others and hostile to the 'uncaring' attitude of certain specialists (for example, surgeons). There is now an interest in 'modern health worries', which is an increased obsession with environmental causes of poor health. Petrie and Wessely believe these worries lead to more psychosomatic illnesses that CAM practitioners seek to treat.[32]

## The role of psychology in complementary and alternative medicine

Psychological theories may be applied to, and tested in, the CAM context. Thus Furnham and Lovett showed the theories of reasoned action and the theory of planned behaviour could be used successfully to investigate factors underlying intentions and actual use of homeopathy over a 1-month period.[33] These theories attempt to explain how attitudes and beliefs about a certain behaviour (that is, using CAM) predict the intention to use it and thence actually doing it. In short, they attempt to explain why and when attitudes do and do not predict behaviour. Similarly, Furnham and Lovett demonstrated how attribution theory (a theory of how individuals attribute causes to their own and others' behaviour) could elucidate patient perceptions of risk.[34] Indeed there are many other psychological theories and models in the health and medical psychology literature (for example, the health beliefs model), which may go a long way to answering some of the fundamental questions in this comparatively new, multi-disciplinary area of research. The health belief model attempts to explain how an individual's beliefs about their own health (that is, seriousness of health problems or susceptibility to illness) leads them to take (or indeed not to take) preventative action. From a theoretical perspective, psychology may be particularly useful in helping understand patient pathways to CAM: the knowledge, attitudes, and beliefs of patients as well as the dynamics of the GP (OM) and CAM consultations.

## Conclusion

People seek CAM because of dissatisfaction with OM and what it can deliver. In particular, patients are dissatisfied with the nature and style of the consultation and its attendant communication, which is regarded as too one-way, with insufficient listening, touching, and attention. The commonality of most CAM is that it delivers all these. Complementary and alternative medicine can also teach OM the importance of eliciting a patient's beliefs about their illness, which will often be related to beliefs about the environment and the patient's life in general. All these factors are addressed within the BPS model. Complementary and alternative medicine is ahead of OM in incorporating psychology into its approach. Orthodox medicine has the advantage of being able to consider biology and the social environment as well. We have a lot to learn from CAM.

## References

1. Ernst E, Furnham A. BMWs and complementary/alternative medicine. *Focus on Alt Comp Ther* 2000; **5**: 253–4.
2. Easthope G, Tranter B, Gill G. General practitioners' attitudes toward complementary therapies. *Soc Sci Med* 2000; **51**: 1555–61.
3. Ernst E. The British House of Lords enquiry into complementary and alternative medicine. *Focus Alt Comp Med* 2000; **5**: 3–5.
4. Abbot N, White A, Ernst E. Complementary medicine. *Nature* 1996; **381**: 361.
5. Vincent C, Furnham A. *Complementary medicine: A research perspective.* Chichester: Wiley; 1997.
6. Vincent C, Furnham A. Complementary medicine: state of the evidence. *J Roy Soc Med* 1999; **92**: 170–7.
7. *JAMA* 1998; **280**(18) (special issue).
8. Eisenberg D, Kessler R, Foster C *et al.* Unconventional medicine in the United States: prevalence, costs and patterns of use. *New Engl J Med* 1993; **328**: 246–52.
9. Eisenberg D, Davis R, Ettner S *et al.* Trends in alternative medicine use in the national survey. *JAMA* 1998; **11**: 1569–75.
10. Fisher P, Ward A. Complementary medicine in Europe. *BMJ* 1994; **309**: 107–11.
11. White A, Ernst E. Economic analysis of complementary medicine: a systematic review. *Comp Ther Med* 2000; **8**: 111–18.
12. Aakster C. Concepts in alternative medicine. *Soc Sci Med* 1986; **22**: 265–73.
13. Furnham A. How the public classify complementary medicine: a factor analytic study. *Comp Ther Med* 2000; **8**: 82–7.
14. Turner R. A proposal for classifying complementary therapies. *Comp Ther Med* 1998; **6**: 141–3.
15. Gray R. Four perspectives on unconventional therapy. *Health* 1998; **2**: 55–74.
16. Ernst E, Pittler M. The effectiveness of acupuncture in treating acute dental pain: a systematic review. *Br Dent J* 1998; **184**: 443–7.
17. Furnham A. Complementary and alternative medicine. *Psychologist* 2002; **15**: 228–31.
18. Furnham A, Kirkaldy B. The health beliefs and behaviours of orthodox and complementary medicine clients. *Br J Clin Psychol* 1995; **25**: 49–61.

19. Borkan J, Neher JO, Soker B. Referrals for alternative therapies. *J Fam Pract* 1994; **39**: 545–50.

20. Wearn AM, Greenfield SM. Access to complementary medicine in general practice: survey in one UK health authority. *J Roy Soc Med* 1998; **91**: 465–70.

21. Wharton R, Lewith E. Complementary medicine and the general practitioner. *Lancet* 1986; **292**: 1498–1500.

22. Anderson E, Anderson P. General practitioners and alternative medicine. *J Roy Coll Gen Pract* 1987; **37**: 52–5.

23. Furnham A, Hanna D, Vincent C. Medical students' attitudes to complementary medicine. *Comp Ther Med* 1995; **3**: 212–19.

24. Visser GJ, Peters L. Alternative medicine and general practitioners in the Netherlands: towards acceptance and integration. *Fam Pract* 1990; **7**: 227–32.

25. Perkin MR, Pearcy R, Fraser JS. A comparison of the attitudes shown by general practitioners, hospital doctors and medical students towards alternative medicine. *J Roy Soc Med* 1994; **87**: 523–5.

26. White AR, Resch KL, Ernst E. Complementary medicine: use and attitudes among GPs. *Fam Pract* 1997; **14**: 302–6.

27. Easthope G, Tranter B, Gill G. General practitioners' attitudes towards complementary therapies. *Soc Sci Med* 2000; **51**: 1555–61.

28. Furnham A. Attitudes to alternative medicine: a study of the perceptions of those studying orthodox medicine. *Comp Ther Med* 1993; **1**: 120–6.

29. Furnham A, Yardley L, Fatimy A *et al.* Health beliefs and preferences for medical treatment. *Comp Ther Med* 1999; **1**: 101–9.

30. Derr S, Shaikh U, Rosen A *et al.* Medical students' attitudes toward, knowledge of, and experience with complementary medicine therapies. *Acad Med* 1998; **73**: 1020.

31. Halliday J, Taylor M, Jenkins A *et al.* Medical students and complementary medicine. *Comp Ther Med* 1990; **1**: 32–3.

32. Petrie, K, Wessely S. Modern worries, new technology, and medicine. *BMJ* 2002; **324**: 690–1.

33. Furnham A, Lovett J. Predicting the use of complementary medicine: a test of the theory of reasoned action and planned behaviour. *J Appl Soc Psychol* 2001; **31**: 2588–620.

34. Furnham A, Lovett J. The perceived efficacy and risks of complementary and conventional medicine: a vignette study. *J Appl Biobehav Res* 2001; **6**: 39–63.

## Discussion

*Wessely*: My immediate reaction is to wonder about the slightly false dichotomy you set up between orthodox and alternative medicine. It is not that I don't recognize the alternative, but I was slightly unsure whether I recognized your construct of orthodox medicine. I see myself as a positive, empirical, Western, educated person and I am extremely sceptical about complementary medicine. But then I also endorse many aspects that you listed as belonging to complementary medicine. How much are you caricaturing conventional medicine?

*Furnham*: I don't know. It is an analysis of variance problem. I think there is more variability within conventional medicine. If you took the specialties, you could tie down some of this variability more. In this sense, is this a useful exercise? I don't know. In one sense it is, because it shakes up our thinking about where the differences lie.

*Wessely*: The question you address is whether the biopsychosocial (BPS) model is the same as the model of alternative medicine. I am absolutely certain it can't possibly be, or otherwise I wouldn't so criticize it. But you have raised interesting speculations about the overlap.

*Furnham*: There is a lot of overlap.

*Drossman*: What I am struck with is the fact that what makes complementary medicine work, in my opinion, is the provider–patient interaction. This shouldn't discriminate it from orthodox medicine. The problem here is not what they are doing, but what practitioners of conventional medicine are not doing. There is a false assumption that it is complementary medicine that is doing something novel.

*Furnham*: You could end complementary medicine tomorrow if you tripled the time of general practioner (GP) consultations.

*Wessely*: The one thing that these patients didn't say is that GPs had no time for them. Everything else they said they didn't like about the GPs, but the one non-significant thing was time.

*Furnham*: I would have thought that most people are not happy with their 7 minutes.

*Wessely*: That wasn't what you showed.

*Drossman*: It could also be a matter of expectation. They may not be expecting the GP to do what the complementary medicine practitioner is doing.

*Furnham*: That is true.

*Sharpe*: I just wonder whether something has been lost in this 'broad-brush' picture that portrays the general public as psychologists. Are there not others who are biologists and who don't want psychological issues raised? They might be expected to prefer narrowly focused biomedicine. Can you see this in your data?

*Furnham*: When I say that people are psychologists, I say this in the sense that they offer explanations that are psychological and they focus on the individual, as opposed to a sociologist who focuses on the society. Is it a question of language, or that they don't know enough about pharmacology or genetics? You will find groups who will put equal emphasis on biological effects. For example, I have studied lay people's attitudes to schizophrenia. The lay public espouse genetic models, whereas relatives of people with schizophrenia are very unhappy with a genetic explanation. To answer your question, what I haven't done is to isolate those with a more biological explanatory perspective from those with a psychological perspective. If you read the popular press, it is all psychological.

*Wessely*: I absolutely disagree. In the field we work in, the alternative views on chronic fatigue syndrome (CFS) are unbelievably reductionist.

*Furnham*: That may be an exception. Is there any other area where that is the case?

*Wessely*: There is a group of people who consult alternative practitioners because they want the most biological explanations about allergies, toxicities, and so on. They see them in a political framework: it is all the fault of governments and industry. But in those models there is no room for any psychosocial element.

*Marien*: Isn't that because they can't have a medical label? If you ask cardiac patients what they believe is the major cause of their heart disease they say stress, whereas if you as a CFS patient they'll seek a biological explanation. This could be because they feel we are rejecting them as a group of people when they want a medical label.

*Fitzpatrick*: I wonder whether we are being presented with a caricature of primary care that is about 20 years out of date. When I started in general practice, the box of tissues on the desk was not mandatory. If you go to see a GP now, they will most likely be a woman, and if they are male they will be wearing a woolly jumper and corduroy trousers. They will have been trained in communication skills. Preoccupation with all these issues has taken over. I don't think you'll find any patients under the age 60 who will use the term 'under the doctor'. People underestimate the impact of Oprah Winfrey-style programmes. Patients come in and emote and speak articulate psychobabble. The doctors emote back.

*Lewin*: There are clear data about this. The government have been interviewing patients around the country and patients complain that doctors don't talk to them. We have just done a survey of 30 randomly chosen heart failure patients from across Yorkshire. None of them knew what the causes of their illness were. Several of their doctors said that they hadn't told the patients that they have got heart failure and asked us not to mention it to them; doctors are often scared to discuss it because it will lead to questions about dying.

*Aylward*: I know you were presenting this with a slightly jovial slant, but the message I got is that most complementary medicine practitioners are being duplicitous at worst and ingenuous at best. In the same way as we find it difficult to find people to interview who are malingering and practising illness deception, has anyone done any work to look at the reasoning of the beliefs of people who do practise complementary medicine? From what you said, it seemed that they were using fairground techniques.

*Furnham*: First, I want to make a distinction between what I call the serious and the non-serious. I think the Gem Johnny's are not serious. They are self-duplicitous. Some of them I respect greatly, but if you interview them and ask them for evidence, they will say it is every day in front of their eyes. People get better and people go back. If you start talking about double-blind trials, which is often impossible, some of the homeopathy people will be more sympathetic, but they don't believe that this is necessary. So in this case I don't think they are being duplicitous.

*Aylward*: To reiterate what Simon Wessely said, many of those complementary medicine techniques are not psychosocial. They allege that they have a specific biological action.

*Furnham*: Although the way they do things is very psychosocial. The interview that goes with most of the procedures is psychosocial.

*Aylward*: That is what we have to learn.

*Salmon*: One of the currents in this discussion is that we are wondering who is more psychological: patients or doctors. In fact, this is an empirical question and there are data we can use to help answer it, such as surveys of the beliefs of patients attending GPs. Stress and psychological factors are at the top of the list of these patients' beliefs about what has caused their symptoms. If we follow this through to secondary care, we have known for a long time that, in patients with cancer, some of the most common beliefs about cause are that they have brought it on themselves. We can see this as a negative side-effect of the psychosocial ideas about illness that have entered the public domain. But it also represents an opportunity because it means that patients are thinking psychologically about their illness. We have done some work looking at GP–patient dialogue when dealing with unexplained symptoms. We approached it from the standard point of view, which is that GPs need to psychologize their patients, helping their patients reattribute their symptoms to psychological causes, for example. What we are finding, however, is almost the opposite. Most of the patients are providing psychological cues. Many are asking what is wrong with them and a great many are using the word 'depression' about their symptoms. A larger number are offering less striking cues, talking about being unhappy or worried, but these are still psychological cues. The other striking thing is that the proportion of times where these cues are taken up by the GP is tiny. Only in a vanishingly small number of cases do we see a GP who uses the fact that the patient is talking about depression or psychological problems and has asked what causes their unexplained symptoms, to weave a psychological explanation of those symptoms. So patients are providing the raw material for the GPs to use, but on the whole, the GPs aren't using that material to weave a sort of explanation that perhaps the complementary medicine practitioners are offering.

*Wessely*: That's deeply depressing, because they've all been on Mike Fitzpatrick's course.

*Davey Smith*: Has there been much research about whether people actually want to be involved in shared decisions about their care? You talk about people going around shopping for their medical practitioners, but perhaps they are shopping around for a practitioner who is then going to decide about their care plan for them.

*Furnham*: That's where the locus of control comes in. There are some people who want to be 'under the doctor': they want the responsibility for their health to be shouldered by other people. What is very noticeable about the complementary people is that they want to have this shared role. They get it with their dentist, accountant, and other professionals they interact with. But they don't seem to get it in the same way with their doctors. But this doesn't apply to everyone and the locus of the control variable is the one that picks this up. This is associated with factors such as social class and education.

*Davey Smith*: There are lots of expositions about why people would want to be involved in shared decision making with their GP. However, if your car breaks down and you take it to the garage, you don't want the engineer to share the decision-making process with you. It seems to me to be entirely legitimate to not want to be involved in shared decision making. I haven't found any studies that have really addressed this issue.

*Lorig*: The second you say, 'I don't want to be involved in shared decision making', you are involved in it. It is only when you are not given that option that you are not. This is sometimes forgotten in the shared decision-making literature.

*Lewin*: To continue with George's motoring analogy, you don't want the mechanic to whip your engine out without discussing the possible bill with you.

*Elwyn*: There is actually a large body of evidence looking at patient preferences for involvement and information. There have been three reviews recently and the conclusion is that 80–90% of patients want more information than they are given and a lesser percentage want involvement in decision making. The problem is that they have been asked about this hypothetical issue of whether they would want to be involved if they were asked. This is a stupid question, because they don't know about the decisions if they don't know the information. This research is very naïve. Coming back to the point about whether GPs open up the cues, Peter Campion and Peter Tate have done a study that has recently been published in the *British Medical Journal* using 3000 videotapes of registrars taking the Royal College of General Practioners exam.[1] One of the criteria for scoring is for them to pick up these cues and almost all of them fail to do it, even after training. We have just done an analysis using a new instrument that asks how much GPs in routine consultations involve patients in decision making. It is very rare indeed. If we increase the time of the consultation from 8 to 12 minutes it goes up by 50%.

*Fitzpatrick*: There is a socially and culturally approved script, which people have acquired through reading magazines and watching television programmes. This conditions the way in which they respond to a lot of these questions. For example, if they are asked if they want to be in control they say 'yes', because it is thought to be good to want to be in control. If they are asked whether they are in favour of science, they say 'yes' because everyone is in favour of science. Glyn Elwyn's point is quite right: we have to distinguish between how people want to respond to that and how they deal with any specific situation they are in. This is why these approaches may be exaggerating how people really feel.

*Wessely*: I think your rather dim post-modernists aren't in favour of science.

*Marien*: I want to reinforce what Glyn was saying. Howie's work shows that simply extending consultation time in general practice improves patient compliance and adherence.[2] Along with this, it improves doctor satisfaction and also reduces prescribing and referral rates. This has huge implications for health costs. The extraordinary system that we have running in general practice with 7-minute consultations is something that really needs to be addressed by health economists. It is complete madness. You can't adopt a BPS approach, addressing fears, anxieties, and expectations in 7 minutes, as well as do a physical examination.

*Furnham*: Patients have the expectations that you can or should. They want it, don't get it, and go to someone who will give it to them.

*Wessely*: General practice consultations are not really just 7 minutes: you are considering this as a one-off situation. This is just a part of a long-term interaction between the patient and doctor spread over months and years.

*Elwyn*: That pattern is changing. In large practices the longitudinal personal relationship is fragmenting a bit.

*Lewin:* We touched earlier on the iatrogenic nature of some of the damaging health beliefs and how they are induced by poor doctor–patient communication. There is a danger that if you double the amount of time you spend with your GP and they are still doing the wrong thing, they will make things twice as bad!

*Stansfeld:* Is it the case that patients don't want so much input into decision making when it comes to issues which are potentially frightening or threatening? Is this where people would rather let the doctors take over?

*Furnham:* There's an interesting literature on repressive coping. There is this idea that there is a group of individuals who don't want to know what goes on; they repress. If you tell people they are going to have a serious operation in 2 weeks' time, the sensitizers talk about it and that's their preference. There is another group who want to completely push it out of their mind. I seem to remember that the repressors get better.

*Lewin:* There was a study which randomized people to either the option they wanted, which was more information or less information, or to the option they didn't want. If you were mismatched with your coping style you did worse.

## References

1. Campion P, Foulkes J, Neighbour R *et al.* Patient centredness in the MRCGP video examination: analysis of large cohort. Membership of the Royal College of General Practitioners. *BMJ* 2002; **325**: 691–2.

2. Howie JGR. Patterns of work. In: *Trends in general practice.* London: Royal College of General Practitioners; 1977.

# 10 A case of irritable bowel syndrome that illustrates the biopsychosocial model of illness

## Doug Drossman

## Summary

This chapter will illustrate how the biopsychosocial (BPS) model might work within the context of medical practice. I also want to discuss its relevance to research. I am going to use a case study as an example of the role of clinical care in developing research strategies for applying psychosocial principles. I will argue that individual illnesses are a legitimate area of research into the BPS model.

## Introduction

In many ways people have interpreted George Engel's seminal paper different-ly, based largely on how it might relate to their own subject. Having worked with Engel, I think his vision was to bring psychosocial issues into medical practice and research. His article was a template.[1] He was very interested in the issues we have already addressed, such as complementary medicine and the physician–patient communication. He was a master interviewer. We would listen to him and see how his interviews frequently obtained psychosocial information that was relevant to the patient.

## Disease versus illness

One issue, challenged by George Davey Smith's chapter, was that of bio-medical reductionism, where everything is reduced to a single aetiology that is necessary and sufficient an explanation and where dualism determines illness to be dichotomized into organic versus functional. At the crux of some of our discussions is the disease versus illness distinction. The disease is the externally verifiable evidence of a pathological state and the illness is the patient's perception of ill health. We have to come to terms with the limitations of psychosocial factors in explaining the aetiology of clearly established chronic disease, such as heart disease or arthritis. Once we have done this, we can focus more on adaptation and management using psychosocial parameters.

I would like to take a moment to respond to Davey Smith's discussion of the peptic ulcer story. The problem here is with the disease and illness paradigm. I see some of my patients treated against *Helicobacter pylori* and they come back complaining of ulcer pain. My guess is that they are *H. pylori* negative and endoscopically have no ulcer, because they have successfully been treated. Yet the pain persists: 'illness without disease'. The fact is that ulcers and pain do not always correlate. Instead, a patient may have functional dyspepsia. Dyspepsia pain is more often explained in terms of motility, sensation, and psychosocial factors and may not be associated with ulcers. In fact, most ulcers demonstrated by endoscopy are asymptomatic. Also, most 'ulcer pain' is not associated with ulcers. If we think about it this way and go back to the 1950s when these papers were being presented,[2,3] doctors were not doing endoscopies but they were diagnosing ulcer-like pain as ulcer disease. Presumably many had functional dyspepsia and they were finding psychosocial correlates with this group. The challenge is to recognize what we mean by illness and disease. When we look at the biomedical model, there is no question that there are biological determinants that explain disease. The assumption is, however, that the disease explains the illness in a linear way, which then explains the outcome. We accept that there could be environmental exposures that will modify this and there might even be psychological overlay that can affect the

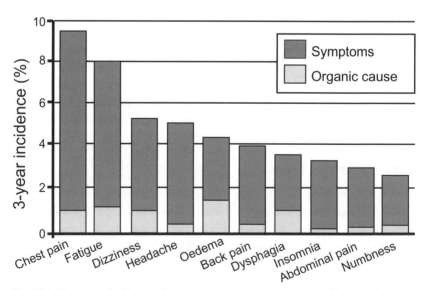

**Fig. 10.1** Three year incidence of most common symptoms reported in ambulatory clinic with proportion (light coloured bar) in which an organic aetiology is found.[4]

outcome. But the point is that it is a linear model, where the disease explains illness.

What about illness without disease? Kroenke and Mangelsdorff published a very important paper in which they followed patients in an ambulatory care centre for several years.[4] They looked at the incidence of established organic disease in the most frequent 10 or 11 complaints. The most common complaints seen over that period of observation included symptoms like fatigue, headache, and abdominal pain and the frequency of established organic disease was on average about 10 per cent (see Fig. 10.1). From a healthcare systems model, physicians are confronted with illness, not disease, particularly in primary care. This is what we have to understand, study, and treat. That is not to say we do not study and treat disease, but we do not want to blur the boundaries.

## The biopsychosocial model and science

The BPS model does not refute science; it incorporates science. It also incorporates relevant psychosocial factors, all of which are of course amenable to study by appropriate scientific methodology. Biological and psychosocial predispositions, along with environmental exposures, can affect both the disease and the illness. Furthermore, illness has effects that can feed back and affect either disease activity or the clinical outcome. Human immunodeficiency virus as a disease causes illness, but it also affects society. Leserman and colleagues showed that life stress affects immune reactivity and the timing of the expression of the disease.[5] Furthermore, the impact on society has had an effect on the disease, with new medications introduced and the large amount of money that has been spent on research. So we are looking at mutually reciprocating factors, consistent with the BPS model, rather than a more linear or biomedical 'cause-and-effect' situation.

I am going to focus here on reciprocating psychosocial factors modifying both the illness and disease of the patient. The model for irritable bowel syndrome (IBS) is that there are genetic and environmental factors that affect physiology and psychosocial factors—the brain–gut connection. This in turn will affect the physiology, which affects symptom behaviour and the outcome. Again, this is all measurable. I will show what we have done over the past few years to look at these factors.

## The example of irritable bowel syndrome

Irritable bowel syndrome involves pain, disturbed defaecation, and bloating, with no clear structural abnormalities. The pathophysiology is four-fold. There is (1) increased motor reactivity, (2) altered sensation or lower pain threshold, (3) a susceptibility to peripheral sensitisation (that is, infection or trauma to the bowel can sensitize the bowel to have a lower pain threshold), and (4) the role of the brain in modulating these visceral afferent signals. If you give someone a fatty meal and stimulate their bowel, people with IBS have greater pressures in their sigmoid colon and there is an enhanced motor response. This is why patients might have cramps and diarrhoea after eating a meal. All of us might have cramps and diarrhoea after eating a big fatty meal with caffeine and alcohol, that is the gastrocolic reflex. As an independent factor, such patients also have a lower pain threshold. With balloon distension in the colon, patients complain of pain after a while. Patients with IBS have a lower pain threshold. This is not motility, it is a secondary effect of a lower pain threshold. The third point is that if you inflame the bowel it will become sensitive and the pain threshold will diminish. In a rat model of IBS, which has an inflamed bowel through mustard oil application, there is a greater firing of the afferent nerves than in controls. Sensitization occurs. This is why patients with IBS continue to have symptoms for a day or two after colonoscopy, whereas patients with polyps do not. This is because the distension may have created some level of sensitization. This comes from the brain in its relationship with the gut.

## A case study

The case I present is a patient with a history of functional bowel symptoms.[6] I choose this case because it demonstrates the BPS model and is amenable to study. The patient has a history of abuse, where the *psychological* impact factor was irrefutable. It involved an interaction with someone, so there was also a negative *social* factor and it involved alterations in brain function, both from a psychological and physiological perspective. This also had *biological* manifestations in the physiology of the brain and how it interacted with the IBS. The other interesting thing about this patient is that this is someone who has had a personal affect on my research career

In 1986 the patient was referred to me, aged 12, with a history of severe constipation and abdominal pain. She was frequently admitted to hospital and this affected her school life and activities. We did a medical evaluation and found she had colonic inertia. This is not IBS, but it is pain associated with slow bowel movements. We put her on a bowel-retraining programme. I followed her for the next 4 or 5 years and saw her every 4–6 months. She had decreased admissions and pain medication; she was doing better. She had good grades, became socially active, and became a cheerleader in junior high school. At the age of 16 she started dating a 19 year old. I remember this clearly because she came in with her mother (her parents were divorced) and the mother asked me to 'set her daughter straight' because she was dating an older man. What she meant was that her daughter was growing up and she was concerned. During the physical examination, when the mother was out of the room, I asked the girl whether she was sexually active (she was) and whether she was using protection (she was not). I told her that I would give her some information about birth control and that I would do a pelvic examination and give her birth control, when she came back in a month. On her return, a month later, she was tearful, had been experiencing sleep disturbance, had lost 4 pounds of weight and was failing in her grades. She began to tell me that from the day she had been told by me that she would come back for a pelvic examination, she had experienced unformed nightmares. During the course of the month she gradually recalled that a friend of the family had sexually abused her between the ages of 3 and 7 years. This was at the time that her physical symptoms began. The perpetrator had left town and the mother had told her daughter to forget about it. The daughter did and the symptoms began. For the next several years, until the age of 16, she had these symptoms but had not recalled the abuse. What probably happened is that, by me being an older man, doing a pelvic examination may have triggered a reactivation of post-traumatic stress disorder. She was referred for very brief counselling and the symptoms resolved for 10 years.

This had a profound effect on me because, having been trained by Engel, I was concerned that a lot of my patients were reporting histories of trauma. I did not know how relevant to their current health this was. The questions in my mind concerned the relationship of abuse history to gastro-intestinal (GI) illness, the effects of abuse on health outcomes, the reasons for the associations of the abuse to GI illness, and the mechanisms for the observed effects.

## The relationship between abuse and gastro-intestinal illness

Over the next 10 years we showed a high prevalence of abuse among patients with severe functional GI disorders. Our first paper showed that 44 per cent of the women in our GI practice gave a history of abuse.[7] There was a relationship between adult and child abuse history. Abuse was more common in functional than organic GI disorders and was associated with a poor health status. Physicians were not aware of this, only 11 per cent of them being aware of the history of abuse in those patients who had been abused.

Later work by Longstreth and Wolde-Tsadik showed that this might be related to severity;[8] the more severe the condition, the more likely a history of abuse was reported. There may have been a self-selection of the patients. Did this abuse lead to greater severity of pain or symptoms, or a greater effect on health behaviour? About 40–50 per cent of patients attending tertiary care centres gave a history of abuse, compared to only about 15% in primary care.

We looked prospectively at psychosocial health outcomes among women in a GI clinic, a standard tertiary care referral setting. We have since validated our abuse measure on three levels of sexual abuse: attempt but no physical contact (making a child watch a sexual act and tried and not succeeded); touch, which is touching genital areas or making them touch the perpetrator; and finally rape, which is actual penetration.[9] We found that each of these three levels of abuse determined significant differences on a variety of outcome measures, including pain, non-GI symptoms, days of disability, number of operations, and higher levels of psychological distress.

Physical abuse was broken down into battering and life threats (feeling that your life is at risk). Similar results were seen. Life threat was associated with poorer health status on these measures compared with battering. Our conclusion was that physical and sexual abuse contributes to poor health status. The major effect is seen with rape and life-threatening physical abuse.

## How does a history of abuse cause bowel illness?

If abuse is more common in both IBS and functional GI illnesses, are the symptoms explained by the abuse history an additive factor or are they unrelated? To address this we did a regression analysis in which we looked at the effect of abuse on these outcome measures, adjusting for diagnosis. We found that they were independent factors. That is, IBS or functional GI illness, independent of the abuse history, was associated with poor health status. Conversely, abuse history, unrelated to diagnosis, was also independently associated with poor health status. Patients with functional GI disorders reported more severe abuse and had a poorer health status when compared to those with organic diagnoses. Functional diagnosis and abuse had independent effects on health status. This all suggests that there was an amplifying or synergistic effect of abuse on the diagnosis. In regression modelling we found that abuse severity was the strongest predictor of a variety of outcomes including abdominal pain, psychological distress physician visits, and quality of life in a GI population, regardless of diagnosis, explaining 41 per cent of the variance.[10] Catastrophizing, ability to decrease symptoms, and low educational attainment were also predictors.

We also looked at associations with disability. Patients with GI symptoms and a history of abuse were more likely to report non-GI somatic symptoms.[11] This is no big surprise. Abuse, somatic symptoms, and disability explained 30 per cent of the variance of visits to the doctor. We were the first to report this in a medical population, but since then other researchers looking at other medical populations have shown that poor prognostic factors are penetration, life threat, serious injury, childhood abuse, and experiences over a long period.[12] For our patient, we do not know if there was life threat or injury, but there was definitely penetration, childhood abuse, and prolonged repetitive experiences.

Now we get to the issue of mechanism: how does this occur? Here are some possibilities. Patients with functional GI illness have high psychosocial co-morbidity. This could be why they do more poorly in their health status. They may have symptom amplification by staying within the healthcare system. Does abuse affect the gut directly, or the brain, or both? I previously mentioned injury and sensitization. Could direct trauma to the vagina or rectum sensitize the bowel in some way to cause a lower pain threshold? Or is it an effect mediated by the brain? We have measured the rectal balloon pressure at which patients report discomfort. People with a history of abuse actually had higher pain thresholds for the same pressure.[13] Therefore it is not happening at the level of the gut.

Let us talk about the brain and its feedback system. Somatic pain messages go to the somatosensory cortex via the thalamus. In contrast, visceral pain messages go to the dorsal horn, cross to the thalamus, and then go to the limbic system and anterior cingulate gyrus. Feedback systems are induced and block the pain. Pain could be amplified through these central phenomena. There could be either facilitation of input to the brain, or failure to inhibit. In other words, if there is a normal inhibiting effect, this could be blocked. This is called disinhibition. For example, if a basketball player sprains their ankle they may continue in the game and not notice the pain. At the end of the game they cannot get up. During the game the afferent signal was the same, but there was inhibition, taking place at the central level. This is the basis for hypnosis. There is a failure to inhibit normal ascending visceral signals. If this occurs, afferent visceral signals can be amplified. The perigenual area of the cingulate cortex is very rich in β endorphin. It appears to be the area that is associated with the descending inhibition. This anterior area of the cingulus turns down the signals from below. It has opioidergic, serotonergic, and noradrenergic effects. But the mid-cingulate cortex is not only associated with attention to physical sensations but also with anxiety and response selection. Why do I tell you this? Naliboff and colleagues studied positron-emission tomography (PET) images in response to rectal distension in patients with IBS and in healthy controls.[14] They found that there was activation of the pre-frontal cortex and this descending inhibitory area involving the pons and peri-aqueductal grey area in controls, but in the IBS patients there was activation of the mid-cingulate (that is, increased attention) area. They proposed rectal distension was associated with disinhibition in IBS patients.

## The relevance to the case report

Let us return to the patient I began to describe. I reported that she did well for 10 years. She came back to me about 2 years ago, at the age of 27. She had severe pain and diarrhoea, consistent with IBS. She developed it after *Clostridium difficile* enterocolitis secondary to antibiotics given for acute asthma. So she had a gut infection that triggered her IBS. At the same time, she had just got married and was involved for the first time in a decade in an abusive relationship with her husband. She felt helpless and vulnerable, with poor self-esteem and catastrophic thoughts. She had repeated admissions and started taking narcotics for pain. I tried to help rehabilitate her. There was a family confrontation, she divorced her husband, stopped narcotics, and went into therapy. The pain remitted and she had an increased sense of control and greater self-confidence and self-esteem. Her quality of life improved. So, she had a clear case of post-infectious IBS in a setting of severe psychosocial disturbance. The reason why people get post-infectious IBS appears to be associated with psychological distress.[15] People who do not have psychological distress at the time of the infection appear to recover sooner. It is truly a BPS effect.

Can we take our understanding further? We did fMRI brain imaging on this patient when she had severe IBS and again 8 months later after her recovery. At the time of the severe IBS, this patient had so much pain during balloon rectal distension that she pushed the panic button and stopped the procedure. She then decided to carry on, but she still scored the pain at a level of 5 out of 5 (the maximum). She showed activation of the anterior and mid-cingulate region of the brain, which replicates Naliboff's findings in IBS (see Fig. 10.2)[14] After recovery, this activation level went down almost to normal (see Fig. 10.2).

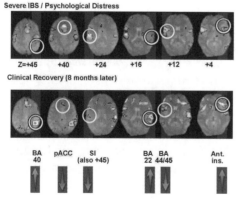

**Fig. 10.2** fMRI of a young woman's brain in response to rectal distension. Top image was taken during an episode of severe IBS, showing activation of anterior and mid-cingulate gyrus and somatosensory cortex. Lower image was taken after clinical improvement, with decreased activation of these areas. From reference 6.

Now let us also look at the psychosocial parameters. At the time of the severe IBS, her pain score was 5 on a scale of 5. When she was doing better she scored her pain with the same amount of rectal distension at a level of 3 and was surprised that we were applying the same amount of distension. Her SCL-90 (a measure of somatic and psychological symptoms) score dropped from the 97th percentile to normal. Her Beck depression score went from 37 to 6. The number of stresses was markedly reduced, as was her catastrophizing score. Her admission frequency went from three in a three-month period to zero and her days in bed dropped by about 50 per cent. So, the fall in brain activation was associated with clinical improvement, reduction in pain reporting, improvement in symptoms, and reduction in psychosocial factors.

We have taken this a step further with a $2 \times 2$ design of patients with IBS and abuse, IBS alone, abuse alone, and normals. The activation area in the cingulate cortex in IBS and abuse is greater compared to activation in those with a history of abuse or IBS alone. Psychosocial factors may be amplifying the pain, with the mean values for pain in those with IBS and abuse being near the maximum.[6,13,16]

## The biopsychosocial model applied to treatment

We have shown that there are many BPS factors in terms of diagnosis, physiology, comorbidity, coping, and cognition and physiological effects on the brain (possibly even structural) that affect outcome. The model we propose for treatment is that in severe IBS, where there is central disinhibition, we need to examine the efficacy of behavioural and antidepressant treatments because they may have more of a role than symptomatic treatments.

We have just completed a study of 400 patients, looking at the efficacy of cognitive behavioural therapy (CBT) and antidepressants in patients with functional bowel disorder.[17,18] Cognitive behavioural therapy was significantly better than education, using a composite outcome score ($P < 0.001$). Desipramine was marginally significantly ($P = 0.15$) better than placebo. However, with regard to treatment effect, there was no significant difference in composite outcome between CBT and desipramine.

We also found that CBT worked equally well with abused and not abused patients. In contrast, desipramine was only better than placebo in those with a history of abuse, but not in those without such a history. We are currently evaluating the reasons for these differential effects.

## References

1. Engel GL. The need for a new medical model: a challenge for biomedicine. *Science* 1977; **196**: 129–36.

2. Weiner H, Thaler M, Reiser M *et al.* Etiology of duodenal ulcer—I. Relation of specific psychological characteristics to rate of gastric secretion. *Psychosom Med* 1957; **19**: 1–10.

3. Alexander F. *Psychosomatic medicine: its principles and applications.* New York: Norton; 1950.

4. Kroenke K, Mangelsdorff AD. Common symptoms in ambulatory care: incidence, evaluation, therapy, and outcome. *Am J Med* 1989; **86**: 262–6.

5. Leserman J, Jackson ED, Petitto JM *et al.* Progression to AIDS: the effects of stress, depressive symptoms, and social support. *Psychosom Med* 1999; **61**: 397–406.

6. Drossman DA, Ringel Y, Vogt B *et al.* Alterations of brain activity associated with resolution of emotional distress and pain in a case of severe IBS. *Gastroenterology* 2003; **124**: 754–61.

7. Drossman DA, Leserman J, Nachman G *et al.* Sexual and physical abuse in women with functional or organic gastrointestinal disorders. *Ann Intern Med* 1990; **113**: 828–33.

8. Longstreth GF, Wolde-Tsadik G. Irritable bowel-type symptoms in HMO examinees. Prevalence, demographics, and clinical correlates. *Dig Dis Sci* 1993; **38**: 1581–9.

9. Leserman J, Li Z, Drossman DA *et al.* Impact of sexual and physical abuse dimensions on health status: development of an abuse severity measure. *Psychosom Med* 1997; **59**: 152–60.

10. Drossman DA, Li Z, Leserman J *et al.* Effects of coping on health outcome among female patients with gastrointestinal disorders. *Psychosom Med* 2000; **62**: 309–17.

11. Leserman J, Li Z, Drossman DA *et al.* Selected symptoms associated with sexual and physical abuse history among female patients with gastrointestinal disorders: the impact on subsequent health care visits. *Psychol Med* 1998; **28**: 417–25.

12. Kilpatrick DG, Saunders BE, Amick-McMillan A *et al.* Victim and crime factors associated with the development of crime-related post-traumatic stress disorder. *Behav Ther* 1990; **20**: 199–214.

13. Ringel Y, Drossman DA, Turkington TG *et al.* Regional brain activation in response to rectal distention in patients with irritable bowel syndrome and the effect of a history of abuse. *Dig Dis Sci* 2003; **48**: 1774–81.

14. Naliboff BD, Derbyshire SWG, Munakata J *et al.* Cerebral activation in irritable bowel syndrome patients and control subjects during rectosigmoid stimulation. *Psychosom Med* 2001; **63**: 365–75.

15. Drossman DA. Mind over matter in the postinfective irritable bowel. *Gut* 1999; **44**: 306–7.

16. Ringel Y, Drossman DA, Leserman J *et al.* IBS diagnosis and a history of abuse have synergistic effect on the perigenual cingulate activation in response to rectal distention. *Gastroenterology* 2003; **124**: A-531.

17. Drossman DA, Toner BB, Whitehead WE *et al.* Cognitive–behavioral therapy vs education and desipramine vs placebo for moderate to severe functional bowel disorders. *Gastroenterology* 2003; **125**: 19–31.

18. Drossman DA, Toner BB, Whitehead WE *et al.* A multi-center randomized trial of cognitive–behavioral treatment (cbt) vs. education (edu) in moderate to severe functional bowel disorder (fbd). *Gastroenterology* 2003; **124**: A-530.

## Discussion

*Creed*: You talked a lot about abuse, but I'm wondering whether the abuse is really being reflected in depression. Depression could be the factor that is crucial to many of the data you have shown us. For example, in the PET scan work, studies have been done in patients with depression that show rather similar findings. It could be that people who have been abused are more likely to have depression.

*Drossman*: We have put in a grant to look at this question. We have data showing a correlation of activation of the brain with psychosocial distress. We didn't look at axis 1 diagnoses, but we did look at Beck depression. The activation seemed to occur with both. We didn't look at the interaction between those two. This is an important issue: abuse may be mediated through other factors. Parenthetically, when we looked at the subgroups, the subgroup with a Beck depression score of over 16 had no benefit from cognitive behavioural therapy (CBT) or desipramine. Our hypothesis was that they would show benefit. One of the negative predictors was high depression and I don't understand this.

*Aylward*: For how many of the people who reported abuse were you able to confirm that this did occur?

*Drossman*: We did not make any effort to do this. We have dealt with this issue from 1990 on in discussions in symposia. From our standpoint, because the reporting of abuse has such a potent effect on outcome, we accept what we are told. We are looking at this from a health outcome model. Questioning the legitimacy of claims of abuse takes us into another realm of issues, such as recovered memories. From my clinical experience with the patients, I believe them.

*Wessely*: As epidemiologists we really are killjoys, but this kind of research does leave itself with some problems. One is the problem of bias: that what you have is poor health outcomes associated with increased recall of adversities, rather than the other way round. The other problem is of confounding because abuse isn't randomly distributed in the population. It comes with a whole host of other adversities. We know this from studies of psychiatric outcome of abuse. It is somewhat non-specific because it correlates with a huge number of different outcomes. In a research context, how much would your model be affected if you changed one of the arrows on your slide: you had it very unidirectional, suggesting that abuse led to these various outcomes. If you put it the other way round and it is the poor outcome that led to increased abuse history, how would this fit?

*Drossman*: I accept that, because I believe that: the arrow should be both ways. The point is, we are identifying markers that are associated with adverse outcome, which we are then looking to modify to improve outcome. We can look at these interactions and no doubt others will. But I also know that when these patients go into CBT and address these issues, we see a real relation between the responses to abuse and similar responses to their illness. We ask the patients what the experience was like when they were abused. They describe feelings of helplessness, vulnerability, and lack of control. When they talk about their IBS they also feel helpless and vulnerable, so there is a homology. We often make that link. They often ask what this has to do with their IBS. We say that we don't know for sure, but they are telling us the same cognitive thoughts and feelings that make them feel unable to control this; we are going to work on helping them to manage these symptoms better.

*Chalder:* How many people were randomized in the study you described?

*Drossman:* 402.

*Chalder:* Have you done a regression analysis putting all the predictors of outcome in?

*Drossman:* We are doing this now. We have had to do a lot of item reduction because all our baseline variables were significant. The question was what psychosocial factors are important over and above treatment?

*Chalder:* I was just wondering whether sexual abuse was put into the model.

*Drossman:* Sexual abuse was present in the first cut, but it wasn't that strong, relative to some others. We use a questionnaire called the 'Implicit model of illness' by Turk,[1] which has to do with a person's belief about whether they can control their illness.

*Chalder:* Irritable bowel syndrome does seem to be one of those conditions that appears to respond to almost anything in terms of a placebo response. Francis Creed compared antidepressants with psychotherapy and found that there was an equivalent effect. We compared CBT plus mebeverine hydrochloride with mebeverine hydrochloride alone. Even though CBT plus drug had some added benefits, the drug alone was also beneficial.

*Drossman:* The placebo response rate in IBS is a real challenge. It is the same thing with the peripherally acting pharmacological drugs. We are going to have a symposium on the placebo effect for this reason. There is something about the way the patients are responding or what the doctors are doing that makes a difference. I have a slide that shows placebo response rate varying from 33% to 88% in 10 different studies. This shows significance with the lower placebo response rate and non-significance in the others. The highest levels were from John Fielding from Ireland who always had negative studies with 80% response rate. He saw the patients in his office, gave them the placebo, and had an interaction with them. The lowest response rate was by

Piai in Italy where the pills were mailed to the patients. It is not the giving of the drug that is crucial, but how the drug is given that makes the difference.

*Chalder*: As I understand, Blanchard conducted a study, as yet unpublished, treating IBS with CBT. He got a negative result, which is difficult to understand given the placebo response we see.

*Drossman*: His earlier work was positive. I think there are real differences. What Francis Creed and I are looking at are the moderate to severe patients. He is working on people self-referred to a psychological treatment programme, which is a different population.

*Wessely*: In your trial you have followed up patients. Do you ever repeat the abuse questionnaire with the same people?

*Drossman*: In our psychosocial outcome study we did repeat it 2–4 weeks later, both in the screening and the intake procedures. The frequency prevalence increased on this repetition. We haven't tried repeating this after a longer interval.

*Wessely*: We have done a cohort study of members of the British armed forces. When we repeated the same question about traumatic events 2 years later, we found their responses changed according to their current mental state. The worse they rated their current health, the more adversities they recalled.

*Drossman*: If your point is that this may be a marker of psychosocial distress, I don't discount that. The critical point is that it seems to correlate with outcome measures and is amenable to modification.

*Salmon*: It's possible that what's happening is that having symptoms that make you feel wretched increases recall of abuse. This would be a strong argument if the IBS patients were being compared with asymptomatic individuals. As I understand it, in this work they are being compared with symptomatic patients, which controls for that possibility and differential recall of abuse is still there.

*Wessely*: But we find it in patients with chronic fatigue syndrome and fibromyalgia as well. It is not specific.

*Salmon*: That was the second point I wanted to make, about specificity. We have been looking at patients from neurology and gastro-intestinal clinics.[2,3] Patients with pseudoseizures also showed a much greater recall of abuse of various kinds than the patients with epilepsy.[2] But when we looked at the variables that might explain the link between abuse and being in the non-epileptic seizure group, depression and anxiety weren't important, but measures of functioning of the family of origin were significant.[3] The particular significant dimension was family over-control (measured by the family environment scale). When this was controlled for, abuse wasn't significantly related to being in the non-epileptic seizure group. This might be an indication that it is not the abuse itself that is related to non-epileptic seizures, but something about the controlling nature of the family in which abuse happens. So we might find more specificity in the link between childhood history and symptoms if we look at the particular characteristics of the abuse or of the family background associated with it.

## References

1. Turk DC, Rudy TE, Salovey P. Implicit models of illness. *J Behav Med* 1986; **9**: 453–74.
2. Reilly J, Baker GA, Rhodes J *et al.* (1999) The association of sexual and physical abuse with somatization: characteristics of patients presenting with irritable bowel and non-epileptic attack disorder. *Psychol Med* 1999; **29**: 399–406.
3. Salmon P, Al-Marzooqi S, Baker G *et al.* Childhood family dysfunction and associated abuse in patients with non-epileptic seizures: towards a causal model. *Psychosom Med* 2003; **65**: 695–700.

# 11 Are the patient-centred and biopsychosocial approaches compatible?

## Francis Creed

## Summary

The question I will be addressing in this chapter is whether the patient-centred and biopsychosocial (BPS) approaches are compatible. First, I will define briefly my understanding of the patient-centred approach. I will look at whether this affects outcome and then I will describe some of Peter Maguire's work, exploring why the BPS approach is not used more widely. I will conclude by saying that we need to encourage particular individual interviewing skills independently of their overall models.

## The patient-centred approach

The doctor who uses this approach responds to patients in a way that allows expression of their reasons for attending, their symptoms, and their thoughts, feelings, and expectations. This approach has also been described as the doctor exploring the illness experience and expectations, while regarding the patient as a whole person, finding common ground between the doctor and patient, taking the opportunity for health promotion and thus enhancing the doctor–patient relationship.[1] In a study of 865 consecutive patients attending their general practitioner (GP), Little and colleagues gave out questionnaires before the consultation to assess the patients' expectations and afterwards to assess reasons for consultation, demographic factors, number of medical problems, and anxiety. The outcome measures were symptom burden, satisfaction and help to cope with illness. They found that a high satisfaction with the GP consultation occurred when the consultation was seen by the patient as one where there was good communication between the doctor and patient and a good partnership. Enabling the patient to cope with the illness correlated with whether the doctor had (1) shown an interest in the effect of the illness on the patient's life, (2) mentioned health promotion, and (3) used a positive approach. Reduced symptom burden was associated with an enhanced doctor–patient relationship.

There were some problems with this study, which need to be recognized. First, there was an important measurement issue, because the study only used self-administered questionnaires. The authors admitted that their satisfaction measure also included a subscale of communication, so there may well have been contamination between predictor and outcome measures. Second, there was a problem, which struck me as a psychiatrist reading this paper, in that the GPs did not appear to have used the BPS model. The results demonstrated that anxiety was very strongly associated with poor satisfaction, poor coping with illness and life, and an increased symptom burden. This appears to have been ignored in the study. Had the GP detected and managed the anxiety successfully these three outcomes could have been improved. Thus this study does not allow us to answer satisfactorily the question of whether using the patient-centred approach affects outcome. One of the difficulties is the fact that the model is not precise and may be used differently in different settings. There are different theoretical perspectives, different types of patients and doctors, different diseases, and difficult measurement issues.

An important review of the area is provided by Mead and Bowers.[2] Their introduction makes clear their view that the patient-centred model was developed in part to differentiate primary care from secondary care and to provide a framework for GP vocational training. They were interested in the model as it might provide a possible measure for the quality of care in primary care. They observed that the lack of theoretical clarity led to a lack of valid and reliable measures, but could discern from the literature five dimensions of patient centredness.[2]

1. *A biopsychosocial perspective.* This is a response to the limitations of the biomedical model. In itself, though, it is inadequate to define patient centredness.

2. *The patient as a person and the personal meaning of illness.* This is an important dimension.

3. *Sharing power and responsibility and recognition of patients' needs and preferences.* This has been associated with certain interview behaviours, particularly encouraging patients to voice their own ideas. Listening is important and by no means universal. Reflecting and offering collaboration also matters.

4. *The therapeutic alliance.* The doctor's role is to achieve the desired emotional context for the consultation. This is a fundamental requirement of the model.

5. *The doctor as a person.* This area has been quite heavily influenced by Balint's work.[3] What the doctor brings to the consultation and how the doctor responds to the patient are important aspects, but they are very difficult to measure.

Mead and Bowers examined the studies that have used verbal coding of patient centredness to identifying doctors' behaviours that encourage patients to talk and promote the discussion of non-medical topics and empathic and affective statements.[2] The reliability of these measures varies greatly. The classification of a topic as medical or non-medical can be made reliably, but the measurement of the doctor's response as appropriately empathic and reassuring is much less reliable. The studies that have assessed these dimensions have demonstrated that patient centredness is associated with certain types of patients. It is more common in patients who are female, older, tense, or distressed and those who are better known to the doctor. It is also associated with the doctor maintaining eye contact, with longer consultations, and the diagnosis of depression. There are so many factors that can influence these measures of patient centredness that studying the area is technically difficult.

## Is the patient-centred approach associated with an improved outcome?

The studies that have used this approach have found evidence of improved patient compliance, satisfaction, and recall of information from the doctor.[4–9] However, there is also evidence of an association between some aspects of this model and dissatisfaction on the part of the doctor.[10] Using better outcome measures, patient centredness was not related to patients' ratings of the consultation, satisfaction, or health outcomes.[11,12]

The five dimensions of patient centredness—the BPS approach, the patient as a person, power-sharing, therapeutic alliance, the doctor as a person—have to be seen in the context of certain barriers to communication. These include time limitations, workloads, government policy initiatives, and priorities. In addition, there is the culture, age, and sex of both the patient and the doctor, the type of problem, the prior knowledge of both the doctor and the patient, and the training of doctors. All of these factors influence outcome, as well as the actual consultation, which can be measured in terms of short-term outcome (satisfaction, compliance, recall) or long-term outcome (health status).

There is evidence that health professionals can influence the way patients think and feel about their illness or its treatment: if this leads to a change in behaviour it can alter the outcome.[5] This seems to be an important thread that we need to continue to work with.

## Improved interview skills

I will now describe Maguire's approach and extend his work to try to answer the question of why improved interviewing is not used more widely. Many of his publications start off with the challenge that doctors and nurses are reluctant to ask patients about the full range of their problems. To some extent this can be attributed to patients, some of whom consider that their concerns are not something a doctor can do much about. Much has to do with the way that doctors and other heath professionals interview patients.

In patients with cancer, Maguire's group have shown that patients who have a large number of concerns, which are not addressed by health professionals, are at risk of developing anxiety and depression.[13] There is a clear opportunity, therefore, for health professional to address the patient's concerns to prevent later anxiety and depression developing.[14]

One relevant study was carried out with nurses working in two hospices in Sheffield.[15] The setting is important, because this study did not include a self-selected group of staff on a training course but a complete set of staff working in one institution. The hospice patients had, on average, seven problems or concerns at baseline, which were elicited at an independent research interview. These concerns were commonly uncontrolled pain, various aspects of anxiety, tiredness, appetite, mobility, and effects on relatives. Most of these were not elicited by the hospice staff, who mostly asked about physical problems. This failure to ask patients' about their concerns was regarded as a deficiency in their assessment.[16] The staff were then trained to improve their interview skills.

## Training to improve interview skills

Maguire's group organize regular workshops for cancer health professionals to improve their interview skills. The aim is to encourage staff to use a patient-centred assessment in which they facilitate patients' talk and enable a discussion of the patient's concerns.[14] This extends as far as desired by the patient. This research group uses a sophisticated system of audiotaping interviews and rating them in terms of the *form* (open or closed questions), the *function* (is it eliciting a psychological response?), the *content* (to what level is feeling explored?), the level at which the health professional uses *blocking* (to stop exploration of feelings), and whether it is *cue based* (does the interviewer use an earlier disclosure to explore certain things?).[17] In the Sheffield hospice study, the researchers calculated the proportion of interviews in which 60 per cent or more of patients' concerns were elicited. Before training 44 per cent of interviews reached this threshold. After training this proportion rose to 70 per cent.[17] So there is good evidence that staff can be trained to identify patients' concerns more accurately.[18]

## What does interview training do to health professionals' behaviour?

The three behaviours demonstrated by health professionals that were associated with promotion of patient disclosures were (1) open directive questions as opposed to closed questions, (2) questions with a psychological focus, and (3) questions that clarified the psychological focus. Disclosure of patients' concerns was also associated with fewer behaviours that blocked disclosure. These blocking behaviours included questions with a specifically physical focus, further questions aimed at clarifying the physical symptoms, and statements by the health professional that were classified by the researcher as 'giving advice prematurely' and 'normalizing'. An example of 'premature reassurance' is as follows:

> *Patient:* 'I'm worried about the operation.'
> *Healthcare professional:* 'Don't worry, it will be fine.'

An example of 'normalization' would be

> *Patient:* 'I'm very upset about having to have a mastectomy.'
> *Healthcare professional:* 'I can see you are upset; you are bound to be. Everyone is when they have this kind of surgery.'

Although the training enabled concerned health professionals to elicit more of the patients' concerns there were problems. Maguire and colleagues found that as healthcare professionals were encouraged and trained to elicit more psychological symptoms or concerns, there was an increase in the blocking behaviour. An example of blocking would be

> *Patient:* 'My husband thinks I should have chemotherapy, but I have three young girls and I don't know how I can explain to them that I might lose my hair and be sick.'
> *Healthcare professional:* 'How old are the children?'
> *Patient:* '11, 9, and 10 months.'
> *Healthcare professional:* 'This actually developed shortly after the pregnancy then?'
> *Patient:* 'Yes.'

The health professional effectively blocks the patient from discussing her concerns about the effect of chemotherapy on her hair by changing the topic of conversation.

Such distancing strategies have been recorded frequently in the interviews collected by this research group. Such strategies include jollying the patient along by explaining away the distress as normal, offering advice before the problem is understood, offering false reassurance, or switching to a safer topic for fear of releasing strong emotions in the patient, which would be difficult to handle.[19]

So why do health professionals block patients discussing their emotional concerns? Going back to the hospice study, eliciting patients' concerns were limited by the nurses' belief in their competence, possible costs to themselves, their perceived value to patients, and the degree of perceived managerial support.[19]

In one instance a patient said, 'I was frightened of coming here to the hospice. It was the word "hospice". It means the end. You imagine all sorts.' The nurse commented, 'A lot of people think that, it is very difficult to educate people.' When the nurse listened to this extract of her interview as part of her training course she said that she had responded like that because the patient would have started to talk about death and the process of dying—she would not have known what to say (belief in her own competence), it would have been upsetting (possible cost to herself), and she would have felt inadequate. Dealing with patients' concerns is seen as a stressful aspect of work with patients. It seems that nurses are more likely to block emotional concerns expressed by patients if they feel a lack of support from senior managers for such a style of interviewing. When supervisors offered lots of support, blocking was rarer. Another reason for blocking is the lack of adequate training for this kind of interview.

## Patient-centredness versus the biopsychosocial approach

Now we come to the perceived conflict of the BPS model with the patient-centred approach. Bartz published a study, which involved qualitative interviews between Dr 'M' and nine native Americans with diabetes.[20] In fact, the whole article was based around the single doctor, who said that she was using a sophisticated BPS approach and was committed to helping underprivileged people in a culturally sensitive way. She regarded her interactions with these patients as imbued with mistrust and misunderstanding. According to Bartz, she used the BPS model to help the patients to understand the way that diet, exercise, medication, and glucose monitoring were the key to self-care. But she observed that health was not a high priority for these nine patients, so she needed to change their values about health.

In response to the patient's question, 'Do you think stress might be doing this?' Dr M said in explanation, 'I have two responses to this. I reassure them about stress and then I get back to a more important issue: their weight, activity, and diet. Patients don't want to talk about their husband's suicide, their bouncing cheques. Often in the diabetic clinic I don't take the opportunity because of time pressure. I am sure I miss a lot of opportunities to figure out what is going on with my patients. I feel this pressure and this desire not to open a can of worms.'

She is commenting on time limitations and workloads. She said she had prior knowledge of these patients. She went on, 'I know family medicine training has emphasized the importance of listening to this material, but it is not medical stuff; it is not stuff I can affect. Knowing my patient well from the medical perspective means that I direct the patient away from problems like stress towards issues like exercise, diet, and medications which are the cornerstone of diabetic care.' In the Bartz paper, there is another extract.

> *Dr M :* 'How is it going, taking your medicines?'
> *Patient:* 'I think I'd better tell the truth, I've never taken them.'
> *Dr M :* 'So you have never taken any of that diabetes medication. Why is that?'
> *Patient:* 'Because I'm scared. I tried the first one but I didn't feel good.'
> *Dr M :* 'That's interesting that you were scared to take the medication. Some people are scared not to take their medication: they worry that they might get sicker'.
> *Patient:* 'I'm scared because I've been seeing the medicine man and he says don't take it. Well he didn't say that to me, he said it to another lady.'
> *Dr M :* 'I've never heard that. I've never heard of a medicine man who said "don't take your diabetes medicine".'
> *Patient:* 'He didn't say it to me; I was copying another lady'.
> *Dr M :* 'I think you need to find out for yourself what you need to do, not what someone else needs to do. My feeling is that you need to take your medicine'.
> *Patient:* 'Which one? I never really took one'.

Bartz says that Dr M's stance blocked her ability to enter into the very dialogue needed potentially to reconstruct the relationship with her patient. 'Dr M strives to change the patient's perspective to adopt the physician's BPS approach.' Is that really what the BPS model is expecting us to do? Bartz continues, 'The BPS model of disease as applied here may conflict with a patient-centred approach to communication'. He calls for greater use of patient-specific narratives being constructed in clinical practice.

## Conclusion

The patient-centred approach and the BPS model have been outlined briefly. In the literature these are often seen as mutually exclusive models but, in fact, they are different models that have been developed as researchers have tried to conceptualize and measure the different ways that health professionals related to patients. They can be depicted better in terms of two overlapping circles as there are a number of features that are common to both and some features that are specific to each (see Fig. 11.1).

I have argued in this chapter that it may be preferable to switch from studying a particular overall model to studying specific interview skills, as Maguire

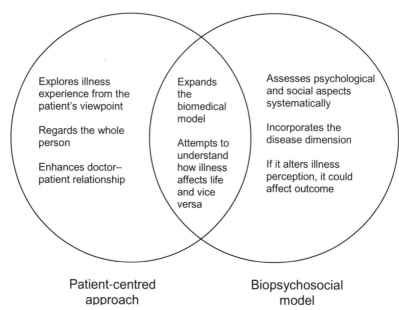

**Fig. 11.1** The common and distinct components of the patient centred approach and biopsychosocial model.

and colleagues have done in health professionals' interactions with cancer patients. The studies that I have discussed concerning both the patient-centred approach and the BPS model are more descriptive than interventional, whereas the Maguire approach has employed a specific training intervention and shown that this leads to changes in the interview styles of health professionals. Whether this leads to improved outcome for patients is the subject of ongoing research.

The evidence that the patient-centred approach or the BPS model improve measurable outcomes is slim and further work is needed. There is evidence that when health professionals influence a patient's beliefs this can affect outcome,[21] but the circumstances in which this occurs are not clear. It seems that whichever approach is adopted health professionals have to work within very considerable time and other constraints. These mean that they may develop the appropriate skills but then not use them in practice, as shown in the Bartz paper. Staff may feel that they are not equipped to deal with the emotional concerns that patients may wish to discuss and there may not be managerial support for spending time in such activity. Thus we need to look at broader aspects of the context in which health professionals work, as well as the specific model they may use in interviewing patients, if we are to successfully introduce more patient-centred approaches.

# References

1. Little P, Everitt H, Williamson I, Warner G, Moore M, Gould C *et al.* Observational study of effect of patient centredness and positive approach on outcomes of general practice consultations. *BMJ* 2001; **323**: 908–11.

2. Mead N, Bowers P. Patient-centredness: a conceptual framework and review of the empirical literature. *Soc Sci Med* 2000; **51**: 1087–110.

3. Balint M. *The doctor, his patient, and the illness.* 2nd edn. London: Pitman Medical; 1971.

4. Stewart M. Patient characteristics which are related to the doctor-patient interaction. *Fam Pract* 1983; **1**: 30–6.

5. Stewart M. What is a successful doctor–patient interview? A study of interactions and outcomes. *Soc Sci Med* 1984; **19**: 167–75.

6. Roter D, Hall J, Katz N. Relations between physicians' behaviours and analogue patients' satisfaction, recall and impressions. *Med Care* 1987; **25**: 437–51.

7. Cecil D, Killeen I. Control, compliance and satisfaction in the family practice encounter. *Fam Med* 1997; **29**: 653–7.

8. Wissow L, Roter D, Bauman L, Crain E, Kercsmar C, Weiss K, *et al.* Patient–provider communication during the emergency department care of children with asthma. *Med Care* 1998; **36**: 1439–50.

9. Street R. Analyzing communication in medical consultations: do behavioural measures correspond to patients' perceptions? *Med Care* 1992; **30**: 976–88.

10. Winefield HR, Murrell TG, Clifford J. Process and outcomes in general practice consultations: problems in defining high quality care. *Soc Sci Med* 1995; **41**: 969–75.

11. Stewart M, Brown J, Donner A, McWhinney I, Oates J, Weston W. *The impact of patient-centred care on patient outcomes in family practice (final report).* Canada: Center for Studies in Family Medicine, University of Western Ontario; 1995.

12. Henbest R, Stewart M. Patient-centredness in the consultation 2: does it really make a difference? *Fam Pract* 1990; **7**: 28–33.

13. Parle M, Jones B, Maguire P. Maladaptive coping and affective disorders among cancer patients. *Psychol Med* 1996; **26**: 735–44.

14. Maguire P. Improving the recognition of concerns and affective disorders in cancer patients. *Ann Oncol* 2002; **13 (suppl 4)**: 177–81.

15. Booth K, Maguire PM, Butterworth T, Hillier VF. Perceived professional support and the use of blocking behaviours by hospice nurses. *J Adv Nurs* 1996; **24**: 522–7.

16. Heaven CM, Maguire P. Disclosure of concerns by hospice patients and their identification by nurses. *Palliative Med* 1997; **2**: 283–90.

17. Maguire P, Booth K, Elliott C, Jones B. Helping health professionals involved in cancer care acquire key interviewing skills—the impact of workshops. *Eur J Cancer* 1996; **32A**: 1486–9.

18. Maguire P, Faulkner A, Booth K. Helping cancer patients disclose their concerns. *Eur J Cancer* 1996; **32A**: 78–81.

19. Wilkinson S. Factors which influence how nurses communicate with cancer patients. *J Adv Nurs* 1991; **16**: 677–88.

20. Bartz R. Beyond the biopsychosocial model: new approaches to doctor–patient interactions. *J Fam Pract* 1999; **48**: 601–7.

21. Di Blasi Z, Harkness E, Ernst E, Georgiou A, Kleijnen J. Influence of context effects on health outcomes: a systematic review. *Lancet* 2001; **357**: 757–62.

## Discussion

*Elwyn*: There are a couple of systematic reviews, which would be worth adding to what you have said. One is by Vicky Entwistle and her colleagues who found 12 randomized controlled trials (RCTs) of the patient-centred approach.[1] Another is by Simon Griffin, who has done a large review of interventions to improve communication, including a lot of patient-centred approaches.[2] The patient-centred approach has been most widely defined and researched by Moira Stewart and her colleagues at McMaster. They would probably take a slight issue with your drawing apart of the biopsychosocial (BPS) approach from patient centredness. I think they see what you had on the other side of the overlapping circle as fitting within it. I don't think they would see illness perception as separate from illness experience. They mention illness ideas, concerns, and expectations very much in the patient-centred approach. They would probably try to use a friendlier phrase for the BPS model. I am not sure how the paper by Bartz you mentioned was published: it doesn't seem to have gone into what Moira Stewart has done with what Levenstein took over and developed in Canada.[3]

*Creed*: I accept that. You touch on one prejudice when you talk about the meta-analysis. It is important to remind ourselves that meta-analysis is not a substitute for good research. You can look at series of poor studies and fail to learn much from them.

*White*: I'd like to echo what Glyn Elwyn has said. I would see the BPS model as more of a template in the doctor's mind of the factors that need to be covered while using a patient-centred approach.

*Creed*: And Dr M didn't use a patient-centred approach.

*Fitzpatrick*: The 'whole person' approach would seem to be synonymous with assessing the psychological and social aspects systematically. Your diagram doesn't seem to me to add any value.

*Creed*: The diagram illustrates the differences between the models.

*White*: They don't conflict.

*Sharpe*: I think there is a point here, though. Whether we consider the patient-centred approach as part of Engel's BPS model or not doesn't matter. But one can imagine an authoritarian use of the BPS model and I'm sure it happens, particularly in psychiatry. We have just completed a study of 100 people with a conversion disorder. These people had 7- or 8-hour interviews and full life-event assessments. Many did *not* appear to have psychological traumas prior to onset of symptoms, although many of them had physical traumas. The orthodoxy is that they are supposed to have psychological trauma. It is not very hard to imagine an interview with a psychiatrist who insists that the patient must volunteer some psychological trauma. One can therefore imagine the doctor forcing the BPS agenda on a patient who has a simple biological problem. In other words training in a rigid or insensitive application of the BPS approach could result in patients being pressured to 'come up with the psychosocial goods' when, in reality, there aren't any.

*Shorter*: Freud's interviews of patients were much like that, in the area of getting at the sexual aetiology.

*Drossman*: One way to look at the BPS model is as a way of *constructing* the information, but the interview is the *process* in which the information is obtained. They are not comparable. The interview is the vehicle with which you get the information.

*Lorig*: The question is whether you take the patient's evidence and place it onto the biological or sociobiological state, or whether you take your knowledge of the sociobiological state and force it onto the patient. It is a difference in perspective more than anything else.

*Marien*: I want to come back to the concept of phobia. Michael Von Korff talked about back pain patients having a phobia about activity, as do chronic fatigue syndrome patients. One of the ways of overcoming this phobia is through behaviour and exposure. Some of what you showed illustrates that we doctors are phobic about emotion and opening a 'cans of worms'. When I went to do a psychology degree, having trained in medicine, one of the psychologists teaching me let out an audible sigh when he heard that I was a doctor. He apologized and said that he had done this because doctors are ineducable. I wanted to quote Balint, who I think summed this up in his book, *The doctor, his patient, and the illness*.

> Every doctor has a vague but almost unshakeably firm idea about how a patient should behave when ill. Although this idea is anything but explicit and concrete, it is immensely powerful and influences practically every detail of the doctor's work. It was almost as if every doctor had revealed knowledge of what was right and wrong for patients to expect and to endure. Further, as if he had a sacred duty to convert to his faith all the ignorant and unbelieving among his patients.[4]

I think what he was saying was that we have a model, a medical model, and we impose it on our patients. I think it is uncomfortable to move out of the system. Professor Byrne who did a lot of work on patient-centred medicine described how the average time it took for a doctor to interrupt a patient was 18 seconds.[5] We have an agenda, time limit, and workload pressure. Everything mitigates against opening this perceived 'can of worms'. We have not been educated to do it, we don't have time to do it, and we don't know how to deal with it if we do open it (the can of worms). It is little wonder that general practitioners and hospice nurses do not address this issue.

*Fitzpatrick*: I disagree. Balint's quote was written in the 1950s. It expressed a relationship between doctor and patient that does not exist any longer. The basic point that seems to be missed here is in relation to the disease/illness problem. There are a vast number of people in general practice who have experience of illness, but do not have any diagnosable disease. The scale of the wider social forces that are encouraging this is enormous. I recently read David Wainwright's book on work-related stress.[6] He makes the point that there is a whole range of problems that people used to experience in the work-place and which used to be dealt with by trade unions. Now they present themselves in the doctor's surgery. There are court cases about work-related stress and people discuss this on TV programmes. The problem that follows on from this is that illness is redefined in terms of disease. People come in with a whole list of conditions; they don't come in and say they have work-related stress. The way in which doctors deal with this is a wider problem. We can't provide people with all sorts of disease labels, which have the effect of intensifying and perpetuating disability.

*Main*: I wonder whether I could broaden the discussion a little to the training of other sorts of professionals when time constraint is not an issue. Sometimes this is used as an excuse. We have been training occupational health nurses and physiotherapists to elicit certain types of BPS information from patients. What we discovered fairly early on were the anxieties amongst staff. People didn't feel they were confident or trained to deal with difficult questions that might come from their patients. The paradigm we developed, as part of the RCT I mentioned earlier, is that we split the physiotherapists into groups of three. Independently, we got them to come up with the worst questions they could imagine a patient would ask them. Each had a set of five questions. Group A's questions were given to group B, who role-played the patient and group C tried to respond. We developed this role-playing routine, incorporating their worst anxieties. This increased their confidence fantastically, because they had discussed the worst things they could imagine a patient could come up with. I think we have vastly underestimated the extent to which all of us, as professionals, hide behind things, when we are faced with distressed and angry patients.

*Creed*: I agree with that and also with the previous comment that there are these barriers. There is evidence to suggest that the time factor is not the most important one. You can do this work without extending the length of the consultation. The other barriers you mentioned that I have listed are real, though, and they stop us implementing the BPS patient-centred approach.

*Chalder*: I was once supervising a mature female nurse doing psychosocial intervention with patients with cancer who were undergoing chemotherapy.

What fascinated me was that she was avoiding quite a lot of emotional issues. When I started to ask about the difficulties she was experiencing, it became clear that she had great difficulty herself in talking about emotional issues, even in her own private life. This is probably a reflection of what is going on in society as a whole. Most people seem to get by, somehow, by not addressing emotional issues.

*Creed*: We have seen this with training general nurses to detect alcohol problems in patients. Some of them say that the patients drink as much as they do and that's not an issue.

*Waddell*: We have been focusing on barriers to people using the BPS model. Looking at a lot of my clinical colleagues, I think the block happens before implementation. Many of them don't even see the need to consider the BPS model, because they are perfectly happy with their biomedical model. It is not that they are blocked or afraid of this; they don't even reach that stage.

*Creed*: The way forward here is to do the kind of work that Michael Von Korff has done, showing that it is possible to improve outcome in this way.

*Waddell*: That is fair enough, but for the colleagues I am talking about, it wouldn't matter because they don't see a need to even consider the BPS model.

## References

1. Lewin SA, Skea ZC, Entwistle V, Zwarenstein M, Dick J. Interventions for providers to promote a patient-centred approach in clinical consultations (Cochrane Review). In: *The Cochrane library. Issue 1*. Chichester: Wiley; 2004.

2. Griffin S, Gillard S, Veltman M, Grant J, Stewart M, Kinmonth AL. A systematic review of trials of interventions to improve the interactions between patients and practitioners. In: *The 29th Annual Scientific Meeting of the Association of University Departments of General Practice*. Bournemouth: CBC Oxford Ltd, on behalf of the AUDGP; 2000.

3. Stewart M, Brown JB, Weston WW, McWhinney IR, McWilliam CL, Freeman TR. *Patient-centred medicine: transforming the clinical method*. Thousands Oaks, California: Sage; 1995.

4. Balint M. *The doctor, his patient and the illness*. 2nd edn. London: Pitman Medical; 1971.

5. Byrne PS, Long B. *Doctors talking to patients*. London: Her Majesty's Stationery Office; 1976.

6. Wainwright D, Calnan M. *Work stress: the making of a modern epidemic*. Buckingham/Philadelphia: Open University; 2002.

# 12 What are the barriers to healthcare systems using a biopsychosocial approach and how might they be overcome?

Kate Lorig

## Summary

This chapter will describe an expert patient-led psychological and behavioural programme aimed at improving health status for those with chronic conditions. I will present its structure, model, outcomes, and the problems that had to be overcome to achieve dissemination

## Introduction

Most of my work comes from a different perspective than the other papers that have been presented at this meeting—the perspective of the patient. For the last 20 years I have been designing self-management programmes for people with chronic illness that involve both psychological and behavioural education. These programmes are different in that they are taught by people who themselves have chronic illnesses. They are not support groups, but instead are highly structured. Every single minute of the courses' 14.5-hour duration is structured according to a manual. This includes both the content of the course and the process or way the programme is presented. To the participant, however, the programme does not appear structured.

## The expert patient programme

We have conducted a series of trials, most of which were randomized with others being longitudinal, involving a total of 3000–4000 patients.[1–9] I am not going to report on these here, except to say that our basic findings have been that people who attend these programmes and then who are followed for 6 months to 2 years have better quality-of-life outcomes: less fatigue, pain, and disability. They end up with less healthcare utilization. The only predictive factor we have been able to find is self-efficacy, or confidence that they can achieve a specific behaviour. Both baseline self-efficacy and changes in self-efficacy are associated with changes in symptoms.[10,11] Our interventions are targeted at helping people with medical management, role management, and emotional management of their chronic conditions. Strategies to enhance self-efficacy are used systematically throughout the programme.

In a recent study we replicated earlier findings in the Kaiser Permanente,[7] the largest non-governmental healthcare system in the USA. It cares for over 8 million people. The purpose of the study, which I will now describe, was to disseminate one of our interventions, taking it out of the mode of experiment and placing it in the context of a large healthcare system. We wanted to examine the dissemination process and learn what happens to such an intervention when it is placed in such a large healthcare system.

The chronic disease self-management programme, known in the UK as the expert patient programme, involved small groups of 10–16 people. We put people with all kinds of different diseases together. In this particular study we had people with conditions such as depression, Parkinson's disease, heart disease, and fibromyalgia all in the same group. The programme was 2.5 hours per week for 6 weeks. It was peer taught and the peers received 4 days of training to teach the programme. The process, which is much more important than the content, was targeted to build self-efficacy and confidence. We did this in a very systematic way[12,13] by improving skills mastery, providing modelling, helping participants to reinterpret the meaning of their symptoms, and encouraging social persuasion. For example, to accomplish skills, mastery participants made a commitment to do something every single week; what participants decided to do was totally up to them. We did not guide this in any way. Some people did exercise, others might have done relaxation techniques, some might have pasted pictures of their children into photograph albums, and others may have abstained from eating chocolate. This action planning process worked pretty well. The second way of enhancing efficacy was by modelling. There are two types of knowledge in healthcare, especially for people with chronic illness. There is medical knowledge and there is patient knowledge: 'I have lived with this disease and I can teach you how to live with this disease.' We tried to combine these things and by using peers we were doing this by modelling. This was accomplished by having patients teach patients and structuring the intervention so that there are many structured way for participants to share patient knowledge.

The third part of the intervention involved changing perceptions. How did we do this? Every time we talked about a symptom, we talked about it as having multiple causes. If someone said that their pain was caused by their disease, we said that this was probably true, but pain can be caused by lots of other things, such as tight muscles, depression, or being overweight. The idea was not to put any value on these things, but to say that there are many reasons why there is pain and hence there are many things that the patient might be able to do to deal with it. What they decide to do is up to them. The fourth way of enhancing self-efficacy was through social persuasion. This was accomplished by having people report back each week on their accomplishments. In addition, any time that anyone had a problem, the group, rather than the leader helped to make suggestions.

## Outcomes of the Kaiser Permanente study

At the time that we started this study, Kaiser Permanente had 12 regions. We then added the Group Health Cooperative of Puget Sound, which made a 13th region. We trained people from each region to then go ahead and train other people within that region. Our work based at Stanford was only to provide the initial training with the people from the different regions. As an outcome, we evaluated all the courses given in 1998, the first year of the study.[7] There were a total of 68 workshops with 703 participants and the results were collated from the pre-test and then the 6-month and 1-year post-tests. There was no randomization. The outcomes here were very similar to our earlier randomized study. The participants tended to be older people who were fairly highly educated. Before you get too concerned about this, bear in mind that our monolingual Spanish speakers with a much lower mean education had the same outcomes and the outcomes from a large randomized trial in Shanghai also look similar.[8,14]

Thus the results seem pretty robust. Most participants were Caucasian. People had an average of 2.3 conditions: I point this out, because if you are dealing with co-morbidities you are not dealing with just depression or heart disease, you are dealing with 2.3 chronic diseases. We saw a range of improvements. The effect sizes ranged from about 0.2 and 0.38. The subjects' quality of life—what we call 'health status'—improved. We did not look at mortality. Visits to both physicians and emergency departments and hospitalizations were reduced, with potential cost savings.

## Patient recruitment

The big question is how do we disseminate this intervention? In the first and second years, we conducted about 500 telephone interviews with those administering and delivering the programme. These were transcribed by hand and then sent off to a medical anthropologist who coded them. On the basis of this coding, in the third year we sent out a semi-structured questionnaire, examining the categories that we picked up in our interviews. These interviews were conducted with all kinds of people: the people who taught the classes, their supervisors, the regional coordinators, the regional directors of psycho-educational interventions, and key administrators and physicians within the system. There were 225 surveys returned.

Recruiting workshop participants proved to be the most difficult problem. If you had asked me at the end of the second year, I would have predicted that the programme would die. The reason for this was that the staff at Kaiser Permanente had started doing most of their recruiting through physicians. There was never any physician opposition to the programme, but there were no referrals. Kaiser staff talked to physicians, Kaiser physicians talked to Kaiser physicians. Physicians were given easy referral forms. When they were asked why they did not refer, their response can be summed up in the reply of one physician who said that unfortunately this was not part of his 'dance'. He said that he could only do so much in a brief office visit with a patient with multiple chronic conditions and that referral to our programme was just not on the radar screen.

Eventually, Kaiser went to a second marketing strategy, direct mailings. Initially, they gave a list to the physicians of all eligible patients on the basis of different criteria (high utilizers, or people with diabetes, for example). They asked the physicians to cross out the names of people they did not want invited. They were given 2 weeks to do this. Direct mailings ended up being the very best means of recruitment, with a response rate of 7–12 per cent (that is, people actually showing up in class). There was some evidence that if this had been done slightly differently by making follow-up phone calls, we could have increased this response rate to as high as 40–50 per cent. Articles in adult media were quite successful and reminder calls helped. Videos originally put together for the physicians were successful with the patients. What did not work were public service announcements, referrals from physicians and other healthcare professionals, and videos in waiting rooms. For videos to be effective, we found out that they needed to be shown with a person to discuss them.

What were some of the dissemination factors? First, leadership buy-in. At the beginning of the project, I made the phone calls to each of the regional directors. Looking back, I can see that there was or was not buy-in as early as the first phone call. The regions that never did anything did not do anything from the first phone call. They talked for a shorter time and they were more negative. The infrastructure was also important: was there staff time, or a champion—someone who really wanted this done? The champions were usually physicians, but not always. The other problem had to do with internal Kaiser transitions. Kaiser Permanente started out with 12 regions. During the time of the study, four of these closed. This caused a huge upheaval in the system. Individual commitment was also an important factor. In most of the regions the people who took on the programme very quickly became champions. There was no extra money put into the system for this programme except for the salary of one national coordinator. A critical mass of trainers was also a requirement. The only original trainers were three of us at Stanford. We trained two people in each region. Looking back I would have done this differently, because what happened was that if a region lost one of its master trainers, it lost the programme. Doing it again, we would develop a core of national trainers, which is what is happening with the expert patient programme in the UK. The other problem was that some of our regions had too many master trainers, which ended up being almost as bad, because they were not fully utilized.

One of the barriers to this intervention was that people did not understand the difference between a generic versus disease-specific course. Healthcare professionals did not understand it and patients did not understand it. We had a real understanding problem. How can you put people with diabetes together with people with heart disease? In reality, the skills for managing the diseases are very similar. There were also a huge number of competing programmes and competing interests. We have talked about this during this meeting. No one wanted to give up their programme to this 'new kid on the block', which no one trusted anyway. Unfamiliarity with working with volunteers was a further obstacle. 'What do you mean; you are bringing peers into our system?' 'What are the legal ramifications?' (this one question stopped the programme dead in one region for 8 months). There was also unfamiliarity with working in the community. 'We only see people in our facilities when we want to see them.' There was also no structure for paying peers. I say this, because when you are disseminating things, rewards and punishments are key components. Even though these volunteers do not get paid much, they do get paid a little and this system had no mechanism for doing this. The lack of reward for trainers was also a problem. Trainers were expected to do their training on top of their regular jobs within this system. Doing 4 days of training is kind of fun the first time, but by the ninth time it is not.

## The long-term outcomes

What happened 5 years later? Against all odds these workshops are continuing. The 13 regions are down to seven. Kaiser Permanente in California has decided to provide the programme as a covered benefit starting in January 2003. It will be free for all patients. Nationwide Kaiser Permanente is giving the programme to over 2500 patients a year and is also helping a number of community agencies to give the programme. In this last year the programme won Kaiser Permanente's highest award for quality and innovation within the organization.

In the context of this meeting, we have been discussing what makes up the biopsychosocial model and what we should be doing. Our experience with this group intervention shows that once we have decided what we should do, there is a whole fresh set of problems: how do we disseminate our interventions?

## References

(For further information and updated bibliography see http://patienteducation.stanford.edu/.)

1. Lorig KR, Mazonson PD, Homan HR. Evidence suggesting that health education for self-management in chronic arthritis has sustained health benefits while reducing health care costs. *Arthr Rheum* 1993; **36**: 439–46.

2. Lorig KR, Sobel D, Stewart AL, Brown BW Jr, Bandura A, Ritter P *et al*. Evidence suggesting that a chronic disease self-management program can improve health status while reducing hospitalisation: A randomised trial. *Med Care* 1999; **37**: 5–14.

3. Lorig K, González VM, Ritter P. Community-based Spanish language arthritis education program: a randomized trial. *Med Care* 1999; **37**: 957–63.

4. Lorig K, González VM. Community-based diabetes self-management education: definition and case study. *Diabetes Spectrum* 2000; **13**: 234–8.

5. Moore JE, Von Korff M, Cherkin D, Saunders K, Lorig K. A randomized trial of a cognitive-behavioral program for enhancing back pain self care in a primary care setting. *Pain* 2000; **88**: 145–53.

6. Lorig K, Ritter P, Stewart A, Sobel D, Brown BW, Bandura A *et al*. 2-year evidence that chronic disease self-management education has sustained health and utilization benefits. *Med Care* 2001; **39**: 1217–23.

7. Lorig KR, Sobel D, Ritter PL, Hobbs M, Laurent D. Effect of a self-management program on patients with chronic disease. *Effect Clin Pract* 2001; **4**: 256–62.

8. Lorig, KR, Ritter PL, González VM. Hispanic chronic disease self-management. A randomized community-based outcome trial. *Nurs Res* 2003; **52**: 361–9.

9. Lorig KR, Ritter PL, Laurent DL, Fries JF. Long-term randomized controlled trials of tailored-print and small-group arthritis self-management interventions. *Med Care* 2004; **42**: 346–54.

10. Bandura A. Self-efficacy: toward a unifying theory of behavioral change. *Psychol Rev* 1977; **84**: 191–215.

11. Bandura A. *Self-efficacy: the exercise of control*. New York: Freeman; 1977.

12. Bodenheimer T, Lorig K, Holman H, Grumbach K. Patient self-management of chronic disease in primary care. *JAMA* 2002; **288**: 2469–75.

13. Lorig KR, Holman HR. Self-management education: History, definition, outcomes, and mechanisms. *Ann Behav Med* 2003; **26**: 1–7.

14. Dongbo F, Hua F, McGowan P, Shen Yi-E, Lizhen Z, Huiqin Y *et al*. Implementation and quantitative evaluation of chronic disease self-management programme in Shanghai, China: Randomized controlled trial. *Bull World Health Org* 2003; **81**: 174–82.

## Discussion

*Aylward*: How did you recruit people?

*Lorig*: If I had the money, I'd put real marketing experts on it. This programme is now being used in about 14 countries and the Australians found out that the way to recruit people is via symptoms. You ask people whether they are tired, for example. As an aside, the commonest symptom across chronic diseases is fatigue. Are they tired, do they have pain? If so, come along.

*Waddell*: You touched briefly on the question of education, which is linked with social class. You did say that the ones that took part got the same results, but from the look of your profile the difficulty is getting lower educational or social class subjects to take part at all. Is there a good answer to that?

*Lorig*: I'll give you two answers. First, in the Kaiser system, you have to be employed to get into it. This is one reason we get a higher educational level. We have been running the same programme with monolingual Spanish speakers. We run it in churches and community halls. The outcome data are exactly the same and they are slightly easier to recruit.[1] An article has recently been published of a randomized study for about 1000 people from Shanghai neighbourhoods.[2] They have very low educational levels. Their outcome data were almost exactly the same.

*Waddell*: How did you recruit them?

*Lorig*: Very differently. This past Easter I went to mass twice; and I'm Jewish. The place to find Spanish speakers in the USA is mass on Easter Sunday. Between myself and the staff we covered 17 masses. We gave a little announcement and had people come to us afterwards. We just take their names and addresses and then call them later. We learned that if we talked to them, many others did not wait around so we lost many potential subjects. We go to where the people are.

*Lewin*: That has been our experience in recruiting Asians into cardiac rehabilitation. There have been a number of innovative schemes where people have gone to community centres and mosques. There is a scheme in Leicester employing trained lay facilitators to bridge the gap and bring people in.

*Lorig*: Yes; the system has to go to them, you don't ask them to go to the system.

*Sharpe*: I am very interested in one issue you raised, which follows from the biopsychosocial (BPS) model. That is, when it comes to intervention, one doesn't have to define the target patient groups in terms of biological disease, but might alternatively define it in terms of psychological or social factors. And if the psychological and social issues are common across chronic biomedically defined diseases, we can apply interventions irrespective of medical diagnosis. I am personally interested in this idea, but you said there was a failure to understand it: how did you overcome that failure of understanding?

*Lorig*: Very slowly. We did several things. One thing we made as part of our programme was to have patients write letters to their physicians. They didn't have to mail them, but a lot of them did. As the physicians start hearing from their patients and when they start seeing the same patients and find that they are easier to handle, something clicks and they realize that this makes a difference. With patients, we have not focused on diseases, but on symptoms. This is what they respond to and they are very much the same across chronic diseases.

*White*: Have you seen a differential effect in outcome by diagnosis or diagnostic group? I ask this because work done in the UK under the aegis of the Department of Health suggested that a particular diagnostic group, chronic fatigue syndrome, did not do at all well.[3] But the big difference from your work was that these poor outcomes occurred in a group solely composed of chronic fatigue syndrome patients. Patients with chronic fatigue syndrome did better when they did the programme with patients with arthritis.[3]

*Lorig*: The answer is yes and no. The people with arthritis ended up having less pain, but for the people with heart disease, pain was not a big issue. With shortness of breath, we saw bigger results in our chronic obstructive pulmonary disease patients. I don't have good data on fibromyalgia. One question I am frequently asked is whether people with depression should be put in their own group. Initially the people with depression wanted to be in their own group, but they ended up being just as happy in mixed groups. We are currently doing two studies, one in arthritis and one in diabetes, to see whether it makes much difference if people are in a disease-specific group as opposed to a general group. Our initial results don't show a great deal of difference.

*Wessely*: I can see lots of reasons why it is a good idea to have mixed groups.

*Lorig*: When people walk into the course, the group leader explains that they are going to ask each person to tell the group their name, their disease, and one or two problems they have because of the disease. I might say, 'My name is Kate, my disease is arthritis, and my biggest problem is that I can't hike any more.' This is all written up on boards. The leader turns to the group and might say, 'Isn't it interesting. You all have different diseases but your problems are all the same' (they always are). 'What we are going to talk about in this class are these problems.' After that we never mention specific diseases. We don't let people play the game, 'my disease is worse than your disease'.

*Creed*: Earlier, we were discussing some of the organizational barriers to instituting the BPS model more widely. You have obviously had to face enormous organizational barriers; it sounds like you have been very successful in overcoming them. What are the most telling things that have made a difference?

*Lorig*: We have proselytized, but we have never tried to convince anyone to do this. Everyone has come to us and we have tried to respond to their needs.

Then what happens is that people who were sceptical decided that perhaps this wasn't so bad after all. There was a theory of dissemination talked about by Rogers.[4] He says that there are different groups of people. The 'innovators' leap out in front and try everything new. These were not the people we want to reach, even though they are important. Instead, we wanted to target the next group of people, the 'early adopters'. These are the people that need to be successful. If they are, the rest of the world will eventually come along. The experience here in the UK is very interesting from my point of view.[5] We started doing this work in arthritis almost 25 years ago. The model was adopted very widely all over the world. The little contact I had with people in the UK was that they were saying it would never work here because we are different. Arthritis Care sent one person to a training session in Denmark 10 years ago. This person came back and was responsible for starting all the activity that is now going on in the UK.

*Waddell*: I'd like to come back to Peter White's point. If I understand you correctly, this is largely a programme for older people with chronic diseases aiming at improving quality of life. Does it work for a younger working-age group with medically unexplained disorders who are on long-term incapacity benefits?

*Lorig*: We don't know whether this model works for medically unexplained disorders. We have used it with back pain and it seemed to work, in a study we did with Michael Von Korff.[6] The results weren't quite as powerful as with some other diseases.

*Von Korff*: For run-of-the mill primary care back pain patients, we saw fear reduction and modest improvements in Roland disability scores.[7] We did this once with lay leaders and in a trial with very experienced psychologists and got very similar results. In neither group did we see results on outcomes such as return to work. This is a really promising intervention modality that is ripe for research. Kate Lorig outlined the sources of resistance. These were sources of resistance that reflect professional prerogatives: referrals, space, hours, and resource allocation. If we want to make the BPS model work, we need to start addressing some different fields than the primary care visit and medical care. We need more research on this to make it work.

*Fitzpatrick*: It is interesting to contrast the approach Kate Lorig is talking about with what we are familiar with about patient campaigns of a self-help character, which often have a very activist feel to them, such as the National Asthma campaign or the ME campaign. There are vast numbers of these self-help groups. It is one of the great growth areas of voluntary activity over the last 20 years. They frequently have an activist, bottom-up character. What Kate has described has a strongly top-down character: the nature of the training seems didactic, with master trainers. How does this sit with the existing self-help campaigns, or voluntary organizations such as Age Concern?

*Lorig*: The two master trainers in the UK both came from patient groups. Most of our master trainers are patients. The pilot that was done here in the UK was run by the Long-term Care Alliance and an alliance of patient groups.[3,5] The reason that patient groups are willing to do this is because the programme is really based on patient concerns. All the stuff we have done is based on many focus groups with patients. We know we are reaching patient concerns. We don't solve problems, but rather teach patients how to solve them. It resonates with patients, so we have had virtually no resistance from patient groups.

*Wessely*: The bit where I can see there might be problems is with the actual interventions that your groups are proposing. You are proposing certain interventions and you have a particular view of the world. You mentioned diet and exercise. But what would happen if your group started to challenge these particular treatment ideologies and, for example, said that they wanted to know how to get more benefits from the state? They might agree that their problem is fatigue, but they may say that they think the solution is something different.

*Lorig*: I would say, 'Right now we are talking about fatigue and we'll be finished in a bit, but then we are going to go on to problem solving. We can use that as an example in problem solving, so if you'll wait just 5 minutes, we'll get there. Whether or not you want to use these techniques for fatigue is OK with me. These are things that might be useful; if not, then don't use them.'

*Wessely*: As you turn over your flip charts you are going to come to some bits where some people in the room fundamentally don't agree. They might say, 'I tried that and it didn't work for me: in fact, it made me worse'.

*Lorig*: I'd say, 'You know, then I really think you shouldn't do it. If other people have had other experiences, that's fine. These are just things that some people have found helpful. If you want to try them, that's fine. If you don't, that's fine also.' I am not going to get into the argument that is called 'you've got to make me'. I will never get into that game. This is part of our leader training.

*Marien*: There is some commonality here with Simon Wessley and Michael Sharpe's paper on functional syndromes and chronic illness.[8] What chronic illness does from a primary care perspective is cause loss of function, role, health, and work. There is a lot of loss. Kabat-Zinn's work using mindfulness meditation is relevant here.[9] He took groups of people with a range of illnesses. He said give me all your chronic disabled and I'll heal them! This was a very risky thing to do, but his outcome data were very good. He created quite a structured programme using mindfulness meditation. He never pushed anyone to do anything. It is very much group work, using the group strength. The people who come to this sort of thing may well be more motivated. My question concerns the mindfulness aspect. You talked about Bandura and self-efficacy and you said it is quite a didactic programme.

*Lorig:* It is not didactic; it's structured. There is a difference.

*Marien:* Could you give us some detail on how you use Bandura's work on self-efficacy and the sort of flavour of what you do?

*Lorig:* I'll get Mike Von Korff to do an action plan with me. This is what happens at the end of every session with every person. Mike, what would you like to do this week?

*Von Korff:* I want to run five times.

*Lorig:* When was the last time you ran?

*Von Korff:* Last Saturday.

*Lorig:* How long do you want to run for?

*Von Korff:* 25 minutes.

*Lorig:* When?

*Von Korff:* In the morning.

*Lorig:* How certain are you that you will run five times in the morning for 25 minutes in the next week, with 0 being totally unsure and 10 being totally sure.

*Von Korff:* About a 4.

*Lorig:* (The cut-off point here is 7 for predicting success.) Mike, what would be the problem?

*Von Korff:* It will be raining, or I'll be tired, or I'll have to go to an early meeting.

*Lorig:* Group: do any of you have suggestions for Mike?

*Wessely:* Don't fly so much.

*White:* Cut down the number of runs.

*Chalder:* What do you think might be more realistic?

*Lorig:* Don't ask a question, just make a suggestion please.

*Waddell:* It doesn't have to be first thing in the morning.

*Sharpe:* It doesn't have to be 25 minutes.

*Marien:* You don't have to run!

*Lorig:* Mike, do any of those things sound like they would be helpful?

*Von Korff:* Cutting down the frequency and perhaps running for a shorter time might help.

*Lorig:* Do you want to re-state an action plan?

*Von Korff:* Three times a week for at least 15 minutes.

*Lorig:* How certain are you that you will do this?

*Von Korff:* 7.

*Lorig*: The answer is pretty much the same at this point, and that is great, go ahead and try it and we'll see how it goes. What happens is that people very quickly learn how to do this. This action plan does a couple of things. First, involves skills mastery. It is very hard for someone to say they can't do something if they have done it. Remember, theory says if you think you are going to do it you probably will.[10,11] That is why we use the efficacy question. Second, it has a role modelling component. As a leader, I will never make a suggestion. All the suggestions come from peers. Every time we talk about a new symptom we will say, for example, that fatigue is a problem for many people with arthritis. We'll either give them a list of the causes of fatigue, or we will get people to suggest where it comes from and construct a list. Given the list, we will ask people what sort of things people might be able to do. A person might say, 'I never thought about it before, but maybe I'll go for a walk, what do you think?' I'll say, 'Try it. One of two things will happen, you'll feel worse, in which case you'll find out that this is not a good thing to do, or you'll feel better. Try it.'

*Chalder*: It is clear that you are a very effective cognitive behavioural psychotherapist and I want to congratulate you on your programme. It sounds marvellous.

*Lorig*: If you are interested in it, I would suggest seeing it in action. Bob Lewin has done this.

*Lewin*: I went along because I got involved through the Department of Health.[5] They wanted to add some disease-specific modules. I was very sceptical: I thought this was going to be a watered down form of cognitive behavioural therapy (CBT), done by people who had been taught by rote how to do this from a set of flip charts. It can sound like this until you go and experience it. In fact this is a new form of therapy, using techniques we already know about in a new context. For example, goal setting is completely different when it is done by lay people. I had to be careful as a fairly experienced therapist to forget that part of me that wanted to guide the process. Patients tend to be stuck and not take techniques further, once they leave the clinic. I wonder if patient-generated goals last longer? As we all know, CBT gains tend to fade over time.

*Chalder*: Not in our 5-year follow-up.[12]

*Lewin*: Most of the time we have to accept that there is attrition. I wonder if self-generated treatment will stick better with patients. In our cardiac programmes we have done things to try to teach patients the methods of goal setting so that they can continue with it after discharge. But still there is always a professional standing in the background even if they don't speak. By not intervening they are tacitly giving permission and saying that what the patient has chosen to do is safe. I think the programme we have heard about is therefore a fascinating and valuable approach.

*Stansfeld*: This is reminiscent in some ways of things like Weight Watchers and Alcoholics Anonymous. Some of the same principles of self-help are there.

*Lorig*: It is not quite as ritualized or structured.

*Stansfeld*: It seems to me that the equality of the people taking part is important. How much is the group dynamic important? How much of the effect is to do with mutual social support for people undergoing adverse experiences?

*Lorig*: Years ago we designed an experiment where we randomized people either to one of our arthritis groups or to a group that was arthritis free in content but emphasized social support. The people in the second group got so mad at us that they would not complete the experiment and left after 3 weeks. I don't really know the answer but something is going on there beyond social support. The reason I say this is because if you look at the history of group programmes, the outcomes are all over the place and mostly negative. If social support were the factor we would have seen more uniform outcomes.

*Stansfeld*: In some ways social support is a very effective form of social control. For instance, with health behaviours it can go either way. If your social network tends to drink or smoke heavily, then you are more at risk. The other way around could also work. This may partly be why married status is protective for men but not so much for women. I can see how your social support intervention was irritating to people, but was this a more focused support?

*Lorig*: I doubt it. These people never see each other after 6 weeks, yet we are still seeing results as much as 4 years later.

*Sharpe*: Can you deliver the intervention a different way other than through a group? If so, how well does it work?

*Lorig*: If I had more time and an internet connection, I could show you. We have just designed a programme which is given in groups lasting for 6 weeks on the internet.[13] People communicated with each other through bulletin boards and e-mail. They got the same key messages and made action plans each week, which they shared through bulletin boards. We don't know whether this will translate yet.

*Sharpe*: What about a book or other form of self-help package?

*Lorig*: When we send them the book it doesn't work.

*Drossman*: A lot of the role play here has been about behaviour around function. Has pain been dealt with effectively?

*Lorig*: We do a lot of work with pain in our arthritis groups, because this is the main symptom. Our entire arthritis course is aimed at pain. In the chronic disease course we have something called a symptom cycle. All these symptoms are related. In the arthritis course it is called the pain cycle: all of these things are related to pain. We consistently show a 12–25 per cent reduction in pain in arthritis.

*Drossman*: What are the suggestions that come up for management in arthritis?

*Lorig*: We do all kinds of things. We do cognitive relaxation, restructuring of the way people talk to themselves and exercise.

*Marien*: Isn't this CBT?

*Von Korff*: It is drawing on the theoretical principles of CBT. There is something different going on, though. First, every healthcare system in the developed world is up against the constraints of resources that society is willing to devote to healthcare. There are more services that clearly need to be provided. We are not going to be able to solve this by throwing more professionals at the problem. Second, the basic problem for chronic illness is in enhancing patient participation. If we don't start looking at some new ways of enhancing patient participation and ways that are more efficient in their use of professional resources, we are not going to get anywhere. This is a really promising avenue for research and innovation and it shouldn't all fall to Kate Lorig to do randomized trials of this.

*Lorig*: I'm slowly coming to the end of my research career. My fondest hope is that 25 years from now someone will give a talk like George Davey Smith's saying weren't those ideas silly because we now know this is the way to do it.

*Marien*: As you say, if we rely on health professionals to do this, we will stay stuck. This does offer a route for reaching more people than we could ever access.

*Von Korff*: But recruitment does need to be tied to healthcare systems.

## References

1. Lorig K, González VM, Ritter P. Community-based Spanish language arthritis education program: a randomized trial. *Med Care* 1999; **37**: 957–63.
2. Dongbo F, Hua F, McGowan P, Shen Yi-E, Lizhen Z, Huiqin Y, *et al.* Implementation and quantitative evaluation of chronic disease self-management programme in Shanghai, China: randomized controlled trial. *Bull World Health Org* 2003; **81**: 174–82.
3. Cooper J. *Partnership for successful self-management: the living with long-term illness (Lill) project report.* London: The Living with Long-term Medical Conditions Alliance (LMCA); 2001 (http://www.lmca.org.uk/pdfs/lill%20report%20.pdf).
4. Rogers E. *Diffusion of innovation.* New York: Free Press; 1995.
5. Department of Health. *The expert patient: a new approach to chronic disease management for the 21st Century.* London: Department of Health; 2001 (www.ohn.gov.uk/ohn/people/ep_report.pdf).

6. Von Korff M, Moore JE, Lorig K, Cherkin D C, Saunders, K, Gonzalez VM, *et al.* A randomized trial of a lay person-led self-management group intervention for back pain patients in primary care. *Spine* 1998; **23**: 2608–15.

7. Deyo RA, Battie M, Beurskens AJ, Bombardier C, Croft I, Koes B, *et al.* Outcome measures for low back pain research: a proposal for standardized use. *Spine* 1998; **23**: 2003–13.

8. Wessely S, Nimnuan C, Sharpe M. Functional somatic syndromes: one or many? *Lancet* 1999; 354: 936–9.

9. Kabat-Zinn J, Lipworth L, Burney R, Sellers W. Four year follow-up of a meditation-based programme for the self-regulation of chronic pain: treatment outcomes and compliance. *Clin J Pain* 1986; **2**: 159–73.

10. Bandura A. Self-efficacy: toward a unifying theory of behavioral change. *Psychol Rev* 1977; **84**: 191–215.

11. Bandura A. *Self-efficacy: the exercise of control.* New York: Freeman; 1977.

12. Deale A, Hussain K, Chalder T, Wessely S. Long term outcome of cognitive behavior therapy versus relaxation for chronic fatigue syndrome: a 5 year follow up study. *Am J Psychiat* 2001; **158**: 2038–42.

13. Lorig KR, Laurent DD, Deyo RA, Marnell ME, Minor MA, Ritter PL. Can a back pain E-mail discussion group improve health status and lower health care costs? A randomised study. *Arch Intern Med* 2002; **162**: 792–6.

# 13 Final discussion: how to overcome the barriers

*White*: In this final discussion I think would be useful would be to outline the barriers that we have identified so far in our discussions and to explore ways round them. I think we have agreed that the aetiological work is not immediately relevant to the biopsychosocial (BPS) model in the healthcare system at the moment. It may be in the future. Therefore what we need to concentrate on pragmatically is the use of the BPS model in healthcare. We have already identified various barriers: lack of resources of time and money, lack of training, emotional inhibition, and patient engagement inhibition. It may be useful to discuss possible solutions to these.

*Drossman*: One element in terms of possible solutions that hasn't been addressed is teaching the teachers. Is there a way to communicate these ideas to the people involved with running medical schools? Can we teach people to take proper histories and integrate psychosocial information into a care plan? I think so. Often, the problem is in changing the behaviours of physicians at practice who are 50 years old. It may be much easier to start with new medical students. We want to begin with them and then follow this through in terms of ongoing support.

*Chalder*: Rather than start with the physicians, which might be quite a difficult task, we could make a start with youngsters in schools. My experience is that they are much easier to educate and to treat. The only barrier is the parents. Once we have the child or older youngster on our side we are in a very good position. They take up the messages up very quickly.

*Lorig*: I'd like to suggest something a little more radical. I think we need some patients to look at how healthcare is delivered. We need to try some new models. A model started in the UK and which has been widely adopted in the USA is group visits. This is where the physician actually sees patients in groups. This is not for their first diagnosis. It would be easy to put the BPS model into this setting. If you wanted to do it I would start with an experimental plan with people who paid for it. The big resistance to this is that doctors want to know how they are going to be paid. There are lots of ways that we could change our medical practice, for example, by using the internet or telephone more.

*Wessely*: Mansel Aylward, you are involved with policy definitions. What have you heard here that might influence your secretary of state?

*Aylward*: I have been given a lot of information that reinforces some of the messages that I have passed on to decision makers. I haven't heard anything startlingly new, but I am happy to have my views confirmed. We have made some significant progress. We had some great difficulty last year persuading certain people that the way forward in the more effective assessment of disability and its management in people on state benefits lay more with a BPS approach to rehabilitation, job retention, and recovery, than a focus on economic disincentives or wielding the stick approach. There seems to be an antipathy in some parts of Government towards anything that is perceived as fuzzy or nebulous, without a hard evidence base. If the BPS approach is perceived in this way and is competing for investment with hard policies focusing on bed occupancy and delivery of acute services, it is very difficult to get the Department of Health, among others in Government, to favour health-focused interventions and rehabilitation adopting the BPS approach. But in recent months I'm beginning to see a change. The Department for Work and Pensions may now have been persuaded to invest in initiating pilot studies in various areas of the country, in particular involving benefit recipients with back pain and fatigue, to see if all the talk about the BPS approach has any basis in improving outcomes.

*Wessely*: What made some of the policy makers change their views?

*Aylward*: Systematic reviews of the literature garnering evidence to support the BPS concept. Identification of best practices in using BPS approaches that improve function and rates of return to work, particularly in people with disability caused by back pain. Recent meetings in the form of focus groups of key opinion makers support with authoritative and expert opinion the value of BPS approaches. There are going to be some developments soon.

*Wessely*: What kind of evidence caused this change?

*Aylward*: The evidence which has been there all along. The key aspect has been effectively communicating this evidence in a far more robust and authoritative way. We also ran a series of workshops where we discussed and evaluated various approaches to facilitate return to work and to address the rising numbers of people in receipt of incapacity benefits. Some £25 billion per year is being spent on state benefits resting either directly or indirectly on a medical basis. The prospect of effective interventions that might reduce that expenditure are powerful catalysts for change.

*Waddell*: To take this a stage further, I am not sure that evidence is what convinces people. We do need an evidence base, but it is ideas that really influence people. People go to war for ideas, not for evidence. When you look at changing practice, it is really about ideas rather than evidence. My hesitation about what was said earlier is that everything seems to show that the behaviour of health professionals is difficult to change. But there are some suggestions from the Australian education campaign, Kate Lorig's work, and our work in Scotland, that it may actually be easier to change patients and the public and they will then force the professionals to change. The information from Australia has helped tremendously.[1,2] Some decision makers were very jaundiced, but this has played a role in convincing them that there is something in this and that it will save money. It is all about money. The main thing was to persuade the treasury that there was an opportunity for keeping costs down, particularly over the longer term.

*Drossman:* One of the efforts in the USA that has had some influence on Congress is the burden of illness study carried out by the American Gastroenterology Association. They identified the costs in terms of direct and indirect costs. Direct costs refer to costs related to the healthcare, such as medication and physician visits and indirect costs are other ways in which the illness impacts on the economy, for example, loss of work productivity or wages due to illness. Using irritable bowel syndrome (IBS) as an example, the prevalence is 15 million in the USA. When you multiply this by the number of dollars spent in terms of physician visits and prescriptions, it exceeds the cost burden of inflammatory bowel disease (IBD). Thus the higher prevalence (about 100 times greater) for IBS offsets the high cost per patient of IBD, yielding a greater cost to society. The cost to the economy is about US$2 billion of direct and US$20 billion of indirect costs. This had some influence on Congress. It is not proving that you can treat it that matters, but proving that the economic burden is there and that efforts must be placed on finding better treatments.

*Wessely:* I once tried to add up the cost burden of a range of conditions and it comes to more than the gross national product of the entire western world!

*Lorig:* Particularly for morbidity.

*Lewin:* One of the other things that Greville Mitchell is helping us do through One Health is an analysis that will look at the lost opportunity costs from not using cognitive behavioural therapy (CBT) approaches. We are doing this in collaboration with Jos Kleijnen. This is a complicated procedure because we haven't even got an agreed definition of CBT. We'd be delighted to have any suggestions for how we might do this.

*Wessely:* Can I clarify? Is Jos also doing a review of more direct psychosocial interventions in this area?

*Lewin:* Yes. The study is looking at the possible cost savings. What would the Government gain if they were to spend more on these areas?

*Mitchell:* People are pretty limited in viewing government future budgets. They will escalate: that is a fact of life. Therefore, if you are going to add to this bill you won't catch the government's attention, even if you say you have the perfect cure, but that it will cost. However, if you go to Gordon Brown (UK Chancellor) and say, 'We can prove to you that if we address this issue, we can save £2 billion', then you will have his full attention.

*Aylward*: That is the approach that has been taken, but not in such a robust fashion.

*Malmgren*: Considering that so many people go to alternative and complementary medicine practitioners, perhaps we should not only confront alternative medicine, but also try to make alliances. In particular, we could try this with practitioners who use brands of alternative medicine that we think have some plausibility.

*Wessely*: In many levels this is happening. We discussed over coffee whether we should call this business 'integrated healthcare'. Unfortunately, Prince Charles has taken this name. There are huge social and political forces almost forcing this on us, sometimes in ways that aren't particularly helpful.

*White*: The idea of making 'integrated healthcare' into integrated healthcare without the inverted commas is a good one.

*Marien*: I'm a little bit surprised that evidence doesn't make any difference to healthcare policy makers. But I stand corrected by people who have been looking at evidence for a long time. Inherently it still upsets me, because I'm a bit of an idealist. The fact that evidence doesn't impact is a bit depressing. But if we then take Gordon Waddell's plan of overcoming the obstacles with ideas, then we have to think carefully. There is a danger that we develop a sort of learned helplessness if evidence doesn't make a difference. We need to think about a strategy of changing people's views. I like Gordon's idea of changing patients, because I don't think we are going to change the professions. We have seen from Kate Lorig how there is a huge resistance to changing practice even if there is an evidence base. It may be a good idea to discuss how we take this forward. There is a huge amount of dualism in medicine, but there is a lot of dualism in the public, too. If they are psychologically minded and generally they are more psychologically minded than the medical professions, then how do we capitalize on this?

*Fitzpatrick*: A recent event at a hospital in Middlesborough bears on the discussions we have had over the last couple of days. In this hospital, 23 people have been exposed to a notional threat of contamination from instruments used in brain biopsy of a woman who turned out to have CJD. They have been informed that they probably haven't been exposed to a risk of contracting this disease, which can have a 30-year incubation period. These patients have already had special counselling and have been offered this on a lifelong basis. This illustrates the very wide context of the therapeutic ethos that has developed in our society. A whole range of social problems have now been reinterpreted in therapeutic terms. Whether we are talking about juvenile delinquency, poor performance in school, or teenage pregnancy, all these are seen as problems of self-esteem and need to be dealt with therapeutically. Stress at work is another example. There is a sense of damaged subjectivity which is very much the flavour of the moment for all sorts of social, cultural, and historical reasons, which is then reinforced in the medical context. This seems to be at the root of many of our problems. In the medical sphere, while we need to take account of the subjective aspect very much, and there is a long history of its neglect, there is now a great risk of becoming over-preoccupied about it and reinforcing the degradation of subjectivity.

Last night I picked up my e-mails and received a summary produced by the ME (myalgic encephalomyelitis) association of the report to the chief medical officer of that celebrated working group. This is of interest. The line from the ME association is that if you as a general practitioner (GP) say you are sceptical about the ME label, the chief medical officer has stipulated how this must be dealt with. This reflects the endorsement at the highest level of policy in the medical sphere of a disease label that is not supported by the evidence—it is a completely irrational formulation.

*Aylward*: It doesn't follow that all of that report is supported completely by everyone in government service. The Department of Work and Pensions doesn't necessarily endorse all that is in the working party's report to the Chief Medical Officer at the Department of Health in England. I am also mindful of the views of those who, as members of that group, distanced themselves from some aspects of the report.

*Fitzpatrick*: Nonetheless this is the line and it is very much promulgated that GPs should follow this. It is a consensus forged by excluding many of the people in this room who have been involved in this area. This illustrates a big problem: the government are linking up with patient activist groups in relation to this very significant area of medical practice to dictate a line of approach which is not actually going to be beneficial to patients.

*Wessely*: This is a problem that would need five separate conferences to address. The fact that the response to the possibly non-existent problem in Middlesborough was lifelong counselling indicates that this course is still extremely popular, even if it might not be necessary in those particular instances. Whereas some of us have worked with patients who are sceptical and frankly hostile to any sniff of psychological or psychosocial interventions, there is a much bigger world where there is sometimes the opposite problem: people are all too keen to make psychological formulations and interventions if only they have the opportunity.

*Von Korff*: Someone said earlier that research isn't going to carry the day. Perhaps in the short term this may be true, but if this field doesn't start to do definitive trials and strengthening of the research base, we are dead in the long run.

*Wessely*: There is no dispute about that. Some of the evidence doesn't translate into policy as quickly as we would like, but without the evidence I am quite sure that there would be no changes. Evidence alone is not enough. George Davey Smith wrote a good paper called 'Policy-driven evidence'. This is when policy changes and people look for evidence to support the change that they have decided to make. Greville Mitchell: I think you should have the last word.

*Mitchell*: I would like to speak as a patient, or member of the public, rather than the sponsor of this meeting. As some of you probably know, I'm a great believer in the 'KISS' philosophy—'keep it simple, stupid'—and I'm happy to be stupid. When I first looked at the list of invitees, I was somewhat intimidated and apprehensive. There were 30 professors on the list and this prompted two thoughts. The first was that the discussion would be way over my head and the second was whether I'd be able to cope with being with 30 professors for 2 days. On both counts, you get 10 out of 10, because the lucidity and clarity of the discussion here has been brilliant. I have found it very stimulating and from the perspective of a patient I have found it very encouraging. The question in the title of this meeting was whether the BPS model is a necessity or a luxury. To me, the answer from this meeting is that it is clearly a necessity. I believe what you have been discussing here will produce massive individual and community benefits.

Let me deal with the community benefit first. Of all patients who attend doctors' surgeries, one accepts that around 70 per cent are not organically ill. But they are unwell and they do have physically manifested symptoms. Currently, the system does not address this. The BPS approach will address this problem. At the moment, the cost to the government, the doctor, and the patient, in time and money, is horrendous. We are getting a revolving door policy. The '70% patient' comes in, his problem is not addressed, there is no cure, and he comes back. There is failure all round. What is being addressed at this meeting will provide substantial benefits on all of these three elements.

What I'd like to leave with you, from my patient's perspective, are some thoughts for your consideration. First, on the subject of the mind, it has always amazed me that doctors fail to use the power of the patient's mind. To me, the power of the mind is many times the power of the body. If you can take that resource which comes into your surgery and turn it to advantage, it would have significant assistance in producing a cure. It has amazed me that doctors have failed to get patients on their side. This could be a massive contribution to assisting the cure. The second thing which I think is important is vocabulary and language. There are words that terrify the public, such as 'mental' and 'mind'. However, some progress has been made because there is one word that the public have accepted as a justifiable cause for illness, which is 'stress'. If you refer to anything else regarding the mind, you have lost them. I'm not suggesting misrepresentation, but language is important and we need to be careful with it. The third factor is that when there are matters of the mind, we should major on the idea of changes in molecules having an effect on behaviour. The public would accept that. If you say to them that they have a mental problem, you have lost them. But if you say that the problem they are suffering is because of a change of molecular structure in the brain, the public will be much more accepting because it is a physical explanation. My last comment concerns complementary medicine. Don't get me wrong: I am in the orthodox camp. But what I do think is important is that we should have an open mind. I am a great believer in communication. I have been fortunate to have a degree of financial independence and one of the prime ingredients that has secured that has been communication. I am a passionate believer in communicating with all parties. It doesn't mean I have to subjugate to them, but I think those options should be open. I would ask you to consider the power of the mind of the patient being co-opted as an aid and utilized by the doctor. Vocabulary and language is important when trying to take this forward with the public and if you are able to talk about molecules, this will overcome a lot of hurdles. It has been a brilliant meeting.

## References

1. Buchbinder R, Jolley D, Wyatt M. Population based intervention to change back pain beliefs and disability: three part evaluation. *BMJ* 2001; **322**: 1516–20.
2. Buchbinder R, Jolley DJ, Wyatt M. Effects of a media campaign on back pain beliefs and its potential influence on the management of low back pain in general practice. *Spine* 2001; **26**: 2535–42.

# 14 Beyond the biomedical to the biopsychosocial: integrated medicine

## Peter White

## Summary

This chapter summarizes the previous ones and draws some conclusions. The jury is still out regarding the importance of both psychological and social factors as direct causes of common and chronic medical diseases. In contrast these factors do seem to be important indirect causes when they are mediated by risky behaviours such as smoking, overeating, and being sedentary. There is considerably stronger evidence regarding the importance of the biopsychosocial (BPS) model in determining disability associated with chronic medical conditions. The BPS model affects disability firstly through a patient's illness beliefs and their consequent coping strategies, including their adherence to medical treatments and advice, and secondly though their emotional reactions, particularly fear and depression with consequent catastrophizing and helplessness.

In order to improve the care of people with chronic ill-health, health-care professionals need to examine or be educated to examine their own illness beliefs and consequent communication with their patients. This should occur in the setting of an integrated understanding of the biology, psychology, and social setting of both the patient and their heath-care provision. Thus, the BPS model should become the routine approach adopted by patients, professionals, and the institutions or systems in which they are treated and work. This is likely to enhance the quality of care, be economically useful, and provide greater professional satisfaction.

## Introduction

George Engel introduced the BPS model as an alternative to the biomedical model of medicine more than 25 years ago.[1] He had high hopes that the BPS approach would replace the more narrow biomedical approach. Despite increasing evidence for the BPS model, this has not happened.

A BPS approach is one that incorporates thoughts, beliefs, feelings, behaviours, and their social context and interactions with biological processes, in order to better understand and manage illness and disability. In contrast, the biomedical approach is a more linear approach that assumes phenomena can be explained solely by biological processes. On superficial examination, the BPS model seems to imply that biological, psychological, and social processes are separate, taking us back to Cartesian dualism. In reality these three processes are integrated and indivisible. For example, thoughts and feelings are impossible without a biological process occurring within the brain.[2]

## Review of previous chapters: history, philosophy, and aetiology

What can we learn from the previous chapters? Shorter reviewed the mixed influence of the BPS model since Engel first described it (Chapter 1), suggesting that inadequate resources, professional jealousies, and misunderstandings hindered its universal adoption. In Chapter 2, Malmgren explained how the BPS model provides a way of better understanding the central mind–body problem of medicine, using the analogy of computer hardware representing the body and software the mind.

It is no surprise that we concentrated on the heart as our organ of interest to tease out the role of psychosocial and biological factors in aetiology.[3] The lay public have no problem in believing that stress causes heart attacks and that people recovering from a heart attack should avoid stress. A review of the evidence for this provides more questions than answers. In Chapter 3, Marmot provided a consummate review of the epidemiological evidence for the relationship between stress, in its broadest sense, and ischaemic heart disease, mostly relying on data from large cohort studies.[4,5] In contrast, Davey Smith (Chapter 5) played the role of the 'devil's advocate' in challenging this orthodox view.[6] He suggested that second-order mechanisms, such as stress causing people to smoke, were irrelevant if first, smoking was the only direct cause of heart disease and second, if removal of the direct cause (not smoking) removed the apparent effect of stress on heart disease. Davey Smith went on to criticize the complexity and two-way pathways of the various BPS models proposed at the meeting. He pointed to the historical examples in which complex models of aetiology have been superseded by major advances of understanding, such as psychosocial models of peptic ulceration giving way to an infectious aetiology.

Some doubt therefore remains about a direct link between stress and heart disease, whereas there is little doubt that how we respond to stress can affect our predilection to heart disease, if smoking, overeating, or other stress-reducing behaviours are involved. The acid test of whether psychosocial factors directly influence either the onset or course of heart disease is to test whether altering those risk factors prevents or alters the prognosis of heart disease. It seems there is a weak but significant effect on prognosis after cardiac rehabilitation in general.[7,8] But when the psychosocial intervention is separated from other educational and rehabilitative interventions (such as exercise and advice on diet and smoking) it seems that there is little or no effect.[9] A recent systematic review of stress reduction interventions found no evidence of its effect on prognosis and only a weak effect on quality of life.[10] In the discussion of Chapter 8, Lewin suggested that non-specific psychological interventions, such as relaxation therapy, are unlikely to affect pathology, but that focused interventions may be more powerful; a view shared by others.[3] It is hard to imagine that interventions to stop people from smoking or take more exercise will be successful without encompassing psychological interventions, such as enhancing motivation and tackling nicotine dependence,[11,12] or social and public health initiatives, such as banning smoking in public places.[13,14]

Up to 50 per cent of the commonest causes of death are related to modifiable health risk behaviours, such as smoking, overeating, and a sedentary life style.[15] Using the BPS model for prevention may help to improve health at both individual and public levels.[11–14] Regarding non-cardiac chronic diseases, there is evidence that using the BPS approach may improve medical outcomes in chronic diseases such as diabetes mellitus[16] and there are plausible mediators of these effects such as improvement of adherence to treatments and life style advice.[17–19] In contrast, the initial promise that simple group psychosocial interventions might improve survival after cancer[20] has not been sustained.[21] The evidence that BPS interventions *directly* affect medical outcomes in chronic diseases is hotly debated, with no clear answer as yet.[22]

If stress does have direct effects on pathology, how might this occur? Steptoe and Lightman (Chapters 4 and 6) reviewed the possible pathophysiological mechanisms by which psychosocial factors might interact with biological processes. Lightman used animal models to show how chronic stress, especially when this occurs early in life, can modify nervous system and endocrine stress responses, sometimes permanently. Steptoe showed how stress can affect the immune response, which in turn can affect the brain in a two-way process.

## Review of previous chapters: the disability of chronic diseases, the power of both placebos and complementary medicine, a patient, and a process

The evidence for the importance of the BPS model in explaining the disability associated with chronic disease is considerably stronger.[23] Von Korff (Chapter 7) reviewed how addressing fear-avoidance beliefs and depression can improve disability for patients with low back pain.[24] He also made the important observation that ' ... doctors usually have no more basis for inferring that psychological illness is the cause of pain than that there is an underlying physical cause. Focusing on what can help the patient feel and do better is more appropriate than convincing patients that pain is a "psychosomatic" disorder.' One effect of the technological advance of medicine has been a decline in the art of rehabilitating our patients.[25] This pragmatic approach to enhancing recovery relies heavily on a BPS approach and seems to be reasonably successful.[26,27] We should now start using new communication technologies to widen access to these approaches.[28]

As Kleijnen demonstrated in Chapter 8, few health-care professionals address the context in which health-care is delivered when treating their patients, in spite of its power in influencing outcomes.[29] Engel rightly pointed out the importance of health-care context in the BPS model.[1] Although it would be unethical to deceive a patient by not being honest when using a placebo,[30] Kleijnen demonstrated how it might be possible to harness the power of the placebo, to help our patients, by addressing the health-enhancing properties of the context of health-care: 'These healthcare contexts include communication by doctors, the expectations of both doctors and patients, and the means of administration of interventions.'

This is amply demonstrated by considering the reasons why so many millions of patients take up complementary and alternative medicine (CAM). In Chapter 9, Furnham shows that patients attend CAM practitioners because orthodox approaches do not satisfy them. 'In particular, patients are dissatisfied with the nature and style of the consultation and its attendant communication, which is regarded as too one-way, with insufficient listening, touching, and attention.' In a lesson to orthodox practitioners, good CAM practitioners elicit and attend to a patient's illness beliefs, which process enhances the context/placebo effect on top of whatever efficacy the specific CAM treatment has.

Drossman (Chapter 10) demonstrates both how a BPS approach can be useful in clinical practice and how it can determine the research agenda. Creed (Chapter 11) argues that the BPS approach is consistent with the patient-centred approach, an approach that has particularly influenced primary care, as outlined by Stewart and others.[31] Creed argues for the primary importance of good interview skills, using Maguire's work with patients with cancer.[32] This should be second nature to a good professional, but is infrequently so.[33] Creed reminds us that a common barrier to eliciting fears and concerns in our patients is our own fear of our own emotions; something picked up in the discussion that followed his presentation. We are not very good at looking after our own and can do better.[34]

Because orthodox practitioners have been slow to incorporate the BPS approach into their routine practice, can either patients themselves or healthcare providers lead the way instead? In Chapter 12, Lorig gives a fascinating account of one such approach to overcoming institutional barriers to such health-care. The American health-care provider Kaiser Permanente offers a 'Healthy living with long-term conditions' programme, which involves 'expert' patients helping other patients to maximize their quality of life in spite of their medical condition.[35] The same approach is currently being encouraged within the UK National Health Service as the 'expert patient programme'.[36] The essence of the programme is to maximize the patient's self-efficacy by actively managing their own illness and disability, using goal setting and problem solving techniques.[35,36] Self-efficacy is the confidence or belief that one can achieve specific behaviours or goals.[37] Biological, psychological, and social factors all influence self-efficacy and vice versa.

What is the evidence for the importance of self-efficacy? Self-efficacy was the strongest predictor of quality of life in a prospective study of asthma sufferers.[38] Self-efficacy was related to an active coping style and consequent quality of life in a large study of patients with diabetes mellitus, with the model explaining 62 per cent of the variance.[39] Self-efficacy was a significant predictor of adherence to a cardiac rehabilitation programme.[40] Lower self-efficacy was associated with both worse mood and quality of life in a study of patients with chronic obstructive pulmonary disease, once disease severity was controlled.[41] Depression and fearful catastrophizing were associated factors in several of these studies, although some prospective studies suggest that self-efficacy is a stronger predictor of subsequent disability.[42]

Self-efficacy can be enhanced through skills mastery, which involves helping people do the things they need to do, modelling, having patients interact with others who have similar problems, and reinterpretation of symptoms by offering multiple causes for symptoms. Maximizing the patient's self-efficacy requires that we adopt a BPS model. The essence of the BPS model is its effect on self-efficacy. Routine management of chronic ill-health should use the BPS model to encourage greater self-efficacy, with both patients and health-care professionals being equally committed.

## Medically unexplained ill-health and mental ill-health

With the exception of Chapter 10, this book has been careful to avoid addressing the issue of medically unexplained ill-health and mental disorders, because the BPS is important in addressing disability and improving quality of life associated with all chronic ill-health, whatever its provenance. Having stated this, there is an overwhelming amount of evidence for the utility of the BPS approach in both understanding and helping patients with mental ill-health and physical symptoms for which no explanation is apparent.[33] The latter includes common disorders such as chronic fatigue syndrome, chronic pain disorders, and functional bowel disorders.[43–45]

## How can the barriers to making the biopsychosocial approach routine for chronic ill-health be removed?

Barriers to implementing this approach exist within patients, professionals, and health-care systems.

### The economic advantages

Health-care systems will routinely incorporate the BPS approach when convinced of its economic advantages.[46,47] There is already some evidence of reduced health-care costs and increased patient satisfaction (and thus less cause for costly complaints).[36,46,47] But a more convincing case may mean considering economic costs across the whole of society, not just the health-care system, because economic gains will be greatest in the reduced costs of disability benefits and economic gains that would follow on from employment.[48]

### Professional education and training

A survey of US medical schools between 1997 and 1999 showed that there was great variation in the teaching of BPS medicine.[49] Teaching the skills necessary for professionals to feel confident that they can address the problems thrown up by a BPS approach is more important than persuading them to ask the appropriate questions.[23,33,36,50] Awareness of the effect of a professional's own specific health beliefs may remove one barrier to the patient's improvement.[51] Demonstrating both the advantages and lack of disadvantages of the BPS approach to the health-care professional is important:

(1)  by improving patient satisfaction (and thus reducing complaints);[36,46,47]

(2)  by increasing professional confidence and job satisfaction;[36,46,50]

(3)  by stressing the importance of quality rather than quantity of time involved;[46]

(4)  by ensuring appropriate care or support of the professionals themselves.[34]

### Patient education and self-management

Because many patients now use the internet for information on their health, we should make greater use of this medium to get the right messages across.[28] Patient education and self-management should be seen as something that patients can increasingly do for themselves,[35–37,52] as well as something to be done at a public level.[53] Above all, patients need to know that the BPS approach is simply an extension of the biomedical approach, and makes no assumptions about original causes.

## The drivers

Because patients, health-care systems, and benefit providers have most to gain, it is probably they who will drive the agenda forward, rather than health-care professionals. That is, unless we take the lead ourselves.

## Acknowledgement

Professors Michael Sharpe and Kate Lorig provided helpful suggestions and feedback on an earlier version of this chapter.

## References

1. Engel GL. The need for a new medical model: a challenge for biomedicine. *Science* 1977; **196:** 129–36.

2. Searle JR. Consciousness. *Ann Rev Neuroscience* 2000; **23:** 557–78.

3. Stansfeld SA, Marmot MG. *Stress and the heart: psychosocial pathways to coronary heart disease.* London: BMJ Books; 2002.

4. Stansfeld SA, Fuhrer R, Shipley MJ, Marmot MG. Psychological distress as a risk factor for coronary heart disease in the Whitehall II study. *Int J Epidemiol* 2002; **31:** 248–55.

5. Kivimäki M, Leino-Arjas P, Luukkonen R, Riihimäki H, Vahtera J, Kirjonen J. Work stress and risk of cardiovascular mortality: prospective cohort study of industrial employees. *BMJ* 2002; **325:** 857–65.

6. Macleod J, Davey Smith G, Heslop P, Metcalfe C, Carroll D, Hart C *et al.* Psychological stress and cardiovascular disease: empirical demonstration of bias in a prospective observational study of Scottish men. *BMJ* 2002; **324:** 1247–51.

7. Linden W, Stossel C, Maurice J. Psychosocial interventions for patients with coronary artery disease: a meta-analysis. *Arch Intern Med* 1996; **156:** 745–52.

8. Dusseldorp E, van Elderen T, Maes S, Meulman J, Kraaij V. A meta-analysis of psychoeducational programs for coronary heart disease patients. *Health Psychol* 1999; **18:** 506–19.

9. Writing Committee for the ENRICHD Investigators. Effects of treating depression and low perceived social support on clinical events after myocardial infarction: the Enhancing Recovery in coronary Heart Disease Patients (ENRICHD) randomized trial. *JAMA* 2003; **289:** 3106–16.

10. Rees K, Bennett P, West R, Davey Smith G, Ebrahim S. Psychological interventions for coronary heart disease (Cochrane Review). In: *The Cochrane library, Issue 2.* Chichester: Wiley; 2004.

11. Miller WR, Rollnik S (ed.). *Motivational interviewing: preparing people to change addictive behavior.* New York: Guildford; 1991.

12. West RE. Assessment of dependence and motivation to stop smoking. *BMJ* 2004: **328:** 338–9.

13. Wakefield MA, Chaloupka FJ, Kaufman NJ, Orleans CT, Barker DC, Ruel EE. Effect of restrictions on smoking at home, at school, and in public places on teenage smoking: cross-sectional study. *BMJ* 2000; **321**: 333–7.

14. Sargent RP, Shepard RM, Glantz SA. Reduced incidence of admissions for myocardial infarction associated with public smoking ban: before and after study. *BMJ* 2004; **328**: 977–83.

15. McGinnis JM, Foege WH. Actual causes of death in the United States. *JAMA* 1993; **270**: 2207–12.

16. Ismail K, Winkley K, Rabe-Hesketh S. Systematic review and meta-analysis of randomised controlled trials of psychological interventions to improve glycaemic control in patients with type 2 diabetes. *Lancet* 2004; **363**: 1589–97.

17. Horne R. Patient's beliefs about treatment: the hidden determinant of treatment outcome? *J Psychosom Res* 1999; **47**: 491–5.

18. Sewitch MJ, Leffondre K, Dobkin PL. Clustering patients according to health perceptions: relationships to psychosocial characteristics and medication nonadherence. *J Psychosom Res* 2004; **56**: 323–32.

19. Bodenheimer T, Wagner EH, Grumbach K. Improving primary care for patients with chronic illness: The chronic care model, part 2. *JAMA* 2002; **288**: 1909–14.

20. Spiegel D, Bloom JR, Kraemer HC, Gottheil E. Effect of psychosocial treatment on survival of patients with metastatic breast cancer. *Lancet* 1989; **2**: 888–91.

21. Goodwin PJ, Leszcz M, Ennis M, Koopmans J, Vincent L, Guther H, *et al.* The effect of group psychosocial support on survival in metastatic breast cancer. *New Engl J Med* 2001; **345**: 1719–26.

22. Markovitz JH, Williams RD, Schneiderman N, Relman AS, Angell M, Lundberg GD. Resolved: psychosocial interventions can improve clinical outcomes in organic disease. *Psychosom Med* 2002; **64**: 549–70.

23. Von Korff M, Glasgow RE, Sharpe M. ABC of psychological medicine: organising care for chronic illness. *BMJ* 2002; **325**: 92–4.

24. Von Korff M, Moore JC. Stepped care for back pain: activating approaches for primary care. *Ann Intern Med* 2001; **134**: 911–17.

25. Grahame R. The decline of rehabilitation services and its impact on disability benefits. *J Roy Soc Med* 2002; **95**: 114–17.

26. Guzman J, Esmail R, Karjalainen K, Malmivaara A, Irvin E, Bombardier C. Multidisciplinary rehabilitation for chronic low back pain: systematic review. *BMJ* 2001; **322**: 1511–16.

27. Karjalainen K, Malmivaara A, van Tulder M, Roine R, Jauhiainen M, Hurri H, *et al.* Multidisciplinary biopsychosocial rehabilitation for subacute low back pain in working-age adults: A systematic review within the framework of the Cochrane collaboration back review group. *Spine* 2001; **26**: 262–9.

28. Lorig KR, Laurent DD, Deyo RA, Marnell ME, Minor MA, Ritter PL. Can a back pain E-mail discussion group improve health status and lower health care costs? A randomised study. *Arch Intern Med* 2002; **162**: 792–6.

29. Di Blasi Z, Harkness E, Ernst E, Georgiou A, Kleijnen J. Influence of context effects on health outcomes: a systematic review. *Lancet* 2001; **357**: 757–62.

30. Hill J. Placebos in clinical care: for whose pleasure? *Lancet* 2003; **362**: 254.

31. Stewart M, Brown JB, Weston WW, McWhinney IR, McWilliam CL, Freeman TR. *Patient-centred medicine: transforming the clinical method*. Thousands Oaks, California: Sage; 1995.

32. Maguire P, Booth K, Elliott C, Jones B. Helping health professionals involved in cancer care acquire key interviewing skills–the impact of workshops. *Eur J Cancer* 1996; **32A:** 1486–9.

33. Royal Colleges of Physicians and Psychiatrists. *The psychological care of medical patients: A practical guide. 2nd edition*. London: Royal College of Physicians; 2003.

34. Frith-Cozens J, Payne R. *Stress in health professionals: Psychological and organizational causes and interventions*. London: Wiley; 1999.

35. Lorig KR, Sobel DS, Ritter PL, Laurent D, Hobbs M. Effect of a self-management program on patients with chronic disease. *Effect Clin Pract* 2001; **4:** 256–61.

36. Department of Health. *The expert patient: a new approach to chronic disease management for the 21st century*. London: Department of Health; 2001 (www.ohn.gov.uk/ohn/people/ep_report.pdf).

37. Schwarzer R (ed.). *Self-efficacy: thought control of action*. Washington, DC: Hemisphere; 1992.

38. Mancuso CA, Rincon M, McCulloch CE, Charlson ME. Self-efficacy, depressive symptoms, and patients' expectations predict outcomes in asthma. *Med Care* 2001; **39:** 1326–38.

39. Rose M, Flege H, Hildebrandt M, Schirop T, Klapp BF. The network of psychological variables in patients with diabetes and their importance for quality of life and metabolic control. *Diabetes Care* 2002; **25:** 35–42.

40. Grace SL, Abbey SE, Shnek ZM, Irvine J, Franche RL, Stewart DE. Cardiac rehabilitation II: referral and participation. *Gen Hosp Psychiat* 2002; **24:** 127–34.

41. McCathie HC, Spence SH, Tate RL. Adjustment to chronic obstructive pulmonary disease: the importance of psychological factors. *Eur Resp J* 2002; **19:** 47–53.

42. Asghari A, Nicholas MK. Pain self-efficacy beliefs and pain behaviour. A prospective study. *Pain* 2001; **94:** 85–100.

43. Masi AT, White KP, Pilcher JJ. Person-centred approach to care, teaching, and research in fibromyalgia syndrome: justification from biopsychosocial perspectives in populations. *Semin Arthr Rheum* 2002; **32:** 71–93.

44. Drossman DA, Toner BB, Whitehead WE, Diamant NE, Dalton CB, Duncan S, *et al.* Cognitive–behavioral therapy vs education and desipramine vs placebo for moderate to severe functional bowel disorders. *Gastroenterology* 2003; **125:** 19–31.

45. Royal Australasian College of Physicians. Chronic fatigue syndrome: clinical practice guidelines. *Med J Austral* 2002; **176:** S17–S55 (http://www.mja.com.au/public/guides/cfs/cfs2.html).

46. Margalit APA, Glick SM, Benbassat J, Cohen A. Effect of a biopsychosocial approach to patient satisfaction and patterns of care. *J Gen Intern Med* 2004; **19 (suppl 5, Pt 2):** 485–91.

47. Lorig KR, Sobel DS, Stewart AL, Brown, BW Jr, Bandura A, Ritter P, *et al.* Evidence suggesting that a chronic diseases self-management program can improve health status while reducing hospitalization: a randomized trial. *Med Care* 1999; **37:** 5–14.

48. Waddell G, Aylward M, Sawney P. *Back pain, incapacity for work and social security benefits: an international literature review and analysis.* London: Royal Society of Medicine Press; 2002.

49. Waldstein SR, Neumann SA, Drossman DA, Novack DH. Teaching psychosomatic (biopsychosocial) medicine in United States medical schools: survey findings. *Psychosom Med* 2001; **63**: 335–43.

50. Poirier MK, Clark MM, Cerhan JH, Pruthi S, Geda YE, Dale LC. Teaching motivational interviewing to first-year medical students to improve counseling skills in health behavior change. *Mayo Clin Proceed* 2004; **79**: 327–31.

51. Daykin AR, Richardson B. Physiotherapists' pain beliefs and their influence on the management of patients with chronic low back pain. *Spine* 2004; **29**: 783–95.

52. McClune T, Burton AK, Waddell G. Evaluation of an evidence based patient educational booklet for management of whiplash associated disorders. *Emerg Med J* 2003; **20**: 514–17.

53. Buchbinder R, Jolley D, Wyatt M. Population based intervention to change back pain beliefs and disability: three part evaluation. *BMJ* 2001; **322**: 1516–20.

# Index